2nd Edition

Legal Studies, To Wit:

Basic Legal Terminology And Transcription

Wanda Walker Roderick

R & W Associates
East Lansing,
Michigan

K36

Published by

SOUTH-WESTERN PUBLISHING CO.

CINCINNATI   WEST CHICAGO, IL   DALLAS   PELHAM MANOR, NY   PALO ALTO, CA

ISBN: 0-538-11360-X
Library of Congress Catalog Card Number: 84-50336

1 2 3 4 5 6 7 8 H 1 0 9 8 7 6 5 4
Printed in the United States of America

⎣⎦ PREFACE

Understanding legal terminology is an essential requirement for the nonlawyer employee in the legal office. In order to be able to transcribe and type legal documents and follow legal procedures, you must understand the tools with which you are working. In the legal field these tools are the legal words which are used. Many misunderstandings and frustrations on the job can be eliminated with a basic understanding of legal terms. The study of legal terminology is only a part of the skills and knowledge necessary for the non-lawyer employee, but it is a very vital and necessary element for success in the legal field. With a good basic understanding of legal vocabulary, the job will be much easier, and you, the legal employee, will be a more effective participant and contributor in the legal profession.

During many years of teaching in the area of court reporting, the frequency of errors in student transcripts resulting from lack of knowledge of legal terms pointed out the need for a systematic approach for the learning of basic legal vocabulary. Errors such as the land was measured by "leaps and bounds" instead of "metes and bounds," "quickclaim deed" instead of "quitclaim deed," and a "causal relationship" transcribed as a "casual relationship" may appear humorous on the surface but are not so funny when the fortunes or the lives of people are at stake.

OBJECTIVES

This textbook-workbook is intended to give you knowledge and understanding of approximately 800 terms commonly used in the legal profession. You will learn to define the terms and to use them in legal context. Pronunciation guides are provided for each word, and the correct pronunciation is reinforced by taped dictation. Typing practice from printed copy will assist you in learning the correct spelling of each term, and all objectives are reinforced as you learn to transcribe the terms from taped dictation. Therefore, upon successful completion of this course, you should be able to:

(1) Correctly spell, pronounce, and define the legal terms presented.
(2) Transcribe the legal terms on the typewriter either directly from the tape or from shorthand notes.

INSTRUCTIONAL LEVEL

This course can be used in a regular classroom, but it is also very adaptable to an individualized instructional system or an office block approach. It will provide a good background for you should you desire to work in a legal office as a receptionist/typist, secretary, stenographer, or research assistant. Should you plan to become a court reporter, note-reader/transcriber, or transcript typist, you can also benefit since the transcription is either from a phonetically written word or from taped dictation. Should you desire work in a legal office or in the court reporting field, you must, of course, have a much broader knowledge of legal vocabulary than this course provides, but it will give you an excellent background for legal typing, legal shorthand, legal procedures, and business law courses.

In order to succeed in legal/terminology transcription, you should be able to type—a prerequisite for any of the named jobs in the legal field. Shorthand is not required, but the course is designed so that if you do use a shorthand system (either pen or machine), you can integrate that skill into the study of this course. In this textbook-workbook, space is provided for writing shorthand; but if that space is not adequate, you may use shorthand paper. If you are using machine shorthand, write all the outlines on your shorthand machine instead of writing them in the textbook-workbook.

Because of the tear-out feature of the textbook-workbook, it was necessary to use side binding. It is suggested that pages to be copied on the typewriter be torn out first and put to the side of the machine. If the shorthand procedure is used, tear out the appropriate page and put it on the desk to write the outlines. In both instances, you will find it easier to work with individual pages than with an open book.

LENGTH OF COURSE

The course consists of 30 lessons each containing approximately 25 terms. If you plan to follow the typing/transcription procedure, the course will take approximately 35 clock hours to complete. It will take approximately 45 clock hours to follow the shorthand/transcription procedure.

QUIZZES AND EVALUATIONS

At the end of each lesson are two short quizzes. Answers to these quizzes begin on page 331 in the

Appendix. This enables you to check on your understanding and comprehension of the subject matter presented in each lesson.

There are also two short written quizzes following each taped evaluation. The evaluations occur after every two textbook-workbook lessons as a partial measurement of your understanding and comprehension of the material.

DICTATION TAPES

Practice Dictation. The practice dictation for each of the 30 lessons is on one side of a cassette. This means there are two lessons on a single cassette (15 practice dictation cassettes all totaled). The rate is around 80 words a minute. Each term presented in a given lesson is included in the dictation material for that lesson.

Evaluation Tapes. In addition to the lesson practice dictation material, there are 8 evaluation cassettes. After every two lessons, there is dictated material on a cassette similar to what you will hear on the practice cassettes. Each cassette has a 10-minute evaluation per side. One of the two evaluations is to be given at the completion of every two textbook lessons. These will be administered by your instructor or a specially designated person. Each evaluation consists of three sections—A, B, and C. Be sure that you complete all three sections before going to the next lesson.

AREAS OF LAW COVERED

The various areas of law are listed and arranged in a logical sequence to provide some continuity as you progress through the course. The general areas are introduced first, followed by the most common specific areas such as criminal and civil. Progression is then made into other specific areas that will give you an understanding of the terminology used in most law firms whether the lawyer happens to be in general law practice or in a specialized area. Two lessons are used to cover the terminology in most of the areas. However, for areas such as bankruptcy and partnerships where the number of specific terms are limited, there is only one lesson. After Lesson 10, the lessons may be rearranged or a specific selection may be made to meet your individual needs.

SELECTION OF TERMINOLOGY

The terminology was selected from books on legal secretarial training, law books, legal dictionaries, legal documents, and court transcripts. Also

various legal personnel were consulted regarding specific terms.

The most commonly used terms, as well as those with special legal meanings in each area, were selected. Terms that are used very infrequently were avoided as one of the main objectives was to develop a general basic background in legal terms. The use of certain terms will vary from state to state and those are identified throughout the course. Some of the most commonly used Latin terms are also included. Even though you will learn some legal procedures from the study of the terminology, it is not intended to be a course in law.

PRONUNCIATIONS

The pronunciations for the terms in this course are based on the pronunciation guide of Webster's Ninth New Collegiate Dictionary, 1983, Merriam-Webster, Inc., Springfield, Massachusetts.

SPECIFIC COMMENTS ON LESSONS AND EVALUATIONS

At the beginning of each lesson there is a general introduction that explains the content of the lesson and gives the objectives that you are to complete for the lesson.

Part A—Terminology and Definitions

The first list of legal terms presented in each lesson consists of 12 to 14 terms. The pronunciation and definition for each term is given. A column is also provided for you to write in the shorthand outline for each term if you are following the shorthand procedure.

You should study the words carefully and be sure that you understand the definition of each term and can spell and pronounce the terms.

Quiz No. 1—Terminology and Definition Recall

This quiz will require you to recall the terms that were presented in Part A. The format will be blanks, multiple choice, or matching. The answers are provided in the Appendix so that you can check the answers as soon as you have completed the quiz. This provides reinforcement for the learning, and you should restudy any incorrect answers.

Part A—Typing Legal Terms

Further reinforcement of the terms and definitions is provided in this part. In the first part, you will type the legal terms presented in the lesson. This will assist you in learning the correct spelling for each of the terms. The sentences in the second part reemphasize the terms and the definitions. The terms are presented in legal context or usage whenever possible. If you are following the shorthand procedure, write the shorthand outlines for the material in the space provided. Then cover the printed words with a sheet of paper and transcribe from your shorthand notes. If you are using machine shorthand, write the words and sentences on your shorthand machine and then transcribe from the machine tape. You will not write the outlines in the textbook-workbook if you are using machine shorthand.

Part A—Transcribing from Dictation

Since the material dictated on the cassette is the same as you just practiced typing from printed copy, your main adaptation in this part will be to transcribe from sound or from your shorthand notes. By practicing the material beforehand, your frustrations will be minimized as you move into this section. Also, the tapes will help you learn the correct pronunciation of the legal terms.

This part of the lesson provides you with the opportunity to transcribe from dictation, make mistakes, and relearn before an evaluation. After you have transcribed the dictation, check your transcript with the printed copy and restudy any part that gave you difficulty.

Part B and Quiz No. 2 are a repeat of the above learning situations using 12-14 more new legal terms.

Evaluations

Section A. This part of the evaluation is taped for you to transcribe either directly on your typewriter or from your shorthand notes. It consists of the same legal terms but the dictation varies in content from that given in the lessons. A form for typing, directions, and scoring record are provided at proper intervals in your textbook-workbook. You will turn in this evaluation to your instructor for checking and grading. Each dictated evaluation is 10 minutes in length and is dictated at about 80 words per minute.

Sections B and C. This part provides a written evaluation of your knowledge of the legal terms and definitions. It is to be turned in to your instructor for checking along with Section A. It recaps the lesson and is an indication, along with the dictation section, of whether or not you have fully comprehended the lesson and are ready to continue. This part of the evaluation consists of multiple choice and matching questions.

INDEX OF TERMS

An index of terms is included at the end of the textbook-workbook. It is an alphabetized listing of the terms including the number of the lesson where the term is presented.

ACKNOWLEDGMENTS

Many students, teachers, secretaries, court reporters, and lawyers assisted with the content and organization of this textbook-workbook. The author expresses thanks to all who contributed time and suggestions and especially to those who used the first edition and made suggestions for this second edition.

Wanda Walker Roderick

⫴ CONTENTS

To Wit:

"The state without law would be like the human body without mind."

—Cicero

 # LESSON 1

To Wit: Courts and Legal Systems

A knowledge of the federal and state court systems, the sources of our laws, and the classifications of law is an essential basis for the understanding of legal terminology. The names of the courts may vary from state to state, but the ones most commonly used are defined. Since our law is an outgrowth of the legal systems of other countries, the most common types of law used in our system are also included. When you complete this lesson, you will have an understanding of the general terms used in reference to our courts and legal systems which will help you learn the terminology taught in the following lessons.

Part A	Terminology and Definitions

Directions: Study the terms, pronunciations, and definitions until you are thoroughly familiar with them. In order to complete this lesson successfully, you must understand the meaning and usage of all the legal terms presented. If you are using shorthand, write your shorthand outline in the space provided or on your shorthand machine for each legal term.

LEGAL TERM	PRONUNCIATION	DEFINITION	SHORTHAND OUTLINE
Federal Court System			
1. U.S. Supreme Court	ū s sə-'prem kōrt	The highest court in the federal judicial system. Composed of a chief justice and eight associate justices.	_____
2. U.S. Court of Appeals	ū s kōrt əv ə-'pels	An appellate court. Reviews cases from lower courts. There is a U.S. Court of Appeals in the 11 judicial circuits.	_____
3. U.S. District Courts	ū s 'dis-trikt kōrts	A federal trial court or a federal court of original jurisdiction.	_____

| 4. special courts | 'spesh-əl korts | There are several special U.S. courts which have limited jurisdiction, including the Court of Claims and Bankruptcy Courts. | _____ |

State Court System:

5. supreme court	sə-'prēm kort	The highest court in most state court systems.	_____
6. courts of appeal	korts əv ə-'pel	Courts which review cases from the trial courts. The highest court in states not having a supreme court.	_____
7. appellate courts	ə-'pel-ət korts	Same as courts of appeal. A court which reviews cases that are appealed from a lower court.	_____
8. trial courts	trīl korts	A court of original jurisdiction. Hears a case the first time it is tried in court.	_____
9. courts of original jurisdiction	korts əv ə-'rij-ən-l jùr-əs-'dik-shən	Courts which hear a case the first time it is tried in court. A trial court.	_____
10. lower or inferior courts	lōr ər in-'fir-ē-ər korts	Courts which have a very limited jurisdiction and whose cases may be appealed to a higher court. A written record is not usually required for the proceedings.	_____
11. probate courts	'prō-bāt korts	Courts which deal with the probate of wills and the settlement of estates. May also be called "orphan's courts" and "surrogate's courts" in some states.	_____
12. courts of record	korts əv ri-'kord	Courts in which all proceedings are recorded for future reference. Trial courts, appellate courts, and supreme courts are usually courts of record.	_____
13. courts not of record	korts nät əv ri-'kord	Courts in which the proceedings are not required to be recorded. Usually the lower or inferior courts are courts not of record.	_____

Turn to page 9 and complete Quiz No. 1 before continuing this lesson.

Typing Legal Terms

Directions: Unless otherwise instructed, use a 70-space line and double spacing. Correct all errors. Follow one of the procedures below.

Words

Typing Procedure

On a separate sheet of paper, type the following words at least two times, concentrating on the correct spelling and pronunciation.

Shorthand Procedure

On a separate sheet of paper, type the following words once, concentrating on the correct spelling and pronunciation. Then write the shorthand outline for each word on the lines to the right or on your shorthand machine. Cover the printed words with a sheet of paper and transcribe from the shorthand outlines one time on your typewriter.

U.S. Supreme Court / U.S. Court of Appeals / U.S. District Courts / special courts / supreme court / courts of appeal / appellate courts / trial courts / courts of original jurisdiction / lower or inferior courts / probate courts / courts of record / courts not of record

Sentences

Typing Procedure

Type each of the following sentences one time. Concentrate on the correct spelling and pronunciation of each underlined legal term.

Shorthand Procedure

Write the correct shorthand outlines for the following sentences on the lines to the right or on your shorthand machine. Cover the printed material with a sheet of paper and transcribe from your shorthand outlines one time on the typewriter.

These sentences will be used for practice dictation on the cassettes.

The federal court system deals with cases involving the federal government, suits between states, and specific matters in the various special courts established for that purpose. The U.S. Supreme Court is the highest court in the federal judicial system and is composed of a chief justice and eight associate justices. The U.S. District Court is a federal trial court or court of original jurisdiction. A case tried in the U.S. District Court may be appealed to the U.S. Court of Appeals. The U.S. Supreme Court may then be petitioned to hear the case. There are several special courts in the federal court system such as the Court of Claims and the Bankruptcy Courts. The highest court in most states is called the supreme court. The trial courts or courts of original jurisdiction hear a case the first time it is tried in court. Most trial courts are courts of record. Cases tried in trial courts may be appealed to the appellate courts or courts of appeal and then to the supreme court. Courts of small or restricted jurisdiction, such as municipal courts, are known generally as lower or inferior courts and, in most cases, are courts not of record. A case tried in a lower or inferior court may be reviewed in the trial courts and could then follow the appellate procedure for cases originally tried in the trial courts. Probate courts have jurisdiction over the probate of wills and the settlement of estates.

_____
_____
_____
_____
_____
_____
_____
_____
_____
_____
_____
_____
_____
_____
_____

Transcribing from Dictation

Directions: This dictation emphasizes and reinforces the legal terms and definitions you have studied. Listen carefully to the pronunciation of each of the legal terms. Unless otherwise directed, use a 70-space line and double spacing. Correct all errors. Follow one of the procedures below.

Typing Procedure

Using the cassette from Lesson 1, Part A, transcribe the dictation directly at your typewriter.

Shorthand Procedure

Using the cassette from Lesson 1, Part A, take the dictation using your shorthand system and then transcribe on the typewriter from your shorthand notes.

When you have finished transcribing Part A of the practice dictation, check your transcript with the printed copy. If you made any mistakes in the transcription, you should practice those words several times before going on.

Part B   Terminology and Definitions

Directions: Study the terms, pronunciations, and definitions until you are thoroughly familiar with them. In order to complete this lesson successfully, you must understand the meaning and usage of all the legal terms presented. If you are using shorthand, write your shorthand outline in the space provided or on your shorthand machine for each legal term.

LEGAL TERMS	PRONUNCIATION	DEFINITION	SHORTHAND OUTLINE

Sources of Law:

1. constitutional law — kä nstətüshənl lȯ — A branch of public law which deals with the interpretation and validity of federal and state constitutions. _____

2. statutory law — 'stach-ə-tōr-ē lȯ — Law which has been created by statute in the legislatures. Sometimes called written law. _____

3. common law — 'käm-ən lȯ — A body of law which originated in England and has been adopted as the major source of law in the United States. Common law operates through the rule of precedent (like cases in the future to be decided in a like manner). _____

4. case law — kās lȯ — Law which is based on cases used as precedents rather than on statutes or other sources of law. _____

5. Napoleonic Code — nə-'pō-lē-ə-nik kōd — Law which originated in France and was adopted by the state of Louisiana. _____

6. administrative law — əd-'min-ə-strāt-iv lȯ — A branch of public law which deals with the various administrative agencies created by the government and defines the scope of their power. _____

Classifications of Law:

7. federal law — fed-rəl lȯ — Law which is created by the federal government and is unaffected by state laws. _____

8. state law — stāt lȯ — Laws which are created by a state and are effective only in that state. _____

9. local and municipal ordinances — 'lō-kəl ən myu-'nis-pəl 'ȯrd-nəns-əs — Laws or rules which are created by a local or municipal government and are effective only in that particular governmental unit. _____

10. public law — 'pəb-lik lȯ — A body of law to which the general public is subject, including constitutional, administrative, and criminal law. _____

11. private law — 'prī-vət lȯ — A body of law which deals with relationships between private individuals such as contracts, civil injuries, domestic relations, and partnerships. _____

12. substantive law — 'səb-stən-tiv lȯ — The body of law which creates and defines our rights and duties. _____

Lesson 1, Part B

13. procedural law   prə-'sēj-rəl
                          lò

The body of law which establishes the procedures to be followed for remedial action in court when one's rights have been violated. Also called adjective law.

Turn to page 10 and complete Quiz No. 2 before continuing this lesson.

Typing Legal Terms

Directions: Unless otherwise instructed, use a 70-space line and double spacing. Correct all errors. Follow one of the procedures below.

Words

Typing Procedure

On a separate sheet of paper, type the following words at least two times, concentrating on the correct spelling and pronunciation.

Shorthand Procedure

On a separate sheet of paper, type the following words once, concentrating on the correct spelling and pronunciation. Then write the shorthand outline for each word on the lines to the right or on your shorthand machine. Cover the printed words with a sheet of paper and transcribe from the shorthand outlines one time on your typewriter.

constitutional law / statutory law / common law / case law / Napoleonic Code / administrative law / federal law / state law / local and municipal ordinances / public law / private law / substantive law/ procedural law /

Sentences

Typing Procedure

Type each of the following sentences one time. Concentrate on the correct spelling and pronunciation of each underlined legal term.

Shorthand Procedure

Write the correct shorthand outlines for the following sentences on the lines to the right or on your shorthand machine. Cover the printed material with a sheet of paper and transcribe from your shorthand outlines one time on the typewriter.

These sentences will be used for practice dictation on the cassettes.

The sources of law are constitutional, statutory, common, Napoleonic Code, case, and administrative. Constitutional law is based on the federal and state constitutions and is classified as public law.

Statutory law is created by statute in the legislatures and is sometimes referred to as written law. Common law originated in England and is the basis for the law in most of our states. Napoleonic Code originated in France and is used in this country as a basis for law only in the state of Louisiana. Case law, which is also known as common law, is based on cases used as precedents rather than on statutes such as statutory law. The various agencies created by the government come under the branch of law known as administrative law. Law may also be classified as public or private law. Public law is that body of law to which the general public is subject. It includes constitutional, administrative, and criminal law. Private law is that law which deals with relationships between private individuals. Other laws may be classified as federal law, state law, or local and municipal ordinances. Two other classifications of law are substantive law and procedural law. Substantive law creates and defines our rights and duties; whereas, procedural law, which is also known as adjective law, establishes the procedures to be followed for remedial action in court when one's rights have been violated.

Transcribing from Dictation

Directions: This dictation emphasizes and reinforces the legal terms and definitions you have studied. Listen carefully to the pronunciation of each of the legal terms. Unless otherwise directed, use a 70-space line and double spacing. Correct all errors. Follow one of the procedures below.

Typing Procedure

Using the cassette from Lesson 1, Part B, transcribe the dictation directly at your typewriter.

Shorthand Procedure

Using the cassette from Lesson 1, Part B, take the dictation using your shorthand system and then transcribe on the typewriter from your shorthand notes.

When you have finished transcribing Part B of the practice dictation, check your transcript with the printed copy. If you have made any mistakes in the transcription, you should practice those words several times before going on to Lesson 2.

I have completed the following for Lesson 1:

	PART A, DATE	PART B, DATE	SUBMITTED TO INSTRUCTOR YES	NO
Terminology and Definitions	_____	_____	_____	_____
*Typing Legal Terms	_____	_____	_____	_____
Words	_____	_____	_____	_____
Sentences	_____	_____	_____	_____
*Transcribing from Dictation	_____	_____	_____	_____
Quiz No. 1	_____	_____	_____	_____
Quiz No. 2	_____	_____	_____	_____

When you have successfully completed all the exercises in this lesson and submitted to your instructor those called for, you are ready to proceed with Lesson 2.

*If you are using a shorthand system, turn in to your instructor your shorthand notes along with your transcript.

Quiz No. 1

Terminology and Definition Recall

Directions: In the Answers column write the legal term that is most representative of the corresponding statement. After you have completed this quiz, check your answers with the key on page 331. Unless otherwise directed, turn in this quiz to your instructor upon completion of this lesson.

ANSWERS

1. The highest court in most states is called the _____.

1. _____

2. The highest court in the federal judicial system is the _____.

2. _____

3. The highest court in the federal judicial system is composed of a chief justice and _____ associate justices.

3. _____

4. A court which hears a case the first time it is tried in court is called a (a) _____. These courts are also known as (b) _____.

4a. _____
4b. _____

5. Courts in which the proceedings are not required to be recorded are referred to as _____.

5. _____

6. A court having jurisdiction over the probate of wills and the settlement of estates is the _____.

6. _____

7. Courts in which all proceedings are recorded for future reference are _____.

7. _____

8. Courts which have very limited jurisdiction and whose cases may be appealed to a higher court are called _____.

8. _____

9. State courts which review cases from the trial courts are referred to as (a) _____ or (b) _____.

9a. _____
9b. _____

10. The appellate court for the U.S. is called the (a) _____ and consists of (b) _____ judicial circuits.

10a. _____
10b. _____

11. A federal trial court or a federal court of original jurisdiction is a _____.

11. _____

12. A case first tried in a lower court (may, may not) be appealed directly to the supreme court.

12. _____

13. In the federal court system, the Court of Claims and the Bankruptcy Courts are examples of _____ courts.

13. _____

14. Lower or inferior courts (are, are not) usually courts of record.

14. _____

15. Trial courts (are, are not) usually courts of record.

15. _____

Turn back to page 2 and continue with this lesson.

Quiz No. 2

Terminology and Definition Recall

Directions: In the Answers column write the legal term that is most representative of the corresponding statement. After you have completed this quiz, check your answers with the key on page 331. Unless otherwise directed, turn in this quiz to your instructor upon completion of this lesson.

ANSWERS

1. The branch of public law which deals with the various administrative agencies created by the government and defines the scope of their power is _____ law.

1. _____

2. Law which originated in England and is the basis for the laws in most of our states is _____ law.

2. _____

3. The body of law which includes constitutional, administrative, and criminal law to which the general public is subject is known as _____ law.

3. _____

4. The form of law which originated in France and was adopted by the state of Louisiana is known as _____.

4. _____

5. _____ law is created by a state and is effective only in that state.

5. _____

6. Law which is created by statute in the legislatures and is sometimes called written law is _____ law.

6. _____

7. (a) _____ law creates and defines our rights and duties as opposed to (b) _____ law (or adjective law) which establishes the procedures to be followed when one's rights have been violated.

7a. _____
7b. _____

8. A branch of public law which deals with the interpretation and validity of federal and state constitutions is _____ law.

8. _____

9. Law which is created by the federal government and is unaffected by state laws is _____ law.

9. _____

10. A law, rule, or ordinance enacted or adopted by a municipal corporation for the proper conduct of its affairs or the government of its inhabitants is referred to as (a) _____ and (b) _____ ordinances.

10a. _____
10b. _____

11. Law which is based on cases used as precedents rather than on statutes or other sources of law is _____ law.

11. _____

12. The part of law which deals with relationships between private individuals is called _____ law.

12. _____

Turn back to page 6 and continue with this lesson.

"When the reason of a rule ceases, so should the rule itself."

—Legal Maxim

LESSON 2

To Wit:
General Legal Terminology

There are many legal terms which apply to the entire field of law. Several of these are presented in this lesson so that you will be familiar with them as you get into the study of the more specific areas of law. Legal terms are mostly everyday English words but many times they have a totally different meaning when used in the legal field. When you complete this lesson, you will have a knowledge of some of the general terminology used in its legal context.

Part A	Terminology and Definitions

Directions: Study the terms, pronunciations, and definitions until you are thoroughly familiar with them. In order to complete this lesson successfully, you must understand the meaning and usage of all the legal terms presented. If you are using shorthand, write your shorthand outline in the space provided or on your shorthand machine for each legal term.

	LEGAL TERM	PRONUNCIATION	DEFINITION	SHORTHAND OUTLINE
1.	statute	'stach-üt	A law created by a state or federal legislature.	_____
2.	code books	kōd bu̇ks	Books which contain the laws that have been created by state and federal legislatures.	_____
3.	Corpus Juris Secundum	'kȯr-pəs 'jür-əs si-'kənd-əm	An encyclopedia of laws commonly used as a reference by lawyers.	_____
4.	lex	leks	Latin term for "law." A system of written or unwritten law for a given jurisdiction.	_____
5.	lexicon	'lek-sə-kän	Latin. A dictionary of legal terms.	_____
6.	jurisprudence	ju̇r-ə-'sprüd-ns	The philosophy or science of law.	_____

7. jurist	júrist	One who has a thorough knowledge of law and has written extensively on legal subjects.	_____
8. prosecuting attorney	'präs-i-kyüt-iŋ ə-'tər-nē	An appointed or elected official who represents the people or the state in criminal cases.	_____
9. defense attorney	di-'fens ə-tər-nē	One who represents the defendant in court cases or legal matters.	_____
10. esquire	'es-kwīr	A title written after the surname of an attorney. Usually abbreviated to Esq. and no personal or professional title is prefixed to the name.	_____
11. bar	bär	The legal profession. Lawyers are members of the bar.	_____
12. judge	jəj	The presiding officer of a court of law.	_____
13. bench	bench	A court of law. Also, the judge's seat in a court of law.	_____
14. in propria persona	in prō-'prē-ə pər-'sō-nə	Latin. In one's own proper person. One who acts without the assistance of an attorney.	_____

Turn to page 19 and complete Quiz No. 1 before continuing this lesson.

Typing Legal Terms

Directions: Unless otherwise instructed, use a 70-space line and double spacing. Correct all errors. Follow one of the procedures below.

Words

Typing Procedure

On a separate sheet of paper, type the following words at least two times, concentrating on the correct spelling and pronunciation.

Shorthand Procedure

On a separate sheet of paper, type the following words once, concentrating on the correct spelling and pronunciation. Then write the shorthand outline for each word on the lines to the right or on your shorthand machine. Cover the printed words with a sheet of paper and transcribe from the shorthand outlines one time on your typewriter.

statute / code books / Corpus Juris Secundum /   _____

lex / lexicon / jurisprudence / jurist / prosecuting   _____

attorney / defense attorney / esquire / bar / judge   _____

/ bench / in propria persona /

Sentences

Typing Procedure

Type each of the following sentences one time. Concentrate on the correct spelling and pronunciation of each underlined legal term.

Shorthand Procedure

Write the correct shorthand outlines for the following sentences on the lines to the right or on your shorthand machine. Cover the printed material with a sheet of paper and transcribe from your shorthand outlines one time on the typewriter.

These sentences will be used for practice dictation on the cassettes.

The Latin term for law is <u>lex</u>. Lex is a system of written or unwritten law for a given jurisdiction. A <u>lexicon</u> is a dictionary of legal terms. The <u>code books</u> contain the laws that have been created by state and federal legislatures. The <u>Corpus Juris Secundum</u> is an encyclopedia of laws. The Corpus Juris Secundum is commonly used as a legal reference by lawyers. The philosophy or science of law is known as <u>jurisprudence</u>. Jurisprudence deals with the principles of law and legal relations. A <u>jurist</u> is one who has a thorough knowledge of law. Usually a jurist refers to one who has written extensively on legal subjects. The <u>prosecuting attorney</u> conducts criminal prosecutions on behalf of the state or the people; whereas, the <u>defense attorney</u> tries cases in court on behalf of the one who is charged with the crime in the case. The title "Esquire" may be used following an attorney's name. <u>In propria persona</u> means one's own proper person. Someone who is in propria persona acts in his or her own person and does not have the assistance of an attorney. All members of the legal profession are collectively referred to as the <u>bar</u>. A <u>judge</u> presides and administers the law in a court of justice. The seat occupied by the judge in court is referred to as the <u>bench</u>. When a <u>statute</u> has been violated, the judge will hear the case as presented by the prosecuting and defense attorneys. A statute is a law created by a state or federal legislature. A jurist is very knowledgeable in the field of _____

jurisprudence. Members of the bar may use code _____

books, the Corpus Juris Secundum, or a lexicon as _____

references. _____

Transcribing from Dictation

Directions: This dictation emphasizes and reinforces the legal terms and definitions you have studied. Listen carefully to the pronunciation of each of the legal terms. Unless otherwise directed, use a 70-space line and double spacing. Correct all errors. Follow one of the procedures below.

Typing Procedure

Using the cassette from Lesson 2, Part A, transcribe the dictation directly at your typewriter.

Shorthand Procedure

Using the cassette from Lesson 2, Part A, take the dictation using your shorthand system and then transcribe on the typewriter from your shorthand notes.

When you have finished transcribing Part A of the practice dictation, check your transcript with the printed copy. If you made any mistakes in the transcription, you should practice those words several times before going on.

Part B | Terminology and Definitions

Directions: Study the terms, pronunciations, and definitions until you are thoroughly familiar with them. In order to complete this lesson successfully, you must understand the meaning and usage of all the legal terms presented. If you are using shorthand, write your shorthand outline in the space provided or on your shorthand machine for each legal term.

LEGAL TERM	PRONUNCIATION	DEFINITION	SHORTHAND OUTLINE
1. client	ˈklī-ənt	One who employs an attorney to represent or advise that person in court cases or legal matters.	_____
2. proceeding	prō-ˈsēd-iŋ	Any action in a court of law.	_____
3. legal procedure	ˈlē-gəl prə-ˈsē-jər	The method or steps to be followed in any action in a court of law.	_____
4. due process	dü prə-ˈses	The legal procedures established which provide that every person has the benefit and protection of the law.	_____
5. justice	ˈjəs-təs	A just and fair application of the law for every person. Also, a judge is referred to as a justice.	_____

6. suit	süt	Any action or proceeding in a court of law whereby one seeks relief or recovery from another who has caused injury to or violated the rights of that person.	_____
7. litigation	lit-ə-'gā-shən	A legal action or suit in a court of law whereby one seeks relief or recovery from another.	_____
8. action	'ak-shən	A legal proceeding or suit in a court of law whereby one seeks relief from another for an injury or a violated right.	_____
9. plaintiff	'plānt-əf	One who starts an action, suit, or proceeding in a court of law.	_____
10. defendant	di-'fen-dənt	The one against whom an action, suit, litigation, or proceeding is started in a court of law.	_____
11. party	'pärt-ē	Any person involved in or affected by a legal proceeding.	_____
12. litigant	'lit-i-gənt	A party to an action, suit, litigation, or legal proceeding.	_____
13. versus	'vər-səs	Latin. "Against." When used in a case title, the plaintiff's name is first, followed by "versus," then the defendant's name; for example, Durand versus Selmar. May be abbreviated as "vs." or "v."	_____
14. et alius	et 'āl-ē-us	Latin. "And others." Abbreviated et al. When et al. is used in a legal document with more than one plaintiff or defendant named, it means all persons previously named are included.	_____

Turn to page 20 and complete Quiz No. 2 before continuing this lesson.

Typing Legal Terms

Directions: Unless otherwise instructed, use a 70-space line and double spacing. Correct all errors. Follow one of the procedures below.

Words

Typing Procedure

On a separate sheet of paper, type the following words at least two times, concentrating on the correct spelling and pronunciation.

Shorthand Procedure

On a separate sheet of paper, type the following words once, concentrating on the correct spelling and pronunciation. Then write the shorthand outline for each word on the lines to the right or on your shorthand machine. Cover the printed words with a sheet of paper and transcribe from the shorthand outlines one time on your typewriter.

client / proceeding / legal procedure / due process / justice / suit / litigation / action / plaintiff / defendant / party / litigant / versus / et alius /

_____

_____

_____

_____

Sentences

Typing Procedure

Type each of the following sentences one time. Concentrate on the correct spelling and pronunciation of each underlined legal term.

Shorthand Procedure

Write the correct shorthand outlines for the following sentences on the lines to the right or on your shorthand machine. Cover the printed material with a sheet of paper and transcribe from your shorthand outlines one time on the typewriter.

These sentences will be used for practice dictation on the cassettes.

A <u>client</u> is one who employs an attorney to represent or advise that person in legal proceedings or other legal matters. A client who hires an attorney to start a legal <u>proceeding</u> becomes known as the <u>plaintiff</u> in the suit. When a legal proceeding is begun, there are certain <u>legal procedures</u> that must be followed to assure that <u>due process</u> is granted to all parties of a suit. Our system of justice strives to apply the law fairly and justly to every person involved in a <u>litigation</u>. When a <u>party</u> starts an <u>action</u>, the person charged with a wrongdoing is called the <u>defendant</u>. A party or <u>litigant</u> can be any person involved in or affected by the legal proceeding. The parties to a litigation are seeking <u>justice</u> by following a course of legal procedures usually referred to

_____

_____

_____

_____

_____

_____

_____

_____

_____

_____

_____

_____

_____

_____

_____

_____

as due process. A <u>suit</u>, litigation, proceeding, and action all refer to a dispute in a court of law whereby one seeks relief or recovery from another who has caused injury to or violated the rights of that person. Every person is entitled to due process in our system of justice. The word <u>versus</u> means against. In the title of a suit, action, litigation, or proceeding, the plaintiff's name is first, followed by "versus," then the defendant's name. Versus may be abbreviated "vs." or "v." <u>Et alius</u>, abbreviated et al., means "and others." A judge may refer to a group of plaintiffs or defendants by using the name of the first one listed followed by et al. This means that all the others are also included.

Transcribing from Dictation

Directions: This dictation emphasizes and reinforces the legal terms and definitions you have studied. Listen carefully to the pronunciation of each of the legal terms. Unless otherwise directed, use a 70-space line and double spacing. Correct all errors. Follow one of the procedures below.

Typing Procedure

Using the cassette from Lesson 2, Part B, transcribe the dictation directly at your typewriter.

Shorthand Procedure

Using the cassette from Lesson 2, Part B, take the dictation using your shorthand system and then transcribe on the typewriter from your shorthand notes.

When you have finished transcribing Part B of the practice dictation, check your transcript with the printed copy. If you have made any mistakes in the transcription, you should practice those words several times before going on to Evaluation 1.

Check List

	PART A, DATE	PART B, DATE	SUBMITTED TO INSTRUCTOR	
			YES	NO
Terminology and Definitions	_____	_____	____	____
*Typing Legal Terms	_____	_____	____	____
Words	_____	_____	____	____
Sentences	_____	_____	____	____
*Transcribing from Dictation	_____	_____	____	____
Quiz No. 1	_____	_____	____	____
Quiz No. 2	_____	_____	____	____

When you have successfully completed all the exercises in this lesson and submitted to your instructor those called for, you are ready to proceed with Evaluation 1.

*If you are using a shorthand system, turn in to your instructor your shorthand notes along with your transcript.

Quiz No. 1

Terminology and Definition Recall

Directions: In the Answers column write the letter from Column I that represents the word or phrase that best matches each item in Column II. After you have completed this quiz, check your answers with the key on page 331. Unless otherwise directed, turn in this quiz to your instructor upon completion of this lesson.

COLUMN I	COLUMN II	ANSWERS
A. bar	**1.** The legal profession as a whole.	1. _____
B. bench	**2.** A dictionary of legal terms.	2. _____
C. code books	**3.** A court of law. Also, the judge's seat in a court of law.	3. _____
D. codes	**4.** The Latin term for law.	4. _____
E. Corpus Juris Secundum	**5.** An encyclopedia of laws commonly used as a reference by lawyers.	5. _____
F. defense attorney	**6.** The philosophy or science of law.	6. _____
G. esquire	**7.** One who acts in his or her own person without the assistance of an attorney.	7. _____
H. in propria persona	**8.** One who has a thorough knowledge of law and has written extensively on legal subjects.	8. _____
I. judge	**9.** Books which contain the laws that have been created by state and federal legislatures.	9. _____
J. jurisprudence	**10.** The presiding officer in a court of law.	10. _____
K. jurist	**11.** A law created by a state or federal legislature.	11. _____
L. lex	**12.** One who represents the defendant in court cases or other legal matters.	12. _____
M. lexicon	**13.** An appointed or elected official who represents the people or the state in criminal cases.	13. _____
N. prosecuting attorney	**14.** A title which is written after the surname of an attorney.	14. _____
O. statute		

Turn back to page 12 and continue with this lesson.

Quiz No. 2

Terminology and Definition Recall

Directions: In the Answers column at the right of each statement, write the letter that represents the word, or group of words, that correctly completes the statement. After you have completed this quiz, check your answers with the key on page 331. Unless otherwise directed, turn in this quiz to your instructor upon completion of this lesson.

ANSWERS

1. The word in the title of a case which means "against" is (a) lexicon, (b) action, (c) versus. . . . .   1. _____

2. The one against whom an action, suit, or proceeding is started in a court of law is the (a) plaintiff, (b) defendant, (c) party. . . . .   2. _____

3. Any person involved in or affected by a legal proceeding is a/an (a) party, (b) defendant, (c) attorney. . . . .   3. _____

4. A legal proceeding or suit in a court of law by which one person seeks recovery from another for an injury or a violated right is a/an (a) legal procedure, (b) action, (c) litigant. . . . .   4. _____

5. One who employs an attorney to represent or advise that person in court cases or legal matters is a (a) plaintiff, (b) jurist, (c) client. . . . .   5. _____

6. One who starts an action, suit, or proceeding in a court of law is a (a) plaintiff, (b) defendant, (c) party. . . . .   6. _____

7. The method to be followed in any action in a court of law is known as a (a) litigation, (b) legal procedure, (c) suit. . . . .   7. _____

8. The legal procedure established which provides that every person has the benefit and protection of the law is (a) due process, (b) action, (c) litigation.   8. _____

9. The legal term meaning "and others" is (a) litigant, (b) versus, (c) et alius.   9. _____

10. A party to an action, suit, or legal proceeding is also called a (a) plaintiff, (b) defendant, (c) litigant. . . . .   10. _____

11. A just and fair application of law for every person is (a) justice, (b) suit, (c) action. . . . .   11. _____

12. Any proceeding whereby one seeks recovery from another who has caused injury to or violated the rights of that person is a (a) suit, (b) party, (c) versus.   12. _____

13. Any action in a court of law whereby one seeks recovery from another who has caused injury to or violated the rights of that person is a (a) legal procedure, (b) proceeding, (c) due process. . . . .   13. _____

14. The legal action or suit in a court of law whereby one seeks recovery from another who has caused injury to or violated the rights of that person is a (a) litigation, (b) party, (c) versus. . . . .   14. _____

Turn back to page 15 and continue with this lesson.

 **EVALUATION No. 1**

Student _____

Class _____ Date _____

SECTION A

Directions: This dictation/transcription evaluation will test your spelling and transcription ability on the legal terms that you studied in the two preceding lessons. Use a 5-space paragraph indention, a 70-space line and double spacing unless otherwise instructed. Correct all errors. Follow one of the procedures below.

Typing Procedure

Using the cassette from Evaluation 1, transcribe the dictation directly at your typewriter.

Shorthand Procedure

Using the cassette from Evaluation 1, take the dictation using your shorthand system and then transcribe on the typewriter from your shorthand notes.

SECTIONS B AND C ARE AVAILABLE FROM YOUR INSTRUCTOR.

LESSON 3

To Wit: General Legal Terms

Terms which describe the various types of pleadings, related terms, and some general legal terms are presented in the following exercises.

When you complete this lesson, you should have a knowledge and understanding of terminology involving pleadings and other general legal activities.

Part A	Terminology and Definitions

Directions: Study the terms, pronunciations, and definitions until you are thoroughly familiar with them. In order to complete this lesson successfully, you must understand the meaning and usage of all the legal terms presented. If you are using shorthand, write your shorthand outline in the space provided or on your shorthand machine for each legal term.

LEGAL TERM	PRONUNCIATION	DEFINITION	SHORTHAND OUTLINE
1. pleadings	′plēd-iŋs	All the claims and defenses of the parties to a lawsuit.	_____
2. complaint	kəm-′plānt	The first pleading filed in a civil action whereby the plaintiff states the facts on which the suit is based.	_____
3. petition	pə-′tish-ən	A written application to the court for action upon a legal matter.	_____
4. declaration	dek-lə-′rā-shən	Another name for a first pleading filed in a civil action whereby the plaintiff states the facts on which the suit is based.	_____
5. bill	bil	Another name for a first pleading filed in a civil action whereby the plaintiff states the facts on which the suit is based.	_____

6. narratio	na-'rā-shē-ō	The Latin word for the first pleading filed in a civil action by the plaintiff in which the facts for the basis of the suit are stated.	_____
7. gravamen	grə-'vā-mən	The grievance or injury specifically complained of in a pleading.	_____
8. count	kau̇nt	The various charges in a complaint or declaration made by the plaintiff against a defendant.	_____
9. retainer	ri-'tā-nər	The fee a client pays to an attorney for representation or assistance in a legal matter.	_____
10. champerty	'cham-pərt-ē	An illegal procedure whereby one not involved in the lawsuit makes a deal with a party to the suit to pay the costs of the litigation in exchange for a share of the proceeds from the suit.	_____
11. adjudicate	ə-'jüd-i-kāt	To decide a case by law.	_____
12. contest	kən-'test	To dispute the plaintiff's claim in a court of law.	_____
13. writ	rit	A written command issued by a court which requires some specified action.	_____
14. tribunal	trī-'byün-l	A court of justice. Also, all the judges in a particular jurisdiction.	_____

Turn to page 31 and complete Quiz No. 1 before continuing this lesson.

Typing Legal Terms

Directions: Unless otherwise instructed, use a 70-space line and double spacing. Correct all errors. Follow one of the procedures below.

Words

Typing Procedure

On a separate sheet of paper, type the following words at least two times, concentrating on the correct spelling and pronunciation.

Shorthand Procedure

On a separate sheet of paper, type the following words once, concentrating on the correct spelling and pronunciation. Then write the shorthand outline for each word on the lines to the right or on your shorthand machine. Cover the printed words with a sheet of paper and transcribe from the shorthand outlines one time on your typewriter.

pleadings / complaint / petition / declaration /

bill / narratio / gravamen / count / retainer /

champerty / adjudicate / contest / writ /

tribunal /

Sentences

Typing Procedure

Type each of the following sentences one time. Concentrate on the correct spelling and pronunciation of each underlined legal term.

Shorthand Procedure

Write the correct shorthand outlines for the following sentences on the lines to the right or on your shorthand machine. Cover the printed material with a sheet of paper and transcribe from your shorthand outlines one time on the typewriter.

These sentences will be used for the practice dictation on the cassettes.

A retainer is the fee which the client pays to an attorney for representation or assistance in a legal matter. The pleadings are the claims and defenses of the parties to a lawsuit. A court of law is also called a tribunal. Tribunal may also refer to all the judges in a particular jurisdiction. A complaint states the facts upon which the plaintiff bases the litigation. Depending upon that state, court, and type of proceeding, an initial pleading in a suit may be referred to as a complaint, a declaration, a petition, a bill, or a narratio. Once a client has retained an attorney for representation in a legal matter, the attorney will prepare a complaint, petition, bill, declaration, or narratio which will state the facts on which the suit is based. A count is one of the various charges in a complaint or declaration made by the plaintiff against a defendant. Gravamen is the grievance or injury specifically complained of in a pleading. Champerty is an illegal procedure whereby one not involved in the lawsuit makes a deal with a party to the suit to pay the costs of the litigation in exchange for a share of the proceeds. To adjudicate a case is to decide or settle it in a court of law or a tribunal. If the defendant disputes the plaintiff's claim in a court of law, the defendant is said to <u>contest</u> the _____

plaintiff's claim. A <u>writ</u> issued by a court is a _____

written command which requires some specified _____

action such as the beginning of a suit or other _____

proceeding. _____

Transcribing from Dictation

Directions: This dictation emphasizes and reinforces the legal terms and definitions you have studied. Listen carefully to the pronunciation of each of the legal terms. Unless otherwise directed, use a 70-space line and double spacing. Correct all errors. Follow one of the procedures below.

Typing Procedure

Using the cassette from Lesson 3, Part A, transcribe the dictation directly at your typewriter.

Shorthand Procedure

Using the cassette from Lesson 3, Part A, take the dictation using your shorthand system and then transcribe on the typewriter from your shorthand notes.

When you have finished transcribing Part A of the practice dictation, check your transcript with the printed copy. If you made any mistakes in the transcription, you should practice those words several times before going on.

Part B | Terminology and Definitions

Directions: Study the terms, pronunciations, and definitions until you are thoroughly familiar with them. In order to complete this lesson successfully, you must understand the meaning and usage of all the legal terms presented. If you are using shorthand, write your shorthand outline in the space provided or on your shorthand machine for each legal term.

LEGAL TERM	PRONUNCIATION	DEFINITION	SHORTHAND OUTLINE
1. ignorantia legis non excusat	'ig-nrən-shē-ə 'lē-jəs nän ik-'skyü-zət	Latin. "Ignorance of the law is no excuse."	_____
2. statute of limitations	'stach-üt əv lim-ə-'tā-shəns	A law that requires an action to be started within a certain length of time after the alleged cause occurred.	_____
3. statute of frauds	'stach-üt əv fröds	An act which requires that certain kinds of contracts must be in writing and signed before an action based on the contracts can be instituted.	_____
4. sui juris	'sü-ī 'jur-əs	Latin. One that is legally capable of managing one's own actions or affairs.	_____

5. minor	'mī-nər	One who is too young to be considered as legally competent. Also referred to as an infant.	_____
6. act of God	akt əv gäd	A disaster which occurs as a result of natural causes unaided by any human action.	_____
7. alias	'ā-lē-əs	Latin. "Otherwise." An assumed name by which one is also known.	_____
8. double jeopardy	'dəb-əl 'jep-ərd-ē	A second prosecution for the same offense. Our laws prohibit double jeopardy.	_____
9. jointly and severally	'joint-lē ən 'sev-rəl-lē	When a liability involves more than one party, they may all be sued together or they may be sued separately.	_____
10. per se	pər-'sā	Latin. "In itself or by itself."	_____
11. malicious prosecution	mə-'lish-əs präs-i-'kyü-shən	An action started by a plaintiff without justification and with the intention of damaging the defendant.	_____
12. feasance	'fēz-ns	The proper performance of a legal act.	_____
13. malfeasance	mal-'fēz-ns	The performance of an illegal act. Misconduct.	_____
14. allege	ə-'lej	To make an allegation or charge.	_____

Turn to page 32 and complete Quiz No. 2 before continuing this lesson.

Typing Legal Terms

Directions: Unless otherwise instructed, use a 70-space line and double spacing. Correct all errors. Follow one of the procedures below.

Words

Typing Procedure

On a separate sheet of paper, type the following words at least two times, concentrating on the correct spelling and pronunciation.

Shorthand Procedure

On a separate sheet of paper, type the following words once, concentrating on the correct spelling and pronunciation. Then write the shorthand outline for each word on the lines to the right or on your shorthand machine. Cover the printed words with a sheet of paper and transcribe from the shorthand outlines one time on your typewriter.

ignorantia legis non excusat / statute of

limitations / statute of frauds / sui juris /

minor / act of God / alias / double jeopardy /

_____

_____

_____

jointly and severally / per se / malicious

prosecution/ feasance / malfeasance / allege

_____

_____

Sentences

Typing Procedure

Type each of the following sentences one time. Concentrate on the correct spelling and pronunciation of each underlined legal term.

Shorthand Procedure

Write the correct shorthand outlines for the following sentences on the lines to the right or on your shorthand machine. Cover the printed material with a sheet of paper and transcribe from your shorthand outlines one time on the typewriter.

These sentences will be used for practice dictation on the cassettes.

The statute of limitations is a law that requires an action to be started within a certain length of time after the alleged cause occurred. The statute of frauds is an act which requires that certain kinds of contracts must be in writing before an action based on the contracts can be instituted. A minor is one who is too young to be considered legally competent, but sui juris refers to one that is legally capable of managing one's own actions. Ignorantia legis non excusat is a Latin phrase meaning that ignorance of the law is no excuse. Just because one does not know the law, it does not excuse him or her from breaking the law. If a person is called by an assumed name, the person is said to have an alias. An act of God is a disaster which occurs as a result of natural causes unaided by any human action. A person cannot be held responsible for an act of God. Double jeopardy, which means a second prosecution for the same offense, is forbidden under our laws. Jointly and severally refers to a situation where there is more than one party responsible for a liability and they may all be sued together or they may be sued separately. Per se is a Latin term meaning by itself or in itself. The proper performance of a legal act is feasance, but the performance of an illegal act or misconduct is called malfeasance. Allege means to make a charge

_____
_____
_____
_____
_____
_____
_____
_____
_____
_____
_____
_____
_____
_____
_____
_____
_____
_____
_____
_____
_____
_____

or allegation. The plaintiffs in the case allege that _____

the defendant is guilty of malfeasance. <u>Malicious</u> _____

<u>prosecution</u> cases terminate in favor of the _____

defendant because the plaintiff started the action _____

without justification and with the intention of _____

damaging the defendant. _____

Transcribing from Dictation

Directions: This dictation emphasizes and reinforces the legal terms and definitions you have studied. Listen carefully to the pronunciation of each of the legal terms. Unless otherwise directed, use a 70-space line and double spacing. Correct all errors. Follow one of the procedures below.

Typing Procedure

Using the cassette from Lesson 3, Part B, transcribe the dictation directly at your typewriter.

Shorthand Procedure

Using the cassette from Lesson 3, Part B, take the dictation using your shorthand system and then transcribe on the typewriter from your shorthand notes.

When you have finished transcribing Part B of the practice dictation, check your transcript with the printed copy. If you have made any mistakes in the transcription, you should practice those words several times before going on to Lesson 4.

Check List

	PART A, DATE	PART B, DATE	SUBMITTED TO INSTRUCTOR	
			YES	NO
Terminology and Definitions				
*Typing Legal Terms				
Words				
Sentences				
*Transcribing from Dictation				
Quiz No. 1				
Quiz No. 2				

When you have successfully completed all the exercises in this lesson and submitted to your instructor those called for, you are ready to proceed with Lesson 4.

*If you are using a shorthand system, turn in to your instructor your shorthand notes along with your transcript.

Quiz No. 1

Terminology and Definition Recall

Directions: In the Answers column at the right of each statement, write the letter that represents the word, or group of words, that correctly completes the statement. After you have completed this quiz, check your answers with the key on page 331. Unless otherwise directed, turn in this quiz to your instructor upon completion of this lesson.

ANSWERS

1. A Latin term which is the first pleading filed in an action by a plaintiff is (a) narratio, (b) tribunal, (c) writ ....

1. _____

2. The grievance or injury specifically complained of in a pleading is (a) count, (b) gravamen, (c) complaint. ....

2. _____

3. A court of justice is also referred to as a (a) champerty, (b) tribunal, (c) contest ....

3. _____

4. The first pleading filed in an action by the plaintiff is a (a) count, (b) champerty, (c) declaration ....

4. _____

5. All the claims and defenses of the parties to a lawsuit are known as the (a) retainers, (b) writs, (c) pleadings ....

5. _____

6. Which of the following is not a form of pleading in a court of law: (a) complaint, (b) writ, (c) declaration ....

6. _____

7. A written command issued by a court which requires a specific action is called a (a) complaint, (b) narratio, (c) writ ....

7. _____

8. An illegal procedure whereby one not involved in the lawsuit makes a deal with a party to the suit to pay the costs of the litigation in exchange for a share of the proceeds is called (a) champerty, (b) declaration, (c) petition..................

8. _____

9. The fee that a client pays to an attorney for representation or assistance in a legal matter is a (a) retainer, (b) writ, (c) bill...

9. _____

10. A complaint filed in court by the plaintiff stating the plaintiff's allegations is a (a) tribunal, (b) bill, (c) retainer...

10. _____

11. To dispute the plaintiff's claim in a court of law is to (a) contest, (b) count, (c) adjudicate ....

11. _____

12. To decide a case by law is to (a) narratio, (b) contest, (c) adjudicate ....

12. _____

13. The first pleading filed in a civil action whereby the plaintiff states facts on which the suit is based is a (a) count, (b) complaint, (c) contest ....

13. _____

14. The charge in a complaint or declaration made by the plaintiff against a defendant is called a (a) count, (b) narratio, (c) pleading ....

14. _____

15. A written application to the court for action upon a legal matter is a (a) writ, (b) contest, (c) petition...

15. _____

Turn back to page 24 and continue with this lesson.

Quiz No. 2

Terminology and Definition Recall

Directions: In the Answers column write the legal term that is most representative of the corresponding statement. After you have completed this quiz, check your answers with the key on page 331. Unless otherwise directed, turn in this quiz to your instructor upon completion of this lesson.

ANSWERS

1. One who is too young to be considered as legally competent is a/an _____.

1. _____

2. An assumed name or a second name by which one is also known is referred to in Latin as a/an _____.

2. _____

3. To make a charge or allegation that someone committed a wrongful act is to _____.

3. _____

4. A law that requires an action to be started within a certain length of time after the alleged cause occurred is the _____.

4. _____

5. Misconduct or the performance of an illegal act is _____.

5. _____

6. A second prosecution for the same offense is called _____.

6. _____

7. Double jeopardy (is, is not) permitted under common law and constitutional law.

7. _____

8. An act which requires that certain kinds of contracts must be in writing and signed before an action based on the contracts can be instituted is the _____.

8. _____

9. The proper performance of a legal act is known as _____.

9. _____

10. When a liability involves more than one party and they may all be sued together or they may be sued separately, it is expressed as _____.

10. _____

11. A Latin term which means that one is legally capable of managing one's own actions or affairs is _____.

11. _____

12. An action started by a plaintiff without justification and with the intention of damaging the defendant is a/an _____.

12. _____

13. The Latin phrase which means that ignorance of the law is no excuse is _____.

13. _____

14. A Latin term meaning "in itself" or "by itself" is _____.

14. _____

15. A disaster which occurs as a result of natural causes unaided by any human action is a/an _____.

15. _____

Turn back to page 27 and continue with this lesson.

"Legal justice is the art of the good and the fair."

—Legal Maxim

LESSON 4

To Wit: General Legal Terms

This lesson continues the study of some of the general legal terms which are applicable to all areas of law. When you have completed these exercises, you will have a knowledge and understanding of the most common general legal terminology. This information will give you a good background for studying the terms dealing with specific legal procedures and the various areas of law.

Part A	Terminology and Definitions

Directions: Study the terms, pronunciations, and definitions until you are thoroughly familiar with them. In order to complete this lesson successfully, you must understand the meaning and usage of all the legal terms presented. If you are using shorthand, write your shorthand outline in the space provided or on your shorthand machine for each legal term.

LEGAL TERM	PRONUNCIATION	DEFINITION	SHORTHAND OUTLINE
1. cause of action	'koz əv 'ak-shən	The facts which are the basis for a lawsuit.	_____
2. ipso facto	'ip-sō 'fak-tō	Latin. "By the fact itself."	_____
3. ancillary	'an-sə-ler-ē	A secondary proceeding which is based upon another proceeding. An example of an ancillary proceeding would be a situation where a person who dies owned property in a state other than the one where the person lived. The will would be probated in the state in which that person had lived, and an ancillary proceeding would be filed in the other state in which property was owned.	_____
4. sui generis	'sü-ī 'jen-ə-rəs	Latin. "Of its own kind." "Unique."	_____
5. to wit	tü wit	Namely. Scilicet. When used in legal documents, it is preceded by a general term and followed by a term which specifically identifies the general term, for example, assault with a deadly weapon, to wit: a gun.	_____

6.	scilicet	'sī-lə-set	Latin. "To wit." "Namely."	_____
7.	seal	sēl	A sign or impression used to certify that a document or instrument is genuine.	_____
8.	locus sigilli	'lō-kəs si-'jil-ī	Latin. The place of the seal. Abbreviation L.S. is often used.	_____
9.	notary public	'nōt-ə-rē 'pəb-lik	A public officer who is authorized to administer oaths and to certify that documents or instruments are genuine.	_____
10.	testimonium clause	tes-tə-'mō-nē-əm klȯz	A clause at the end of a document which states that the parties have signed under oath as to the document's contents.	_____
11.	acknowledgment	ik-'näl-ij-mənt	A formal statement made before an authorized person, usually a notary public, whereby one states that the instrument was signed willfully and freely.	_____
12.	endorsement	in-'dȯr-smənt	Information written on the back of a legal document.	_____
13.	legal back	'lē-gəl bak	A cover prepared for legal documents on which the endorsement is usually typed. Usually includes the names of the parties, the document title, the date executed, and the attorney's name or law firm which prepared it.	_____
14.	interpolate	in-'tər-pə-lāt	To alter a document by adding an additional word or words.	_____

Turn to page 41 and complete Quiz No. 1 before continuing this lesson.

Typing Legal Terms

Directions: Unless otherwise instructed, use a 70-space line and double spacing. Correct all errors. Follow one of the procedures below.

Words

Typing Procedure

On a separate sheet of paper, type the following words at least two times, concentrating on the correct spelling and pronunciation.

Shorthand Procedure

On a separate sheet of paper, type the following words once, concentrating on the correct spelling and pronunciation. Then write the shorthand outline for each word on the lines to the right or on your shorthand machine. Cover the printed words with a sheet of paper and transcribe from the shorthand outlines one time on your typewriter.

cause of action / ipso facto / ancillary / sui
generis / to wit / scilicet / seal / locus sigilli /
notary public / testimonium clause /
acknowledgment / endorsement / legal back /
interpolate /

Sentences

Typing Procedure

Type each of the following sentences one time.
Concentrate on the correct spelling and pronunciation of each underlined legal term.

Shorthand Procedure

Write the correct shorthand outlines for the following sentences on the lines to the right or on your
shorthand machine. Cover the printed material with
a sheet of paper and transcribe from your shorthand
outlines one time on the typewriter.

These sentences will be used for practice dictation on the cassettes.

Cause of action refers to the facts which are the
basis for a lawsuit. An ancillary proceeding is a
secondary proceeding which is based upon another
proceeding. Ipso facto is a Latin term meaning "by
the fact itself." To wit and scilicet are synonymous
terms. Scilicet is the Latin word for to wit. Scilicet
and to wit mean "that is to say" or "namely" and
are used in legal documents preceded by a general
term and followed by a term which specifically
identifies the general term. Documents or
instruments are certified as genuine by a notary
public. A notary public may also administer oaths.
The notary public seal is a sign or impression used
to certify that a document or an instrument is
genuine. Locus sigilli is a Latin term meaning the
place of the seal. The place where the seal is on a
legal document is usually indicated by L.S., the
abbreviation for locus sigilli. The testimonium
clause is a clause at the end of a document which
states that the parties have signed under oath as to
the document's contents. An acknowledgment,
made before an authorized person, usually states
that the party willfully and freely signed the
instrument. To interpolate is to alter a document by

adding an additional word or words. An _____
endorsement is information written on the back of a _____
legal document. Legal backs are covers prepared for _____
legal documents and provide a place for the _____
endorsement. The endorsement on the back of a _____
legal document usually includes the names of the _____
parties, the title of the document, the date _____
executed, and the attorney's name. The Latin term _____
sui generis means "of its own kind" or "unique."

Transcribing from Dictation

Directions: This dictation emphasizes and reinforces the legal terms and definitions you have studied. Listen carefully to the pronunciation of each of the legal terms. Unless otherwise directed, use a 70-space line and double spacing. Correct all errors. Follow one of the procedures below.

Typing Procedure

Using the cassette from Lesson 4, Part A, transcribe the dictation directly at your typewriter.

Shorthand Procedure

Using the cassette from Lesson 4, Part A, take the dictation using your shorthand system and then transcribe on the typewriter from your shorthand notes.

When you have finished transcribing Part A of the practice dictation, check your transcript with the printed copy. If you made any mistakes in the transcription, you should practice those words several times before going on.

Part B Terminology and Definitions

Directions: Study the terms, pronunciations, and definitions until you are thoroughly familiar with them. In order to complete this lesson successfully, you must understand the meaning and usage of all the legal terms presented. If you are using shorthand, write your shorthand outline in the space provided or on your shorthand machine for each legal term.

LEGAL TERM	PRONUNCIATION	DEFINITION	SHORTHAND OUTLINE
1. chose in action	'shōz in 'ak-shən	Personal property which one has a right to but which is in the possession of another. Such property may be recovered through a lawsuit.	_____
2. quasi	'kwā-zī	Latin. Almost but not actually the same as. This term is usually used with another term, for example, quasi ex contractu which means "as if from a contract."	_____

3. fraud	frȯd	A misrepresentation of the facts done intentionally to deceive or mislead another.	_____
4. collusion	kə-ʹlü-zhən	When two or more persons secretly agree to participate in a fraudulent act.	_____
5. duress	du̇-ʹres	The use of force to get someone to do something unwillingly.	_____
6. irrevocable	ir-ʹev-ə-kə-bəl	Something that is final and cannot be undone or taken back.	_____
7. penal	ʹpēn-l	Having to do with punishment or a penalty.	_____
8. ensue	in-ʹsü	To follow or to come after.	_____
9. recidivist	ri-ʹsid-ə-vəst	One who repeats criminal acts and cannot be reformed.	_____
10. incriminate	in-ʹkrim-ə-nāt	To accuse one of a crime. Also to put oneself or another in danger of being charged with a crime.	_____
11. malice	ʹmal-əs	Purposely doing something which will harm another. An evil intent.	_____
12. turpitude	ʹtər-pə-tüd	Something which is corrupt, shameful, wicked, or immoral.	_____
13. mens rea	menz ʹrē-ə	Latin. A guilty mind or a criminal intent.	_____

Turn to page 42 and complete Quiz No. 2 before continuing this lesson.

Typing Legal Terms

Directions: Unless otherwise instructed, use a 70-space line and double spacing. Correct all errors. Follow one of the procedures below.

Words

Typing Procedure

On a sheet of paper, type the following words at least two times, concentrating on the correct spelling and pronunciation.

Shorthand Procedure

On a separate sheet of paper, type the following words once, concentrating on the correct spelling and pronunciation. Then write the shorthand outline for each word on the lines to the right or on your shorthand machine. Cover the printed words with a sheet of paper and transcribe from the shorthand outlines one time on your typewriter.

chose in action / quasi / fraud / collusion /

_____

duress / irrevocable / penal / ensue /

_____

recidivist / incriminate / malice / turpitude /

_____

mens rea /

_____

Sentences

Typing Procedure

Type each of the following sentences one time. Concentrate on the correct spelling and pronunciation of each underlined legal term.

Shorthand Procedure

Write the correct shorthand outlines for the following sentences on the lines to the right or on your shorthand machine. Cover the printed material with a sheet of paper and transcribe from your shorthand outlines one time on the typewriter.

These sentences will be used for practice dictation on the cassettes.

Collusion, fraud, duress, malice, turpitude, and mens rea are all terms that refer to some kind of an illegal act. If you make an agreement with another person to defraud someone of their rights or to obtain an object forbidden by law, it is collusion. If a person intentionally lies for the purpose of deceiving or misleading another, that person is guilty of fraud. Therefore, if only one person is involved in committing the illegal act, it is fraud. If two or more persons are involved, it is collusion. Duress is the use of force to get someone to do something unwillingly. Duress, fraud, and collusion all involve malice and mens rea because the intent is evil and wrongful. Turpitude also applies to something which is corrupt, shameful, wicked, or immoral. Quasi is used to indicate that something is almost but not actually the same as. Quasi-legal matter would refer to one that is almost but not entirely a legal matter. A chose in action is a right to personal property which is in the possession of another. A chose in action may be recovered through a lawsuit. If an act or deed is final and cannot be undone or changed, it is said to be irrevocable. Incriminate is

_____
_____
_____
_____
_____
_____
_____
_____
_____
_____
_____
_____
_____
_____
_____
_____
_____
_____
_____
_____
_____

38

a term which means to accuse one of a crime or to put onself or another in danger of being charged with a crime. Penal refers to something having to do with punishment or a penalty. A recidivist, one who repeats criminal acts and cannot be reformed, would probably spend many years in a penal institution. To ensue is to follow or to come after.

_____

_____

_____

_____

_____

_____

_____

_____

Transcribing from Dictation

Directions: This dictation emphasizes and reinforces the legal terms and definitions you have studied. Listen carefully to the pronunciation of each of the legal terms. Unless otherwise directed, use a 70-space line and double spacing. Correct all errors. Follow one of the procedures below.

Typing Procedure

Using the cassette from Lesson 4, Part B, transcribe the dictation directly at your typewriter.

Shorthand Procedure

Using the cassette from Lesson 4, Part B, take the dictation using your shorthand system and then transcribe on the typewriter from your shorthand notes.

When you have finished transcribing Part B of the practice dictation, check your transcript with the printed copy. If you have made any mistakes in the transcription, you should practice those words several times before going on to Evaluation 2.

Check List

	PART A, DATE	PART B, DATE	SUBMITTED TO INSTRUCTOR	
			YES	NO
Terminology and Definitions	_____	_____	_____	_____
*Typing Legal Terms	_____	_____	_____	_____
Words	_____	_____	_____	_____
Sentences	_____	_____	_____	_____
*Transcribing from Dictation	_____	_____	_____	_____
Quiz No. 1	_____	_____	_____	_____
Quiz No. 2	_____	_____	_____	_____

When you have successfully completed all the exercises in this lesson and submitted to your instructor those called for, you are ready to proceed with Evaluation 2.

*If you are using a shorthand system, turn in to your instructor your shorthand notes along with your transcript.

Quiz No. 1

Terminology and Definition Recall

Directions: In the Answers column write the letter from Column I that represents the word or phrase that best matches each item in Column II. After you have completed this quiz, check your answers with the key on page 332. Unless otherwise directed, turn in this quiz to your instructor upon completion of this lesson.

COLUMN I	COLUMN II	ANSWERS
A. acknowledgment	**1.** A sign or impression used to certify that a document or instrument is genuine.	**1.** _____
B. ancilliary	**2.** The facts which are the basis for a lawsuit.	**2.** _____
C. cause of action	**3.** To alter a document by adding an additional word or words.	**3.** _____
D. endorsement	**4.** Latin term for to wit.	**4.** _____
E. interpolate	**5.** A secondary proceeding which is based upon another proceeding.	**5.** _____
F. ipso facto	**6.** A public officer who is authorized to administer oaths and to certify that documents or instruments are genuine.	**6.** _____
G. legal back	**7.** Information written on the back of a legal document.	**7.** _____
H. locus sigilli	**8.** Namely, scilicet; when used in legal documents, it is preceded by a general term and followed by a term which specifically identifies the general term.	**8.** _____
I. notary public		
J. scilicet	**9.** A cover prepared for legal documents on which the endorsement is typed.	**9.** _____
K. seal	**10.** The place of the seal.	**10.** _____
L. sui generis	**11.** Of its own kind; unique.	**11.** _____
M. sui juris	**12.** A formal statement made before an authorized person, usually a notary public, whereby one states that the instrument was signed willfully and freely.	**12.** _____
N. testimonium clause		
O. to wit	**13.** A clause at the end of a document which states that the parties have signed under oath as to the document's contents.	**13.** _____
	14. By the fact itself.	**14.** _____

Turn back to page 34 and continue with this lesson.

Quiz No. 2

Terminology and Definition Recall

Directions: In the Answers column write the legal term that is most representative of the corresponding statement. After you have completed this quiz, check your answers with the key on page 332. Unless otherwise directed, turn in this quiz to your instructor upon completion of this lesson.

ANSWERS

1. Intangible personal property which one has a right to but which is in the possession of another and may be recovered through a lawsuit is _____.

1. _____

2. Purposely doing something which will harm another or an evil intent is _____.

2. _____

3. A legal term which refers to punishment or a penalty is _____.

3. _____

4. A misrepresentation of the facts done intentionally to deceive or mislead another is _____.

4. _____

5. When two or more persons secretly agree to participate in a fraudulent act, it is called _____.

5. _____

6. Something which is corrupt, shameful, wicked, or immoral is _____.

6. _____

7. To follow or to come after is to _____.

7. _____

8. Something that is final and cannot be undone or taken back is _____.

8. _____

9. A Latin term which means "almost but not actually the same as" is _____.

9. _____

10. One who repeats criminal acts and cannot be reformed is a/an _____.

10. _____

11. The use of force to get someone to do something unwillingly is _____.

11. _____

12. A guilty mind or a criminal intent expressed in Latin is _____.

12. _____

13. To accuse one of a crime or to put oneself or another in danger of being charged with a crime is to _____.

13. _____

Turn back to page 37 and continue with this lesson.

╚╚╚EVALUATION No. 2

Student_____

Class _____ Date_____

SCORING RECORD

	Perfect Score	Student's Score
Section A	50	
Section B	20	
Section C	30	
Total	100	

SECTION A

Directions: This dictation/transcription evaluation will test your spelling and transcription ability on the legal terms that you studied in the two preceding lessons. Use a 5-space paragraph indention, a 70-space line and double spacing unless otherwise instructed. Correct all errors. Follow one of the procedures below.

Typing Procedure

Using the cassette from Evaluation 2, transcribe the dictation directly at your typewriter.

Shorthand Procedure

Using the cassette from Evaluation 2, take the dictation using your shorthand system and then transcribe on the typewriter from your shorthand notes.

SECTIONS B AND C ARE AVAILABLE FROM YOUR INSTRUCTOR.

LESSON 5

To Wit: Litigation—Pretrial

There are many pretrial activities which precede the actual trial in a lawsuit. The terms to be studied in the following exercises will acquaint you with the terminology involved with pretrial activities. To successfully complete this lesson, you should be able to correctly spell, define, pronounce, and transcribe from dictation each of the terms presented.

Part A	Terminology and Definitions

Directions: Study the terms, pronunciations, and definitions until you are thoroughly familiar with them. In order to complete this lesson successfully, you must understand the meaning and usage of all the legal terms presented. If you are using shorthand, write your shorthand outline in the space provided or on your shorthand machine for each legal term.

LEGAL TERM	PRONUNCIATION	DEFINITION	SHORTHAND OUTLINE
1. case title	kās 'tit-l	The part of a legal document that contains the names of the parties to the suit.	_____
2. Doe clause	dō klòz	Fictitious names in a case title. When the name or names of all defendants involved are not known, the unknown defendants are usually referred to as John and Mary Doe.	_____
3. caption	'kap-shən	The title page of a court document which includes the case title, the jurisdiction, the venue, the court number, and the document title.	_____
4. jurisdiction	jùr-əs-'dik-shən	The right or authority of a court to hear and adjudge cases.	_____
5. venue	'ven-yü	The geographical location where a case is tried.	_____
6. filed	fīld	Papers which are placed with the clerk of a court.	_____

7. summons	'səm-ənz	A writ which notifies a defendant that a lawsuit has been filed and an appearance must be made before the court at a specified time to answer to the charges.	_____
8. service	'sər-vəs	The delivery of a summons to the person named therein.	_____
9. appearance	ə-'pir-əns	To be present in court as a party to a law-suit.	_____
10. answer	'an-sər	A pleading which states the defendant's defense against the plaintiff's claims.	_____
11. demurrer to complaint	di-'mər-ər tü kəm-'plānt	Disputes the sufficiency in law of the pleading of the other side.	_____
12. bill of particulars	bil əv pə-'tik-ə-lərs	The detailed facts upon which a complaint is based. Usually supplied by the plaintiff upon the request of the defendant.	_____
13. prayer for relief	'prā-ər fər ri-'lēf	The summary at the end of a complaint which requests the court to grant the plaintiff's demands.	_____
14. ad damnum clause	ad 'dam-nən klòz	Latin. A clause in a complaint which states the plaintiff's damage.	_____

Turn to page 53 and complete Quiz No. 1 before continuing this lesson.

Typing Legal Terms

Directions: Unless otherwise instructed, use a 70-space line and double spacing. Correct all errors. Follow one of the procedures below.

Words

Typing Procedure

On a separate sheet of paper, type the following words at least two times, concentrating on the correct spelling and pronunciation.

Shorthand Procedure

On a separate sheet of paper, type the following words once, concentrating on the correct spelling and pronunciation. Then write the shorthand outline for each word on the lines to the right or on your shorthand machine. Cover the printed words with a sheet of paper and transcribe from the shorthand outlines one time on your typewriter.

case title / doe clause / caption / jurisdiction /
venue / filed / summons / service / appearance /
answer / demurrer to complaint / bill of
particulars / prayer for relief / ad damnum
clause /

_____

_____

_____

_____

_____

Lesson 5, Part A

Sentences

Typing Procedure

Type each of the following sentences one time. Concentrate on the correct spelling and pronunciation of each underlined legal term.

Shorthand Procedure

Write the correct shorthand outlines for the following sentences on the lines to the right or on your shorthand machine. Cover the printed material with a sheet of paper and transcribe from your shorthand outlines one time on the typewriter.

These sentences will be used for practice dictation on the cassettes.

The <u>caption</u> is the title page of a court document and includes the case title, the <u>jurisdiction</u>, the venue, the court number, and the document title. The caption includes the <u>case title</u> which names the parties to the lawsuit. If the names of one or more of the defendants to a suit are not known, a Doe clause is used in the case title. The unknown defendants are referred to as John or Mary Doe. The jurisdiction is the right or authority of a court to hear and adjudge cases. Courts can only hear and decide cases which fall within their jurisdiction. The <u>venue</u> is the geographical location where a case is tried. A request for a change of venue would be a request to have the case tried in another court in a different geographical area. Court documents are <u>filed</u> with the clerk of the court. If a person is served with a summons, that person is a defendant in a lawsuit and must make an appearance before the court at a specified time to answer the charges. The delivery of a <u>summons</u> to the person named therein is known as the <u>service</u>. When the defendant has received the summons, the defendant is said to have been served. An <u>appearance</u> is to be present in court as a party to a lawsuit. If one makes an appearance, the person comes into court as a party to a suit. The pleading by which the defendant states the defense against plaintiff's claims is an <u>answer</u>. A <u>demurrer to complaint</u> is a formal method of saying that the claims of the other side are not sufficient in law for a legal action. The bill of particulars supplies the defendant with the detailed facts upon which a complaint is based. The statement of plaintiff's damages in the complaint is called the ad damnum clause. The summary at the end of a complaint which requests the court to grant the plaintiff's demands is the prayer for relief.

_____

_____

_____

_____

_____

_____

_____

Transcribing from Dictation

Directions: This dictation emphasizes and reinforces the legal terms and definitions you have studied. Listen carefully to the pronunciation of each of the legal terms. Unless otherwise directed, use a 70-space line and double spacing. Correct all errors. Follow one of the procedures below.

Typing Procedure

Using the cassette from Lesson 5, Part A, transcribe the dictation directly at your typewriter.

Shorthand Procedure

Using the cassette from Lesson 5, Part A, take the dictation using your shorthand system and then transcribe on the typewriter from your shorthand notes.

When you have finished transcribing Part A of the practice dictation, check your transcript with the printed copy. If you made any mistakes in the transcription, you should practice those words several times before going on.

Part B

Terminology and Definitions

Directions: Study the terms, pronunciations, and definitions until you are thoroughly familiar with them. In order to complete this lesson successfully, you must understand the meaning and usage of all the legal terms presented. If you are using shorthand, write your shorthand outline in the space provided or on your shorthand machine for each legal term.

LEGAL TERM	PRONUNCIATION	DEFINITION	SHORTHAND OUTLINE
1. affidavit	af-ə-'dā-vət	A voluntary written statement made under oath before a notary public or other qualified official.	_____
2. affiant	ə-'fī-ənt	A person who makes an affidavit.	_____

3. jurat	ˈju̇r-at	A clause at the end of an affidavit which verifies the time, place, and person before whom the affidavit was made.	_____
4. verification	ver-ə-fə-ˈkā-shən	Confirmation of the truth of a document.	_____
5. counterclaim	ˈkau̇nt-ər-klām	A claim made by the defendant as a result of the plaintiff's charges in the lawsuit.	_____
6. crossclaim	ˈkrȯs-klām	A claim brought by a defendant against a plaintiff and/or a codefendant seeking relief against either in the event that there is recovery.	_____
7. cross defendant	krȯs di-ˈfen-dənt	The plaintiff who is named as defendant in a crossclaim.	_____
8. cross complainant	krȯs kəm-ˈplā-nənt	A defendant who brings a crossclaim against a plaintiff in the same action. Also referred to as cross plaintiff.	_____
9. reply	ri-ˈplī	The plaintiff's answer to the defendant's answer or counterclaim.	_____
10. intervenor	int-ər-ˈvē-nər	A person not originally a party to a suit who voluntarily enters into the action to protect some interest which that person claims to have in the case.	_____
11. recrimination	ri-krim-ə-ˈnā-shən	A countercharge or a counterclaim.	_____
12. motion	ˈmō-shən	A written or oral application made to a court or judge for a rule or order.	_____
13. court docket	kōrt ˈdäk-ət	A record of the dates and times that cases are to be tried in court.	_____
14. omnibus clause	ˈäm-ni-bəs klȯz	A clause at the end of the prayer for relief in a complaint which makes it possible for the court to award relief other than that specifically requested by the plaintiff.	_____

Turn to page 54 and complete Quiz No. 2 before continuing this lesson.

Directions: Unless otherwise instructed, use a 70-space line and double spacing. Correct all errors. Follow one of the procedures below.

Words

Typing Procedure

On a separate sheet of paper, type the following words at least two times, concentrating on the correct spelling and pronunciation.

Shorthand Procedure

On a separate sheet of paper, type the following words once, concentrating on the correct spelling and pronunciation. Then write the shorthand outline for each word on the lines to the right or on your shorthand machine. Cover the printed words with a sheet of paper and transcribe from the shorthand outlines one time on your typewriter.

affidavit / affiant / jurat / verification /

counterclaim / crossclaim / cross defendant /

cross complainant / reply / intervenor /

recrimination / motion / court docket / omnibus

clause /

Sentences

Typing Procedure

Type each of the following sentences one time. Concentrate on the correct spelling and pronunciation of each underlined legal term.

Shorthand Procedure

Write the correct shorthand outlines for the following sentences on the lines to the right or on your shorthand machine. Cover the printed material with a sheet of paper and transcribe from your shorthand outlines one time on the typewriter.

These sentences will be used for practice dictation on the cassettes.

An affidavit, which is a voluntary written statement made under oath before a notary public or other qualified official, has a jurat clause at the end which verifies the time, place, and person before whom the affidavit was made. The person who makes an affidavit is an affiant. A verification may be attached to a document to confirm the truthfulness of the contents of the document. The defendant may file a counterclaim against the plaintiff in a proceeding. When the defendant files a counterclaim against the plaintiff in the same proceeding, the defendant becomes the <u>cross complainant</u> or cross plaintiff and the plaintiff then becomes the <u>cross defendant</u>. A defendant may bring a <u>crossclaim</u> against a codefendant, or the plaintiff, or both seeking relief from either in the event there is a recovery in the suit. The plaintiff files a <u>reply</u> which is an answer to the defendant's counterclaim. An <u>intervenor</u> is a person not originally a party to a suit who voluntarily enters into the action to protect some interest which that person claims to have in the case. A countercharge or a counterclaim is also called <u>recrimination</u>. Recrimination would be a countercharge against the person who made the original charge. A written or oral <u>motion</u> may be made to the court to have the trial date set. If the motion is honored, the trial date will be set and will be entered on the <u>court docket</u>. An <u>omnibus clause</u> makes it possible for the court to award relief other than that specifically requested by the plaintiff.

Transcribing from Dictation

Directions: This dictation emphasizes and reinforces the legal terms and definitions you have studied. Listen carefully to the pronunciation of each of the legal terms. Unless otherwise directed, use a 70-space line and double spacing. Correct all errors. Follow one of the procedures below.

Typing Procedure

Using the cassette from Lesson 5, Part B, transcribe the dictation directly at your typewriter.

Shorthand Procedure

Using the cassette from Lesson 5, Part B, take the dictation using your shorthand system and then transcribe on the typewriter from your shorthand notes.

When you have finished transcribing Part B of the practice dictation, check your transcript with the printed copy. If you have made any mistakes in the transcription, you should practice those words several times before going on to Lesson 6.

034769

	PART A, DATE	PART B, DATE	SUBMITTED TO INSTRUCTOR	
			YES	NO
Terminology and Definitions	_____	_____	____	____
*Typing Legal Terms	_____	_____	____	____
Words	_____	_____	____	____
Sentences	_____	_____	____	____
*Transcribing from Dictation	_____	_____	____	____
Quiz No. 1	_____	_____	____	____
Quiz No. 2	_____	_____	____	____

When you have successfully completed all the exercises in this lesson and submitted to your instructor those called for, you are ready to proceed with Lesson 6.

*If you are using a shorthand system, turn in to your instructor your shorthand notes along with your transcript.

Quiz No. 1

Terminology and Definition Recall

Directions: In the Answers column write the legal term that is most representative of the corresponding statement. After you have completed this quiz, check your answers with the key on page 332. Unless otherwise directed turn in this quiz to your instructor upon completion of this lesson.

ANSWERS

1. When the names of one or more defendants in a suit are not known, a _____ is used in the case title.

1. _____

2. The summary at the end of a complaint which requests the court to grant the plaintiff's demands is the _____.

2. _____

3. The delivery of a summons to the person named therein is called _____.

3. _____

4. The part of a legal document that contains the names of the parties to the suit is called the _____.

4. _____

5. The title page of a court document which includes the case title, the jurisdiction, the venue, the court number, and the document title is the _____.

5. _____

6. A writ which notifies a defendant that a lawsuit has been filed and an appearance must be made before the court at a specified time to answer the charges is a/an _____.

6. _____

7. A pleading which states the defendant's defense against the plaintiff's claims is a/an _____.

7. _____

8. If the defendant answers the claims of the plaintiff by stating that the claims are not sufficient for a legal action, the answer is called a/an _____.

8. _____

9. The right or authority of a court to hear and adjudge cases is the _____.

9. _____

10. Papers which are placed with the clerk of a court are said to be _____.

10. _____

11. The geographical location where a case is tried is the _____.

11. _____

12. The detailed facts upon which a complaint is based which are usually supplied by the plaintiff upon the request of the defendant are contained in a document called a/an _____.

12. _____

13. To be present in a court as a party to a lawsuit is to make a/an _____.

13. _____

14. A clause in a complaint which states the plaintiff's damages is the _____.

14. _____

Turn back to page 46 and continue with this lesson.

Quiz No. 2

Terminology and Definition Recall

Directions: In the Answers column write the legal term that is most representative of the corresponding statement. After you have completed this quiz, check your answers with the key on page 332. Unless otherwise directed, turn in this quiz to your instructor upon completion of this lesson.

ANSWERS

1. A claim brought by a defendant against a plaintiff and/or a codefendant seeking relief against either in the event there is recovery in the suit is a/an _____.

1. _____

2. A claim made by the defendant as a result of the plaintiff's charges in the lawsuit is a/an _____.

2. _____

3. A written or oral application made to a court or judge for a rule or order is called a/an _____.

3. _____

4. A countercharge or a counterclaim may also be called _____.

4. _____

5. The person who makes an affidavit is called a/an _____.

5. _____

6. A person not originally a party to a suit who voluntarily enters into the action to protect some interest which that person claims to have in the case is a/an _____.

6. _____

7. When the defendant brings a crossclaim against the plaintiff in the same proceeding, the defendant is then known as the _____.

7. _____

8. The truth of a document is confirmed by the _____.

8. _____

9. A clause at the end of the prayer for relief in a complaint which makes it possible for the court to award relief other than that specifically requested by the plaintiff is a/an _____.

9. _____

10. The plaintiff's response to the defendant's answer or counterclaim is a/an _____.

10. _____

11. When the plaintiff is named as defendant in a crossclaim, the plaintiff then becomes known as the _____.

11. _____

12. A clause at the end of an affidavit which verifies the time, place, and person before whom the affidavit was made is a/an _____.

12. _____

13. A record of the dates and times that cases are to be tried in court is a/an _____.

13. _____

14. A voluntary written statement made under oath before a notary public or other qualified official is a/an _____.

14. _____

Turn back to page 49 and continue with this lesson.

LESSON 6

To Wit: Litigation—Pretrial

This lesson continues the study of the terminology involved in pretrial litigation activities. Upon completion of these exercises you should be able to correctly spell, define, pronounce, and transcribe from dictation each of the terms presented.

Part A	Terminology and Definitions

Directions: Study the terms, pronunciations, and definitions until you are thoroughly familiar with them. In order to complete this lesson successfully, you must understand the meaning and usage of all the legal terms presented. If you are using shorthand, write your shorthand outline in the space provided or on your shorthand machine for each legal term.

LEGAL TERM	PRONUNCIATION	DEFINITION	SHORTHAND OUTLINE
1. interrogatories	int-ə-'räg-ə-tor-ēs	Written questions which a witness must answer under oath as a part of the discovery process.	_____
2. deposition	dep-ə-'zish-ən	Part of the discovery process whereby the witness answers questions under oath outside of court, and a verbatim transcript is prepared of the questions asked and the answers given. The witness is called a deponent.	_____
3. verbatim	vər-'bāt-əm	Something which is stated in exactly the same words or word for word.	_____
4. transcript	'trans-kript	A typewritten verbatim copy of a deposition or a court proceeding usually prepared by a court reporter.	_____
5. court reporter	kōrt ri-'pōrt-ər	One who records verbatim the deposition of a witness or the proceedings in court and produces a written transcript thereof.	_____

6. pretrial stipulations	prē-'trīl stip-yə-'lā-shəns	Agreements made between the attorneys as to the conditions or procedures that will be followed in the taking of a deposition.	_____
7. disclosure	dis-'klō-zhər	Making known all the facts that one has about a case.	_____
8. fishing expedition	'fish-iŋ ek-spə-'dish-ən	A tactic used by some attorneys in the discovery process to try to obtain information from a witness that is not based upon or supported by the allegations.	_____
9. concealment	kən-'sēl-mənt	The failure to disclose or reveal the facts one has about a case which the law requires one to make known.	_____
10. contempt of court	kən-'temt əv kōrt	Intentionally doing something which is against the court rules or which interferes with the administration of justice.	_____
11. bench warrant	bench 'wor-ənt	A warrant issued by a judge or the court for the arrest of one charged with contempt of court or one who has been indicted for a crime.	_____
12. subpoena	sə-'pē-nə	A document compelling a witness to appear in court and give testimony at a specified time for the party named therein. A bench warrant may be issued for the arrest of one who does not obey a subpoena.	_____
13. subpoena duces tecum	sə-'pē-nə dü-səs 'tē-kəm	Latin. A writ commanding the person named to produce in court certain designated documents.	_____

Turn to page 63 and complete Quiz No. 1 before continuing this lesson.

Typing Legal Terms

Directions: Unless otherwise instructed, use a 70-space line and double spacing. Correct all errors. Follow one of the procedures below.

Words

Typing Procedure

On a separate sheet of paper, type the following words at least two times, concentrating on the correct spelling and pronunciation.

Shorthand Procedure

On a sheet of paper, type the following words once, concentrating on the correct spelling and pronunciation. Then write the shorthand outline for each word on the lines to the right or on your shorthand machine. Cover the printed words with a sheet of paper and transcribe from the shorthand outlines one time on your typewriter.

interrogatories / deposition / verbatim /

transcript / court reporter / pretrial stipulations /

disclosure / fishing expedition / concealment /

contempt of court / bench warrant / subpoena /

subpoena duces tecum /

Sentences

Typing Procedure

Type each of the following sentences one time. Concentrate on the correct spelling and pronunciation of each underlined legal term.

Shorthand Procedure

Write the correct shorthand outlines for the following sentences on the lines to the right or on your shorthand machine. Cover the printed material with a sheet of paper and transcribe from your shorthand outlines one time on the typewriter.

These sentences will be used for practice dictation on the cassettes.

A witness may be required to answer interrogatories outside of the court under oath to be recorded by a court reporter. A deposition is a part of the discovery process whereby the witness answers questions under oath outside of court. The court reporter prepares a verbatim transcript of the deposition. Opposing counsel may agree to certain pretrial stipulations in a pending action which may affect certain procedures in the taking of a deposition. A party is required to make a disclosure of facts known about a case, but the party seeking the disclosure may not go on a fishing expedition. A "fishing expedition" refers to a tactic used by some attorneys in the discovery process to try to obtain information from a witness that is not based upon or supported by the allegations. If a party does not disclose the known facts about a case and withholds information which the law requires one to make known, the party is guilty of concealment. Concealment can be termed as the intentionally doing of something which interferes with the administration of justice and could lead to a contempt of court charge against the party. In cases of contempt of court, or if a witness does not obey a subpoena, the judge may issue a bench warrant. The subpoena is a document which compels a witness to appear in court and give testimony at a specified time for the party named therein. If a party has certain designated documents which are required in court, a subpoena duces tecum is issued commanding the person to bring those documents into court. If the party fails to do so, a bench warrant may be issued for the party's arrest.

_____

_____

_____

_____

_____

_____

_____

_____

_____

Transcribing from Dictation

Directions: This dictation emphasizes and reinforces the legal terms and definitions you have studied. Listen carefully to the pronunciation of each of the legal terms. Unless otherwise directed, use a 70-space line and double spacing. Correct all errors. Follow one of the procedures below.

Typing Procedure

Using the cassette from Lesson 6, Part A, transcribe the dictation directly at your typewriter.

Shorthand Procedure

Using the cassette from Lesson 6, Part A, take the dictation using your shorthand system and then transcribe on the typewriter from your shorthand notes.

When you have finished transcribing Part A of the practice dictation, check your transcript with the printed copy. If you made any mistakes in the transcription, you should practice those words several times before going on.

Part B | Terminology and Definitions

Directions: Study the terms, pronunciations, and definitions until you are thoroughly familiar with them. In order to complete this lesson successfully, you must understand the meaning and usage of all the legal terms presented. If you are using shorthand, write your shorthand outline in the space provided or on your shorthand machine for each legal term.

LEGAL TERM	PRONUNCIATION	DEFINITION	SHORTHAND OUTLINE
1. examination before trial	ig-zam-ə-'nā-shən bi-'fŏr trīl	Inquiry into the facts prior to the trial of a case so as to obtain the information needed to prosecute or defend the action. Sometimes abbreviated to EBT.	_____

2. pretrial conference	prē-'trīl 'kän-frəns	An informal conference between judge and counsel to discuss a case before it is tried in court in an effort to clarify and expedite its disposition. It is also used to determine if there is adequate evidence to justify proceeding to trial.	_____
3. chambers	'chām-bərs	The private office of the judge where business outside of the courtroom is conducted.	_____
4. notice of lis pendens	'nōt-əs əv lis 'pen-dəns	Latin. A notice issued to inform persons that there is a litigation pending in regard to certain property.	_____
5. attachment	ə-'tach-mənt	A document issued so that persons or property may be legally taken and held in the custody of the law.	_____
6. surety bond	'shu̇r-ət-ē bänd	A bond which insures that a debt or obligation will be paid.	_____
7. garnishment	'gär-nish-mənt	A legal notice to a person who holds property belonging to a defendant that said property is the subject of a garnishment, or the act of withholding a defendant's property by the order of the court.	_____
8. garnishee	gär-nə-'shē	The one who is in possession of the defendant's property which is the subject of a garnishment.	_____
9. bond	bänd	A document which certifies that one will pay a certain amount of money if certain acts are not performed. A bond may be posted to assure the appearance of a defendant in court.	_____
10. recognizance	ri-'käg-nə-zəns	A commitment made and recorded before a court that a certain act will be done. Serves as a bond in some states and is referred to as "released on personal recognizance."	_____
11. moot	mūt	Something which can be debated, argued, or discussed. A moot point is one which can be argued.	_____
12. precedent	'pres-əd-ənt	A judicial decision which serves as a guide for future cases which are similar in nature.	_____
13. recusation	rē-kyü-'zā-shən	An exception or plea that a particular judge is disqualified from hearing a cause because he or she is prejudiced or has a personal interest in the cause.	_____

Turn to page 64 and complete Quiz No. 2 before continuing this lesson.

Lesson 6, Part B

Directions: Unless otherwise instructed, use a 70-space line and double spacing. Correct all errors. Follow one of the procedures below.

Words

Typing Procedure

On a separate sheet of paper, type the following words at least two times, concentrating on the correct spelling and pronunciation.

Shorthand Procedure

On a separate sheet of paper, type the following words once, concentrating on the correct spelling and pronunciation. Then write the shorthand outline for each word on the lines to the right or on your shorthand machine. Cover the printed words with a sheet of paper and transcribe from the shorthand outlines one time on your typewriter.

examination before trial / pretrial conference /

chambers / notice of lis pendens / attachment /

surety bond / garnishment / garnishee / bond /

recognizance / moot / precedent / recusation /

Sentences

Typing Procedure

Type each of the following sentences one time. Concentrate on the correct spelling and pronunciation of each underlined legal term.

Shorthand Procedure

Write the correct shorthand outlines for the following sentences on the lines to the right or on your shorthand machine. Cover the printed material with a sheet of paper and transcribe from your shorthand outlines one time on the typewriter.

These sentences will be used for practice dictation on the cassettes.

The judge may schedule a pretrial conference with the attorneys in a case before it is tried in court in an effort to determine if there is adequate evidence to justify proceeding to trial. An examination before trial, commonly referred to as an EBT, is an inquiry into the facts prior to the trial of a case so as to obtain the information needed to prosecute or defend the action. The judge may hold the pretrial conference in chambers rather than the courtroom. If the title to property is involved in litigation, a notice of lis pendens is filed. An attachment is issued so that persons or property may be legally taken and held in the custody of the law. In some cases, a plaintiff must post a surety bond before attaching property owned by a defendant. If defendant's property is being held by another party, plaintiff may acquire the property by filing a garnishment. To garnishee a defendant's property, a legal notice is issued to the person holding said property stating that it is to be held for the payment of a debt to the plaintiff. A bond is a document which certifies that one will pay a certain amount of money if certain acts are not performed. A bond may be posted to assure the appearance of the defendant in court, or the court may release the person on personal recognizance. A moot point is one which can be debated, argued, or discussed. A precedent is a judicial decision which serves as a guide for future cases which are similar in nature. Recusation is an exception or plea that a particular judge is disqualified from hearing a cause because he or she is prejudiced or has a personal interest in the matter.

Transcribing from Dictation

Directions: This dictation emphasizes and reinforces the legal terms and definitions you have studied. Listen carefully to the pronunciation of each of the legal terms. Unless otherwise directed, use a 70-space line and double spacing. Correct all errors. Follow one of the procedures below.

Typing Procedure

Using the cassette from Lesson 6, Part B, transcribe the dictation directly at your typewriter.

Shorthand Procedure

Using the cassette from Lesson 6, Part B, take the dictation using your shorthand system and then transcribe on the typewriter from your shorthand notes.

When you have finished transcribing Part B of the practice dictation, check your transcript with the printed copy. If you have made any mistakes in the transcription, you should practice those words several times before going on to Evaluation 3.

Check List

	PART A, DATE	PART B, DATE	SUBMITTED TO INSTRUCTOR	
			YES	NO
Terminology and Definitions	_____	_____	_____	_____
*Typing Legal Terms	_____	_____	_____	_____
Words	_____	_____	_____	_____
Sentences	_____	_____	_____	_____
*Transcribing from Dictation	_____	_____	_____	_____
Quiz No. 1	_____	_____	_____	_____
Quiz No. 2	_____	_____	_____	_____

When you have successfully completed all the exercises in this lesson and submitted to your instructor those called for, you are ready to proceed with Evaluation 3.

*If you are using a shorthand system, turn in to your instructor your shorthand notes along with your transcript.

Quiz No. 1

Terminology and Definition Recall

Directions: In the Answers column at the right of each statement, write the letter that represents the word, or group of words, that correctly completes the statement. After you have completed this quiz, check your answers with the key on page 332. Unless otherwise directed, turn in this quiz to your instructor upon completion of this lesson.

ANSWERS

1. A tactic used by some attorneys in the discovery process to try to obtain information from a witness that is not based upon or supported by the allegations is called a (a) contempt of court, (b) concealment, (c) fishing expedition.

1. _____

2. The making known of all the facts that one has about a case is (a) disclosure, (b) verbatim, (c) fishing expedition.

2. _____

3. The intentionally doing of something which is against the court rules or which interferes with the administration of justice is (a) concealment, (b) contempt of court, (c) interrogatories.

3. _____

4. Written questions which a witness must answer under oath as a part of the discovery process are (a) disclosures, (b) interrogatories, (c) depositions.

4. _____

5. Agreements made between the attorneys as to the conditions or procedures that will be followed in the taking of a deposition are (a) disclosures, (b) interrogatories, (c) pretrial stipulations.

5. _____

6. The part of the discovery process whereby the witness answers questions under oath outside of court and a verbatim transcript is prepared of the questions asked and the answers given is a/an (a) transcript, (b) deposition, (c) interrogatory.

6. _____

7. One who records verbatim the deposition of a witness or the proceedings in court and produces a written transcript thereof is a/an (a) court reporter, (b) attorney, (c) court clerk.

7. _____

8. A document compelling a witness to appear in court and give testimony at a specified time for the party named therein is a (a) subpoena, (b) subpoena duces tecum, (c) bench warrant.

8. _____

9. Something which is stated in exactly the same words, or word for word, is (a) verbatim, (b) subpoena, (c) concealment.

9. _____

10. A typewritten verbatim copy of a deposition or a court proceeding usually prepared by a court reporter is a (a) pretrial stipulation, (b) subpoena, (c) transcript.

10. _____

11. The failure to disclose or reveal the facts one has about a case which the law requires one to make known is referred to as (a) pretrial stipulation, (b) concealment, (c) subpoena.

11. _____

12. A writ commanding the person named therein to produce in court certain designated documents is a (a) subpoena, (b) bench warrant, (c) subpoena duces tecum.

12. _____

Turn back to page 56 and continue with this lesson.

Quiz No. 2

Terminology and Definition Recall

Directions: In the Answers column write the letter from Column I that represents the word or phrase that best matches each item in Column II. After you have completed this quiz, check your answers with the key on page 332. Unless otherwise directed, turn in this quiz to your instructor upon completion of this lesson.

COLUMN I	COLUMN II	ANSWERS
A. attachment	**1.** A document issued so that persons or property may be legally taken and held in the custody of the law.	1. _____
B. bond		
C. chambers	**2.** A legal notice to a person who holds property belonging to a defendant that said property is to be held for the payment of a debt to the plaintiff.	2. _____
D. examination before trial		
E. garnishee	**3.** A judicial decision which serves as a guide for future cases which are similar in nature.	3. _____
F. garnishment		
G. moot	**4.** Something which can be debated, argued, or discussed.	4. _____
H. notice of lis pendens	**5.** An exception or plea that a judge is disqualified from hearing a cause because of prejudice or a personal interest in the cause.	5. _____
I. precedent		
J. pretrial conference	**6.** A bond which insures that a debt or obligation will be paid.	6. _____
K. recognizance	**7.** An informal conference between judge and counsel to discuss a case before it is tried in court in an effort to clarify and expedite its disposition or to determine if there is adequate evidence to justify proceeding to trial.	7. _____
L. recusation		
M. subpoena		
N. surety bond		

8. A commitment made and recorded before a court that a certain act will be done and which serves in some states as a bond.   8. _____

9. A notice to inform persons that there is a litigation pending in regard to a certain property.   9. _____

10. The private office of the judge where business outside of the courtroom is conducted.   10. _____

11. Inquiry into the facts prior to the trial of a case so as to obtain the information needed to prosecute or defend the action.   11. _____

12. The one who is in possession of the defendant's property which is the subject of a garnishment, or the act of withholding a defendant's property by the order of the court.   12. _____

13. A document which certifies that one will pay a certain amount of money if certain acts are not performed, such as the appearance of a defendant in court.   13. _____

Turn back to page 60 and continue with this lesson.

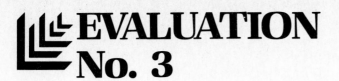# EVALUATION No. 3

Student _____

Class _____ Date _____

SCORING RECORD

	Perfect Score	Student's Score
Section A	50	
Section B	20	
Section C	30	
Total	100	

SECTION A

Directions: This dictation/transcription evaluation will test your spelling and transcription ability on the legal terms that you studied in the two preceding lessons. Use a 5-space paragraph indention, a 70-space line and double spacing unless otherwise instructed. Correct all errors. Follow one of the procedures below.

Typing Procedure

Using the cassette from Evaluation 3, transcribe the dictation directly at your typewriter.

Shorthand Procedure

Using the cassette from Evaluation 3, take the dictation using your shorthand system and then transcribe on the typewriter from your shorthand notes.

SECTIONS B AND C ARE AVAILABLE FROM YOUR INSTRUCTOR.

"The law is not concerned with trifles."

—Legal Maxim

LESSON 7

To Wit: Litigation—
Trial and Proceedings

Many nonlawyer personnel do not have an opportunity to observe the proceedings that take place in a courtroom. However, regardless of your legal position, having a knowledge of what transpires once a case goes to trial will help you to understand the importance of the various aspects of your particular involvement in the case. This lesson introduces legal terms that are used in the courtroom during a trial or legal proceeding.

Part A		**Terminology and Definitions**

Directions: Study the terms, pronunciations, and definitions until you are thoroughly familiar with them. In order to complete this lesson successfully, you must understand the meaning and usage of all the legal terms presented. If you are using shorthand, write your shorthand outline in the space provided or on your shorthand machine for each legal term.

LEGAL TERM	PRONUNCIATION	DEFINITION	SHORTHAND OUTLINE
1. trial	trīl	The examination of civil or criminal cases in a court of law with the purpose of deciding the issue.	_____
2. counsel	′kaủn-səl	An attorney who represents or assists a client in court cases.	_____
3. juror	′jủr-ər	One who is a member of a jury.	_____
4. petit jury	′pet-ē ′jủr-ē	A group of persons selected to hear cases in a court of law and sworn to render a verdict based upon the evidence presented in the case. Usually referred to as "the jury."	_____
5. oath	ōth	A swearing or affirming that one will act faithfully and truthfully.	_____

6.	voir dire	vwä dir	French. A preliminary examination by the court of a prospective juror to determine if the person is competent to serve as a juror.	_____
7.	impanel	im-ˈpan-l	The process of selecting a jury.	_____
8.	challenge	ˈchal-ənj	To object to a certain person serving as a juror.	_____
9.	veniremen	və-ˈnī-rē-mən	Jurors.	_____
10.	foreman or forewoman	ˈfōr-mən or ˈfōr-wu̇m-ən	A juror selected by the other members of the jury to preside over the deliberations and to speak for the jury.	_____
11.	challenge to the array	ˈchal-ənj tü thē ə-ˈrā	An objection made to the entire panel of jurors.	_____
12.	challenge for cause	ˈchahl-ənj fər koz	An objection made to a juror based on a specified reason.	_____
13.	peremptory challenge	pə-ˈrem-trē ˈchal-ənj	An objection made to a juror for which no cause is given. There is a limited number of peremptory challenges allowed to each party in a case.	_____

Turn to page 75 and complete Quiz No. 1 before continuing this lesson.

Typing Legal Terms

Directions: Unless otherwise instructed, use a 70-space line and double spacing. Correct all errors. Follow one of the procedures below.

Words

Typing Procedure

On a separate sheet of paper, type the following words at least two times, concentrating on the correct spelling and pronunciation.

Shorthand Procedure

On a separate sheet of paper, type the following words once, concentrating on the correct spelling and pronunciation. Then write the shorthand outline for each word on the lines to the right or on your shorthand machine. Cover the printed words with a sheet of paper and transcribe from the shorthand outlines one time on your typewriter.

trial / counsel / juror / petit jury / oath / voir dire / impanel / challenge / veniremen / foreman or forewoman / challenge to the array / challenge for cause / peremptory challenge /

_____

_____

_____

_____

Sentences

Typing Procedure

Type each of the following sentences one time. Concentrate on the correct spelling and pronunciation of each underlined legal term.

Shorthand Procedure

Write the correct shorthand outlines for the following sentences on the lines to the right or on your shorthand machine. Cover the printed material with a sheet of paper and transcribe from your shorthand outlines one time on the typewriter.

These sentences will be used for practice dictation on the cassettes.

A trial is the examination of civil and criminal cases in a court of law with the purpose of deciding the issue. Counsel is an attorney who represents or assists a client in court cases. Cases tried in courts of original jurisdiction or trial courts may be decided by a petit jury. A petit jury is a group of persons who are selected to hear cases in a court of law and who have sworn to render a verdict based upon the evidence presented in the case. A juror is one who is a member of a jury. Each juror must take an oath to act truthfully and faithfully. To impanel a jury is to select the jurors who will decide the issue. Part of the impaneling process is the voir dire, which is the preliminary examination by the court of a prospective juror to determine if the person is competent to serve as a juror. During the voir dire, counsel may challenge the capability of a juror or jurors. There are three common types of challenges which counsel may exercise. They are challenge to the array, challenge for cause, and peremptory challenge. A challenge to the array is a challenge to the entire panel of jurors. A challenge to a juror based on a specific reason is a challenge for cause. A peremptory challenge is one for which no cause is given. Each party has a certain number of peremptory challenges. Another name for jurors is veniremen. The veniremen will select a foreman or forewoman to preside over the deliberations and to speak for the jury.

Directions: This dictation emphasizes and reinforces the legal terms and definitions you have studied. Listen carefully to the pronunciation of each of the legal terms. Unless otherwise directed, use a 70-space line and double spacing. Correct all errors. Follow one of the procedures below.

Typing Procedure

Using a cassette from Lesson 7, Part A, transcribe the dictation directly at your typewriter.

Shorthand Procedure

Using the cassette from Lesson 7, Part A, take the dictation using your shorthand system and then transcribe on the typewriter from your shorthand notes.

When you have finished transcribing Part A of the practice dictation, check your transcript with the printed copy. If you made any mistakes in the transcription, you should practice those words several times before going on.

Part B — Terminology and Definitions

Directions: Study the terms, pronunciations, and definitions until you are thoroughly familiar with them. In order to complete this lesson successfully, you must understand the meaning and usage of all the legal terms presented. If you are using shorthand, write your shorthand outline in the space provided or on your shorthand machine for each legal term.

LEGAL TERM	PRONUNCIATION	DEFINITION	SHORTHAND OUTLINE
1. opening statement	′ōp-niŋ ′stāt-mənt	The first step in a jury trial after the jury has been selected whereby the attorneys make a statement to the jury as to what they plan to prove in the trial.	_____
2. witness	′wit-nəs	One who is called to give testimony under oath in court as to any facts that pertain to the case.	_____
3. testimony	′tes-tə-mō-nē	Evidence presented by a witness under oath in a court of law.	_____
4. direct examination	də-′rekt ig-zam-ə-′nā-shən	The first questioning of a witness in court by the attorney for the party who called the witness to testify.	_____
5. cross examination	krȯs ig-zam-ə-′nā-shən	The questioning of a witness by counsel for the party who is in opposition to the party who called the witness to testify.	_____

6. colloquy	′käl-ə-kwē	A talking together, conference, or conversation between the judge and counsel or the judge and witness. Could be in the form of an objection. Deviates from the normal question and answer that takes place between counsel and witness.	_____
7. objections	əb-′jek-shəns	Protests made by counsel to the judge pertaining to certain evidence or procedure in the trial.	_____
8. overruled	ō-və-′rüld	The answer of the court when refusing to support an objection made by counsel.	_____
9. sustained	sə-′stānd	The answer of the court when supporting an objection made by counsel.	_____
10. irrelevant	ir-′el-ə-vənt	Evidence presented which is not applicable or related to the issues in the case. An attorney may make an objection to irrelevant evidence.	_____
11. admissible	əd-′mis-ə-bəl	Evidence that is relevant to the case and may, therefore, be presented in court.	_____
12. motion to strike out	′mō-shən tü strīk aüt	A request made by counsel to eliminate improper evidence from consideration in deciding the issue. Evidence which is ordered stricken cannot be considered but remains as a part of the record in the event the case is appealed.	_____
13. physically expunge	′fiz-i-kəl-lē ik-′spənj	To completely remove certain evidence from the record.	_____
14. mistrial	mis-′trīl	A trial which is declared invalid because of an error in the proceedings or the failure of a jury to reach a verdict.	_____

Turn to page 76 and complete Quiz No. 2 before continuing this lesson.

Typing Legal Terms

Directions: Unless otherwise instructed, use a 70-space line and double spacing. Correct all errors. Follow one of the procedures below.

Words

Typing Procedure

On a separate sheet of paper, type the following words at least two times, concentrating on the correct spelling and pronunciation.

Shorthand Procedure

On a separate sheet of paper, type the following words once, concentrating on the correct spelling and pronunciation. Then write the shorthand outline for each word on the lines to the right or on your shorthand machine. Cover the printed words with a sheet of paper and transcribe from the shorthand outlines one time on your typewriter.

opening statement / witness / testimony / direct examination / cross examination /colloquy / objections / overruled / sustained / irrelevant / admissible / motion to strike out / physically expunge / mistrial

Sentences

Typing Procedure

Type each of the following sentences one time. Concentrate on the correct spelling and pronunciation of each underlined legal term.

Shorthand Procedure

Write the correct shorthand outlines for the following sentences on the lines to the right or on your shorthand machine. Cover the printed material with a sheet of paper and transcribe from your shorthand outlines one time on the typewriter.

These sentences will be used for practice dictation on the cassettes.

At the beginning of a trial, counsel for both sides usually presents an opening statement to the jury which is a statement as to what they plan to prove in the trial. A witness is one who is called to give testimony under oath in court as to any facts that pertain to the case. The first questioning of a witness in court by the attorney for the party who called the witness to testify is the direct examination. After the direct examination, the witness may be subjected to a cross examination by the counsel for the opposing party. During the direct examination or the cross examination, counsel and judge may engage in colloquy or conversation relevant to the case. Objections to the testimony or evidence by counsel is a form of colloquy. An objection must be either sustained or overruled by the judge. If an objection is sustained, the judge agrees with the counsel who made the objection; if the objection is overruled, the judge does not agree with the counsel who made the objection. The counsel making the objection may contend that certain evidence is irrelevant in that it is not applicable or related to the issues in the case. Evidence that is admissible in court is evidence that is relevant to the case. Counsel may make a motion to strike out certain

irrelevant testimony or evidence. The judge may
rule in favor of the motion to strike out and order
that the testimony or evidence be physically
expunged from the record. To physically expunge
testimony from the record means to strike it totally
from the record. A mistrial or dismissal of the case
may result if a fundamental legal procedure is
violated during the trial.

_____

_____

_____

_____

_____

_____

_____

Transcribing from Dictation

Directions: This dictation emphasizes and reinforces the legal terms and definitions you have studied. Listen carefully to the pronunciation of each of the legal terms. Unless otherwise directed, use a 70-space line and double spacing. Correct all errors. Follow one of the procedures below.

Typing Procedure

Using the cassette from Lesson 7, Part B, transcribe the dictation directly at your typewriter.

Shorthand Procedure

Using the cassette from Lesson 7, Part B, take the dictation using your shorthand system and then transcribe on the typewriter from your shorthand notes.

When you have finished transcribing Part B of the practice dictation, check your transcript with the printed copy. If you have made any mistakes in the transcription, you should practice those words several times before going on to Lesson 8.

Check List

	PART A, DATE	PART B, DATE	SUBMITTED TO INSTRUCTOR	
			YES	NO
Terminology and Definitions	_____	_____	_____	_____
*Typing Legal Terms	_____	_____	_____	_____
Words	_____	_____	_____	_____
Sentences	_____	_____	_____	_____
*Transcribing from Dictation	_____	_____	_____	_____
Quiz No. 1	_____	_____	_____	_____
Quiz No. 2	_____	_____	_____	_____

When you have successfully completed all the exercises in this lesson and submitted to your instructor those called for, you are ready to proceed with Lesson 8.

*If you are using a shorthand system, turn in to your instructor your shorthand notes along with your transcript.

Quiz No. 1

Terminology and Definition Recall

Directions: In the Answers column write the legal term that is most representative of the corresponding statement. After you have completed this quiz, check your answers with the key on page 333. Unless otherwise directed, turn in this quiz to your instructor upon completion of this lesson.

ANSWERS

1. An objection made to a juror for which no cause is given is a/an _____.

   1. _____

2. To object to a certain person serving as a juror is to _____ that person.

   2. _____

3. A swearing or affirming that one will act faithfully and truthfully is a/an _____.

   3. _____

4. A preliminary examination by the court of a prospective juror to determine if the person is competent to serve as a juror is a/an _____.

   4. _____

5. A group of persons selected to hear cases in a court of law and sworn to render a verdict based upon the evidence presented in the case is a/an _____.

   5. _____

6. An objection made to a juror based on a specified reason is a/an _____.

   6. _____

7. A juror selected by the other members of the jury to preside over the deliberations and to speak for the jury is the _____ or _____.

   7. _____

8. To go through the steps or process of selecting a jury is to _____ the jury.

   8. _____

9. The examination of civil or criminal cases in a court of law with the purpose of deciding the issues is a/an _____.

   9. _____

10. An objection made to the entire panel of jurors is a/an _____.

    10. _____

11. Jurors are also referred to as _____.

    11. _____

12. One who is a member of a jury is called a/an _____.

    12. _____

13. An attorney who represents or assists a client in court cases is referred to as _____.

    13. _____

Turn back to page 68 and continue with this lesson.

Quiz No. 2

Terminology and Definition Recall

Directions: In the Answers column write the letter from Column I that represents the word or phrase that best matches each item in Column II. After you have completed this quiz, check your answers with the key on page 333. Unless otherwise directed, turn in this quiz to your instructor upon completion of this lesson.

COLUMN I

A. admissible
B. colloquy
C. cross examination
D. direct examination
E. evidence
F. irrelevant
G. mistrial
H. motion to strike out
I. objections
J. opening statement
K. overruled
L. physically expunge
M. sustained
N. testimony
O. witness

COLUMN II

1. The first questioning of a witness in court by the attorney for the party who called the witness to testify.

2. The first step in a jury trial after the jury has been selected whereby the attorneys make a statement to the jury as to what they plan to prove in the trial.

3. A talking together, conference, or conversation between the judge and counsel or the judge and witness.

4. The answer of the court when supporting an objection made by counsel.

5. To completely remove certain evidence from the record.

6. Evidence that is relevant to the case and therefore may be presented in court.

7. One who is called to give testimony under oath in court as to any facts that pertain to the case.

8. The questioning of a witness by counsel for the party who is in opposition to the party who called the witness to testify.

9. Protests made by counsel to the judge pertaining to certain evidence or procedure in the trial.

10. A trial which is declared invalid because of an error in the proceedings or the failure of a jury to reach a verdict.

11. Evidence presented by a witness under oath in a court of law.

12. The answer of the court in refusing to support an objection made by counsel.

13. Evidence presented which is not applicable or related to the issues in the case.

14. A request made by counsel to eliminate improper evidence from consideration in deciding the issue.

ANSWERS

1. _____

2. _____

3. _____

4. _____

5. _____

6. _____

7. _____

8. _____

9. _____

10. _____

11. _____

12. _____

13. _____

14. _____

Turn back to page 71 and continue with this lesson.

LESSON 8

To Wit: Litigation— Trial and Proceedings

Additional legal terms relating to the proceedings that take place in the courtroom are introduced in these exercises. When you have completed this lesson, you should have a better knowledge and understanding of the terminology used during the trial of a case.

Part A	Terminology and Definitions

Directions: Study the terms, pronunciations, and definitions until you are thoroughly familiar with them. In order to complete this lesson successfully, you must understand the meaning and usage of all the legal terms presented. If you are using shorthand, write your shorthand outline in the space provided or on your shorthand machine for each legal term.

LEGAL TERM	PRONUNCIATION	DEFINITION	SHORTHAND OUTLINE
1. evidence	'ev-əd-əns	Testimony, exhibits, or other matter presented in the trial of a case to prove the alleged facts.	_____
2. opinion evidence	ə-'pin-yən 'ev-əd-əns	Testimony given by a witness (usually an expert) as to what that witness thinks or believes about the facts in the case.	_____
3. expert evidence	'ek-spərt 'ev-əd-əns	Testimony given by a person who has special qualifications to testify in regard to specific facts in the case.	_____
4. circumstantial evidence	sər-kəm-'stan-chəl 'ev-əd-əns	Indirect evidence. An inference which may be made from other facts proven in the case.	_____
5. exhibit	ig-'zib-ət	Any document or object presented to the court as evidence in a case. Exhibits must be accepted by the court before they become a part of the evidence. An exhibit is marked for identification (usually by the court reporter) when it is introduced.	_____

6.	hostile witness	ˈhäs-tl ˈwit-nəs	A witness who is openly prejudiced against the party who called the witness to testify in the case. A hostile witness may be cross examined by the party who called the witness to testify.	_____
7.	impeach	im-ˈpēch	To prove in a trial that a witness cannot or should not be believed.	_____
8.	perjury	ˈpərj-rē	Intentionally or knowingly giving false testimony under oath.	_____
9.	incompetent	in-ˈkam-pət-ənt	Not qualified legally. Pertains to evidence which is not admissible in a court case.	_____
10.	hearsay	hir-ˈsā	The repeating of what one heard another say. Hearsay evidence is generally not admissible in court.	_____
11.	res gestae	rēz ˈjes-tē	Latin. "Things done." Things which are a part of the case. Hearsay evidence may be admitted if it can be shown that it is res gestae.	_____
12.	rebuttal	ri-ˈbət-l	An attempt to disprove the evidence presented by the other side.	_____
13.	averment	ə-ˈvər-mənt	A declaration positively stating that the facts are true.	_____
14.	adduce	ə-ˈdüs	To present or introduce evidence in a case.	_____

Turn to page 85 and complete Quiz No. 1 before continuing this lesson.

Typing Legal Terms

Directions: Unless otherwise instructed, use a 70-space line and double spacing. Correct all errors. Follow one of the procedures below.

Words

Typing Procedure

On a separate sheet of paper, type the following words at least two times, concentrating on the correct spelling and pronunciation.

Shorthand Procedure

On a separate sheet of paper, type the following words once, concentrating on the correct spelling and pronunciation. Then write the shorthand outline for each word on the lines to the right or on your shorthand machine. Cover the printed words with a sheet of paper and transcribe from the shorthand outlines one time on your typewriter.

evidence / opinion evidence / expert evidence / _____

circumstantial evidence / exhibit / hostile _____

witness / impeach / perjury / incompetent / hearsay / _____

res gestae / rebuttal / averment / adduce / _____

Sentences

Typing Procedure

Type each of the following sentences one time. Concentrate on the correct spelling and pronunciation of each underlined legal term.

Shorthand Procedure

Write the correct shorthand outlines for the following sentences on the lines to the right or on your shorthand machine. Cover the printed material with a sheet of paper and transcribe from your shorthand outlines one time on the typewriter.

These sentences will be used for practice dictation on the cassettes.

Evidence consists of testimony, exhibits, or other matter presented in the trial of a case to prove the alleged facts. Opinion evidence, expert evidence, and circumstantial evidence are some of the various types of evidence that may be presented in a trial. Opinion evidence is testimony given by a witness, usually an expert, as to what the witness thinks or believes about the facts in the case. Testimony given by a person who has special qualifications to testify in regard to specific facts in a case is called expert evidence. Indirect evidence or an inference which may be made based on other facts proven in the case is referred to as circumstantial evidence. An exhibit is any document or object presented to the court as evidence in a case. An exhibit which has been accepted by the court as evidence is marked for identification and made part of the case. A hostile witness is one who is openly prejudiced against the party who called the witness to testify in the case and may be cross-examined by that party. To impeach a witness is to prove in a trial that the witness cannot or should not be believed. A witness who intentionally or knowingly gives false testimony under oath is guilty of perjury. An expert witness may be deemed incompetent to testify if knowledge is lacking in the specified field. Hearsay evidence is what the witness heard another person say. Hearsay evidence may be admitted if it can be shown that it is part of the res gestae. Res gestae means things that are a part of the case. Rebuttal is an attempt to disprove the evidence presented by the other side. An averment is a positive declaration or assertion as to the facts in a case. Adduce is to present or introduce evidence in a case.

_____
_____
_____
_____
_____
_____

Transcribing from Dictation

Directions: This dictation emphasizes and reinforces the legal terms and definitions you have studied. Listen carefully to the pronunciation of each of the legal terms. Unless otherwise directed, use a 70-space line and double spacing. Correct all errors. Follow one of the procedures below.

Typing Procedure

Using the cassette from Lesson 8, Part A, transcribe the dictation directly at your typewriter.

Shorthand Procedure

Using the cassette from Lesson 8, Part A, take the dictation using your shorthand system and then transcribe on the typewriter from your shorthand notes.

When you have finished transcribing Part A of the practice dictation, check your transcript with the printed copy. If you made any mistakes in the transcription, you should practice those words several times before going on.

Part B | Terminology and Definitions

Directions: Study the terms, pronunciations, and definitions until you are thoroughly familiar with them. In order to complete this lesson successfully, you must understand the meaning and usage of all the legal terms presented. If you are using shorthand, write your shorthand outline in the space provided or on your shorthand machine for each legal term.

LEGAL TERM	PRONUNCIATION	DEFINITION	SHORTHAND OUTLINE
1. pendente lite	ˈpen-dən-tē ˈlī-tē	Latin. "Pending litigation." During the time the case is in court.	_____
2. alibi	ˈal-ə-bī	Latin. "Elsewhere." An excuse. In a criminal case, if the defendant presents proof of being in another place at the time the crime was committed, the defendant has an alibi.	_____
3. amicus curiae	ə-ˈme-kəs ˈkur-ē-ī	Latin. "Friend of the court." A person who has no interest in a case but is called in by the judge to give advice regarding some matter of law.	_____
4. closing arguments	ˈklōz-iŋ ˈär-gyə-mənts	The speeches given by counsel at the end of a case in an effort to persuade the jury to decide the case in favor of their client.	_____

5.	charge to the jury	'chärj tü _thə_ 'jur-ē	The instructions given by the judge to the jury before deliberations as to the rules of law which apply to the case.	_____
6.	deliberations	di-lib-ə-'rā-shəns	The process of the jury discussing the case in an effort to reach a verdict.	_____
7.	sequestered	si-'kwes-tərd	Latin. "Secluded." The seclusion of witnesses or evidence during a case, or the seclusion of the jury until a verdict is reached.	_____
8.	preponderance of evidence	pri-'pän-drəns əv 'ev-əd-əns	Greater weight of evidence. Evidence which has greater value.	_____
9.	burden of proof	'bərd-n əv prüf	The plaintiff in a case has the duty of proving that the defendant is guilty.	_____
10.	credible evidence	'kred-ə-bəl 'ev-əd-əns	Evidence presented in a case that is believable.	_____
11.	prima facie	prī-mə 'fā-shə	Latin. "At first view." Evidence which is sufficient to prove or establish a fact unless contrary evidence is presented.	_____
12.	causal	'kȯ-zəl	Implying a cause. Having to do with cause and effect.	_____
13.	bailiff	'bā-ləf	An officer of the court who is in charge of the jury. May also guard prisoners when they appear in court.	_____

Turn to page 86 and complete Quiz No. 2 before continuing this lesson.

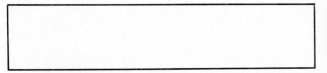

Typing Legal Terms

Directions: Unless otherwise instructed, use a 70-space line and double spacing. Correct all errors. Follow one of the procedures below.

Words

Typing Procedure

On a separate sheet of paper, type the following words at least two times, concentrating on the correct spelling and pronunciation.

Shorthand Procedure

On a separate sheet of paper, type the following words once, concentrating on the correct spelling and pronunciation. Then write the shorthand outline for each word on the lines to the right or on your shorthand machine. Cover the printed words with a sheet of paper and transcribe from the shorthand outlines one time on your typewriter.

pendente lite / alibi / amicus curiae / closing arguments / charge to the jury / deliberations / sequestered / preponderance of evidence / burden of proof / credible evidence / prima facie / causal / bailiff /

_____
_____
_____
_____
_____

Sentences

Typing Procedure

Type each of the following sentences one time. Concentrate on the correct spelling and pronunciation of each underlined legal term.

Shorthand Procedure

Write the correct shorthand outlines for the following sentences on the lines to the right or on your shorthand machine. Cover the printed material with a sheet of paper and transcribe from your shorthand outlines one time on the typewriter.

These sentences will be used for practice dictation on the cassettes.

Pendente lite is a Latin term meaning pending litigation or during the time the case is in court. If a defendant was somewhere else at the time the crime was committed, the defendant is said to have an alibi. A person who has no interest in a case but is called in by the judge to give advice regarding some matter of law is an amicus curiae. Amicus curiae is also referred to as a friend of the court. After all evidence in a case is presented, the opposing counsel gives speeches called closing arguments. In the closing arguments, counsel states their side of the case in an effort to persuade the jury to decide the case in favor of their client. The charge to the jury is given by the judge. When giving the charge to the jury, the judge instructs the jury as to the rules of law they must follow in their deliberations. The deliberations consist of the jury weighing and examining all the evidence in the case. During the course of the trial or deliberations, the jury may be sequestered from the public. Among the things that must be considered by the jury is which party has the greater weight of evi-

dence or the preponderance of evidence. The burden of proof or the proving of the facts which are
disputed is usually the duty of the plaintiff. Evidence that is believable is referred to as credible
evidence. Prima facie is evidence which is sufficient to prove or establish a fact unless contrary
evidence is presented. Causal implies a cause or
having to do with cause and effect. The bailiff is a
court attendant who is in charge of keeping the
jury sequestered during deliberations.

_____

_____

_____

_____

_____

_____

_____

_____

_____

Transcribing from Dictation

Directions: This dictation emphasizes and reinforces the legal terms and definitions you have studied. Listen carefully to the pronunciation of each of the legal terms. Unless otherwise directed, use a 70-space line and double spacing. Correct all errors. Follow one of the procedures below.

Typing Procedure

Using the cassette from Lesson 8, Part B, transcribe the dictation directly at your typewriter.

Shorthand Procedure

Using the cassette from Lesson 8, Part B, take the dictation using your shorthand system and then transcribe on the typewriter from your shorthand notes.

When you have finished transcribing Part B of the practice dictation, check your transcript with the printed copy. If you have made any mistakes in the transcription, you should practice those words several times before going on to Evaluation 4.

Check List

I have completed the following for Lesson 8.

| | PART A, DATE | PART B, DATE | SUBMITTED TO INSTRUCTOR | |
			YES	NO
Terminology and Definitions	_____	_____	_____	_____
*Typing Legal Terms	_____	_____	_____	_____
Words	_____	_____	_____	_____
Sentences	_____	_____	_____	_____
*Transcribing from Dictation	_____	_____	_____	_____
Quiz No. 1	_____	_____	_____	_____
Quiz No. 2	_____	_____	_____	_____

When you have successfully completed all the exercises in this lesson and submitted to your instructor those called for, you are ready to proceed with Evaluation 4.

*If you are using a shorthand system, turn in to your instructor your shorthand notes along with your transcript.

Quiz No. 1

Terminology and Definition Recall

Directions: In the Answers column at the right of each statement, write the letter that represents the word, or group of words, that correctly completes the statement. After you have completed this quiz, check your answers with the key on page 333. Unless otherwise directed, turn in this quiz to your instructor upon completion of this lesson.

ANSWERS

1. Any document or object presented to the court as evidence in a case is a/an (a) rebuttal, (b) averment, (c) exhibit . . . .

1. _____

2. Indirect evidence or an inference which may be made from other facts proven in the case is called (a) circumstantial evidence, (b) opinion evidence, (c) expert evidence . . . .

2. _____

3. Testimony given by a witness, usually an expert, as to what the witness thinks or believes about the facts in the case is (a) circumstantial evidence, (b) opinion evidence, (c) rebuttal . . . .

3. _____

4. The repeating of what one heard another say is (a) hearsay, (b) perjury, (c) opinion evidence . . . .

4. _____

5. A positive declaration or assertion as to the facts in a case is a/an (a) averment, (b) evidence, (c) rebuttal . . . .

5. _____

6. A witness who intentionally or knowingly gives false testimony under oath is guilty of (a) perjury, (b) hearsay, (c) averment . . . .

6. _____

7. A witness who is openly prejudiced against the party who called the witness to testify in the case and who may be cross examined by the party who called the witness is referred to as a/an (a) hostile witness, (b) incompetent, (c) averment

7. _____

8. Testimony given by a person who has special qualifications to testify in regard to specific facts in the case is (a) expert evidence, (b) circumstantial evidence, (c) perjury . . . .

8. _____

9. Testimony, exhibits, or other matter presented in the trial of a case to prove the alleged facts are (a) hearsay, (b) perjury, (c) evidence . . . .

9. _____

10. An attempt to disprove the evidence presented by the other side is a/an (a) hearsay, (b) rebuttal, (c) exhibit . . . .

10. _____

11. An exception to the hearsay rule and a term meaning things done is (a) impeach, (b) perjury, (c) res gestae . . . .

11. _____

12. A term meaning to introduce or present evidence in a case is (a) exhibit, (b) hearsay, (c) adduce . . . .

12. _____

13. To prove in a trial that a witness cannot or should not be believed is to (a) res gestae, (b) impeach, (c) exhibit . . . .

13. _____

14. A word which means not qualified legally and pertains to evidence which is not admissible in court is (a) res gestae, (b) incompetent, (c) hearsay . . . .

14. _____

Turn back to page 78 and continue with this lesson.

Quiz No. 2

Terminology and Definition Recall

Directions: In the Answers column write the legal term that is most representative of the corresponding statement. After you have completed this quiz, check your answers with the key on page 333. Unless otherwise directed, turn in this quiz to your instructor upon completion of this lesson.

ANSWERS

1. A person who has no interest in a case but is called in by the judge to give advice regarding some matter of law is a/an _____.

   1. _____

2. In a criminal case, if the defendant presents proof of being in another place at the time the crime was committed, the defendant is said to have a/an _____.

   2. _____

3. A Latin term meaning pending litigation or during the time the case is in court is _____.

   3. _____

4. Evidence presented in a case that is believable is _____.

   4. _____

5. An officer of the court who is in charge of the jury or who may also guard prisoners when they appear in court is a/an _____.

   5. _____

6. Implying a cause or having to do with cause and effect is _____.

   6. _____

7. Evidence which has greater weight or greater value is referred to as the _____.

   7. _____

8. If a jury is secluded from the public until a verdict is reached, it is said to be _____.

   8. _____

9. The instructions given by the judge to the jury before deliberations as to the rules of law which apply to the case is the _____.

   9. _____

10. A Latin term which means at first view or evidence which is sufficient to prove or establish a fact unless contrary evidence is presented is _____.

    10. _____

11. The duty which the plaintiff has in a case to prove the defendant guilty is the _____.

    11. _____

12. The process of the jury discussing the case in an effort to reach a verdict is called _____.

    12. _____

13. The speeches given by counsel at the end of the case in an effort to persuade the jury to decide the case in favor of their client are the _____.

    13. _____

Turn back to page 81 and continue with this lesson.

Lesson 8, Quiz No. 2

# EVALUATION
No. 4

Student _____

Class _____ Date_____

SCORING RECORD

	Perfect Score	Student's Score
Section A	50	
Section B	20	
Section C	30	
Total	100	

SECTION A

Directions: This dictation/transcription evaluation will test your spelling and transcription ability on the legal terms that you studied in the two preceding lessons. Use a 5-space paragraph indention, a 70-space line and double spacing unless otherwise instructed. Correct all errors. Follow one of the procedures below.

Typing Procedure

Using the cassette from Evaluation 4, transcribe the dictation directly at your typewriter.

Shorthand Procedure

Using the cassette from Evaluation 4, take the dictation using your shorthand system and then transcribe on the typewriter from your shorthand notes.

SECTIONS B AND C ARE AVAILABLE FROM YOUR INSTRUCTOR.

"A matter which has been decided is considered true."
—Legal Maxim

LESSON 9

To Wit: Litigation—
Verdicts and Judgments

Verdicts by a jury and judgments by the presiding judge involve certain basic legal terminology with which all nonlawyer personnel should be familiar. The terminology in this lesson covers the most common types of verdicts and judgments. Upon completion of the exercises, you should be able to spell, pronounce, define, and transcribe the litigation terms that are presented.

Part A	Terminology and Definitions

Directions: Study the terms, pronunciations, and definitions until you are thoroughly familiar with them. In order to complete this lesson successfully, you must understand the meaning and usage of all the legal terms presented. If you are using shorthand, write your shorthand outline in the space provided or on your shorthand machine for each legal term.

LEGAL TERM	PRONUNCIATION	DEFINITION	SHORTHAND OUTLINE
1. verdict	'vər-dikt	The decision of a jury on a case submitted to them for their determination.	_____
2. polling the jury	'pōl-iŋ thə 'jür-ē	After the foreman or forewoman presents the verdict of the jury to the court, each juror may be asked what the juror's individual verdict is in the case.	_____
3. hung jury	'hüŋ 'jür-ē	A jury that cannot reach a verdict.	_____
4. exonerate	ig-'zän-ə-rāt	To prove or declare a person innocent of the charges made against that person.	_____
5. guilty	'gil-tē	Convicted of committing a crime. Not innocent.	_____
6. acquittal	ə-'kwit-l	The verdict that declares one innocent of a crime.	_____

7. opinion	ə-ˈpin-yən	A statement by a judge which gives the reasons for the decision made in a case.	_____
8. advisement	əd-ˈvīz-mənt	The consideration and thought which a case is given by the judge before the decision is made. The case is said to be "under advisement."	_____
9. per curiam	pər ˈkū-rē-am	Latin. "By the court." Indicates an opinion by the entire court.	_____
10. dictum	ˈdik-təm	Latin. An authoritative opinion by a judge on points other than the actual issue in the case.	_____
11. judgment	ˈjej-mənt	The decision of the court.	_____
12. res judicata	rēz jüd-i-ˈkät-ə	Latin. "A thing decided." Something that has been decided in a court of law.	_____
13. judgment by default	ˈjej-mənt bī di-ˈfolt	A judgment given against a party in a suit who fails to make an appearance in court.	_____

Turn to page 97 and complete Quiz No. 1 before continuing this lesson.

Typing Legal Terms

Directions: Unless otherwise instructed, use a 70-space line and double spacing. Correct all errors. Follow one of the procedures below.

Words

Typing Procedure

On a separate sheet of paper, type the following words at least two times, concentrating on the correct spelling and pronunciation.

Shorthand Procedure

On a separate sheet of paper, type the following words once, concentrating on the correct spelling and pronunciation. Then write the shorthand outline for each word on the lines to the right or on your shorthand machine. Cover the printed words with a sheet of paper and transcribe from the shorthand outlines one time on your typewriter.

verdict / polling the jury / hung jury / exonerate /   _____

guilty / acquittal / opinion / advisement / per   _____

curiam / dictum / judgment / res judicata /   _____

judgment by default /   _____

Sentences

Typing Procedure

Type each of the following sentences one time. Concentrate on the correct spelling and pronunciation of each underlined legal term.

Shorthand Procedure

Write the correct shorthand outlines for the following sentences on the lines to the right or on your shorthand machine. Cover the printed material with a sheet of paper and transcribe from your shorthand outlines one time on the typewriter.

These sentences will be used for practice dictation on the cassettes.

The verdict is the decision of a jury on a case submitted to them for their determination. Polling the jury is asking each juror if the verdict announced by the foreman or forewoman is that juror's individual verdict. An attorney may request that a jury be polled. A jury that cannot reach a verdict is referred to as a hung jury. To exonerate means to prove or declare a person innocent of the charges. A verdict of acquittal is the proving or declaring a person innocent of the charges. If the verdict of the jury is guilty, then the jury is convinced that the person so charged did commit the crime. If a judge hears a case instead of a jury, the judge may give an opinion which gives the reasons for the decision made in a case. Before rendering an opinion, the court takes the case under consideration and thought, which is referred to as taking the case under advisement. If an opinion represents the opinion of the entire court rather than just one judge, it is referred to as per curiam. Per curiam can also refer to an opinion written by the chief justice or presiding judge of the court. A dictum is an authoritative opinion by a judge on points other than the actual issue involved in the case. The decision of the court is a judgment. A judgment which is rendered because one of the parties failed to appear at the time specified by the court is a judgment by default. Res judicata is a Latin term meaning "a thing decided" or something that has been decided in a court of law.

Directions: This dictation emphasizes and reinforces the legal terms and definitions you have studied. Listen carefully to the pronunciation of each of the legal terms. Unless otherwise directed, use a 70-space line and double spacing. Correct all errors. Follow one of the procedures below.

Typing Procedure

Using the cassette from Lesson 9, Part A, transcribe the dictation directly at your typewriter.

Shorthand Procedure

Using the cassette from Lesson 9, Part A, take the dictation using your shorthand system and then transcribe on the typewriter from your shorthand notes.

When you have finished transcribing Part A of the practice dictation, check your transcript with the printed copy. If you made any mistakes in the transcription, you should practice those words several times before going on.

Part B | Terminology and Definitions

Directions: Study the terms, pronunciations, and definitions until you are thoroughly familiar with them. In order to complete this lesson successfully, you must understand the meaning and usage of all the legal terms presented. If you are using shorthand, write your shorthand outline in the space provided or on your shorthand machine for each legal term.

LEGAL TERM	PRONUNCIATION	DEFINITION	SHORTHAND OUTLINE
1. adjudge	ə-'jəj	To decide, settle, or sentence by law.	_____
2. dismiss	dis-'mis	To refuse to consider a case in court.	_____
3. dismissal without prejudice	dis-'mis-əl with-'aut 'prej-əd-əs	The plaintiff is not prevented from suing again on the same cause of action.	_____
4. dismissal with prejudice	dis-'mis-əl with 'prej-əd-əs	The plaintiff cannot sue again on the same cause of action.	_____
5. stare decisis	'ster-ē di-'si-səs	Latin. "Let the decision stand." Pertains to the policy of a court to follow precedent when deciding cases.	_____
6. nonsuit	'nän-süt	A judgment which terminates a lawsuit because the plaintiff is unable or refuses to prove the case.	_____
7. decision	di-'sizh-ən	The judgment of the court rendered in a case brought before it.	_____
8. decree	di-'krē	An official decision or order made by a court or a judge.	_____

9.	final decree	'fīn-l di-'krē	A final decision of the court which resolves all issues in a case.	_____
10.	interlocutory decree	int-ər-'läk-yə-tōr-ē di-'krē	A temporary decree. Not final.	_____
11.	decree nisi	di-'krē 'nī-sī	Latin. A decree which will take effect unless it is successfully contested.	_____
12.	order	'ȯrd-ər	A rule of law. A command issued in writing by a court. Not a judgment.	_____
13.	restraining order	ri-'strān-iŋ 'ȯrd-ər	An order issued by the court to prevent someone from doing something until the court decides whether or not to issue an injunction.	_____
14.	sine die	sī-ni 'dī	Latin. Without day. The final adjournment or dismissal of a case against a defendant.	_____

Turn to page 98 and complete Quiz No. 2 before continuing this lesson.

Typing Legal Terms

Directions: Unless otherwise instructed, use a 70-space line and double spacing. Correct all errors. Follow one of the procedures below.

Words

Typing Procedure

On a separate sheet of paper, type the following words at least two times, concentrating on the correct spelling and pronunciation.

Shorthand Procedure

On a separate sheet of paper, type the following words once, concentrating on the correct spelling and pronunciation. Then write the shorthand outline for each word on the lines to the right or on your shorthand machine. Cover the printed words with a sheet of paper and transcribe from the shorthand outlines one time on your typewriter.

adjudge / dismiss / dismissal without prejudice / _____

dismissal with prejudice / stare decisis / nonsuit / _____

decision / decree / final decree / interlocutory _____

decree / decree nisi / order / restraining order / _____

sine die / _____

Sentences

Type each of the following sentences one time. Concentrate on the correct spelling and pronunciation of each underlined legal term.

Write the correct shorthand outlines for the following sentences on the lines to the right or on your shorthand machine. Cover the printed material with a sheet of paper and transcribe from your shorthand outlines one time on the typewriter.

These sentences will be used for practice dictation on the cassettes.

To adjudge a case is to decide or settle it by law. To dismiss an action or suit is to refuse to consider the case in court. A dismissal without prejudice permits the plaintiff to sue again on the same cause of action; whereas, a dismissal with prejudice prevents the plaintiff from suing again on the same cause of action. Stare decisis is a Latin term meaning "let the decision stand." Stare decisis pertains to the policy of a court to follow precedent when deciding cases. Nonsuit is a judgment which terminates a lawsuit in the defendant's favor because the plaintiff is unable or refuses to prove the case. A decree is an official decision or order made by a court or judge. A decree is final and is made when the case is heard in court. The words judgment and decree are sometimes used synonymously. A decision is a judgment of the court rendered in a case brought before it. An order is a rule of law or a command issued in writing by the court. A restraining order is an order issued by the court to prevent a person from doing something until the court decides whether or not to issue an injunction. An interlocutory decree is a temporary decree which is issued prior to a final decree. The final decree is a final decision of the court which resolves all the issues in a case. A decree nisi is a temporary decree which will be made final on motion unless it is successfully contested. Sine die is a Latin term meaning without day. When a case is adjourned

sine die, it means the case is dismissed and no
future date is set to hear it.

_____

_____

_____

Directions: This dictation emphasizes and reinforces the legal terms and definitions you have studied. Listen carefully to the pronunciation of each of the legal terms. Unless otherwise directed, use a 70-space line and double spacing. Correct all errors. Follow one of the procedures below.

Typing Procedure

Using the cassette from Lesson 9, Part B, transcribe the dictation directly at your typewriter.

Shorthand Procedure

Using the cassette from Lesson 9, Part B, take the dictation using your shorthand system and then transcribe on the typewriter from your shorthand notes.

When you have finished transcribing Part B of the practice dictation, check your transcript with the printed copy. If you have made any mistakes in the transcription, you should practice those words several times before going on to Lesson 10.

Check List

	PART A, DATE	PART B, DATE	SUBMITTED TO INSTRUCTOR	
			YES	NO
Terminology and Definitions	_____	_____	_____	_____
*Typing Legal Terms	_____	_____	_____	_____
Words	_____	_____	_____	_____
Sentences	_____	_____	_____	_____
*Transcribing from Dictation	_____	_____	_____	_____
Quiz No. 1	_____	_____	_____	_____
Quiz No. 2	_____	_____	_____	_____

When you have successfully completed all the exercises in this lesson and submitted to your instructor those called for, you are ready to proceed with Lesson 10.

*If you are using a shorthand system, turn in to your instructor your shorthand notes along with your transcript.

Quiz No. 1

Terminology and Definition Recall

Directions: In the Answers column write the legal term that is most representative of the corresponding statement. After you have completed this quiz, check your answers with the key on page 333. Unless otherwise directed, turn in this quiz to your instructor upon completion of this lesson.

ANSWERS

1. A Latin term which means "a thing decided" or something that has been decided in a court of law is _____.

1. _____

2. An authoritative opinion by a judge on points other than the actual issue involved in the case is a/an _____.

2. _____

3. The consideration and thought which a case is given by the judge before the decision is made is called _____.

3. _____

4. The decision of a jury on a case submitted to them for their determination is called the _____.

4. _____

5. To prove or declare a person innocent of the charges made against that person is to _____.

5. _____

6. The decision of the court is a/an _____.

6. _____

7. A statement by a judge which gives the reasons for the decision made in a case is a/an _____.

7. _____

8. When each individual juror is asked what that juror's verdict is in the case, the process is known as _____.

8. _____

9. A jury that cannot reach a verdict is referred to as a/an _____.

9. _____

10. A judgment given against a party in a suit who fails to make an appearance in court is called a/an _____.

10. _____

11. A Latin term which means "by the court" and indicates an opinion by the entire court is _____.

11. _____

12. A person convicted of a crime is said to be _____.

12. _____

13. Declaring one innocent of a crime is a/an _____.

13. _____

Turn back to page 90 and continue with this lesson.

Quiz No. 2

Terminology and Definition Recall

Directions: In the Answers column write the letter from Column I that represents the word or phrase that best matches each item in Column II. After you have completed this quiz, check your answers with the key on page 333. Unless otherwise directed, turn in this quiz to your instructor upon completion of this lesson.

COLUMN I	COLUMN II	ANSWERS
A. adjudge	**1.** An order issued by the court to prevent someone from doing something until the court decides whether or not to issue an injunction.	1. _____
B. decision		
C. decree	**2.** A Latin term which means "let the decision stand" and pertains to the policy of a court to follow precedent when deciding cases.	2. _____
D. decree nisi		
E. dismiss	**3.** The adjournment or dismissal of a case in which no future date is set to hear it.	3. _____
F. dismissal with prejudice	**4.** To decide, settle, or sentence by law.	4. _____
G. dismissal without prejudice	**5.** A temporary decree.	5. _____
H. final decree	**6.** A dismissal which states that a plaintiff cannot sue again on the same cause of action.	6. _____
I. injunction		
J. interlocutory decree	**7.** A decree which will take effect unless it is successfully contested.	7. _____
K. nonsuit	**8.** A judgment which terminates a lawsuit because the plaintiff is unable or refuses to prove the case.	8. _____
L. order		
M. restraining order	**9.** A rule of law. A command issued in writing by a court.	9. _____
N. sine die	**10.** The judgment of the court which is rendered in a case brought before it.	10. _____
O. stare decisis	**11.** An official decision or order made by a court or a judge.	11. _____
	12. To refuse to consider a case in court.	12. _____
	13. A dismissal which does not prevent the plaintiff from suing again on the same cause of action.	13. _____
	14. A final decision of the court which resolves all issues in a case.	14. _____

Turn back to page 93 and continue with this lesson.

"Extreme justice is extreme injustice."

—Legal Maxim

LESSON 10

To Wit: Litigation— Judgments and Appeals

Litigation activities in the courtroom usually terminate in a judgment in favor of one of the parties to the action. If the party against whom judgment is rendered is not satisfied with the outcome of the case, that party may file an appeal to a higher court to have the case reviewed. The appellate court may reverse the decision of the lower court, uphold the decision, or order a new trial. Additional terminology dealing with judgments and terms involved in the appellate process are introduced in this lesson. Upon completion of the following exercises, you should be able to spell, pronounce, define, and transcribe the litigation terms that are presented.

Part A	Terminology and Definitions

Directions: Study the terms, pronunciations, and definitions until you are thoroughly familiar with them. In order to complete this lesson successfully, you must understand the meaning and usage of all the legal terms presented. If you are using shorthand, write your shorthand outline in the space provided or on your shorthand machine for each legal term.

LEGAL TERM	PRONUNCIATION	DEFINITION	SHORTHAND OUTLINE
1. stay	stā	A delay or stopping of a legal proceeding by the court.	_____
2. supersedeas	sü-pər-'sēd-ē-əs	Latin. A writ issued by a judge to stay a legal proceeding.	_____
3. injunction	in-'jəŋ-shən	A writ issued by a court commanding a person to do or not to do some act.	_____
4. suppress	sə-'pres	To hold back or stop something.	_____
5. conclusion of fact	kən-'klü-zhən əv fakt	An assumption or conclusion based on the facts as presented in a case.	_____
6. conclusion of law	kən-'klü-zhən əv lo	An assumption or conclusion arrived at by applying the law to the facts as presented in the case.	_____

7.	enjoin	in-'join	To require or forbid an act to be or not to be done.	_____
8.	damages	'dam-ijs	An amount of money awarded by a court to one who was injured by another.	_____
9.	compensatory damages	kəm-'pen-sə-tōr-ē 'dam-ijs	Damages awarded which are equal to and no more than the amount of the actual loss.	_____
10.	award	ə-'wȯrd	To grant or to give. To decide or settle by law.	_____
11.	redress	'rē-dres	To correct a wrong. To provide satisfaction or relief for one who has been injured by another.	_____
12.	nunc pro tunc	nunk prō tunk	Latin. "Now for then." A decision or order of the court which is retroactive.	_____
13.	status quo	'stāt-əs kwō	Latin. The way things are or their existing state at a given time.	_____

Turn to page 107 and complete Quiz No. 1 before continuing this lesson.

Typing Legal Terms

Directions: Unless otherwise instructed, use a 70-space line and double spacing. Correct all errors. Follow one of the procedures below.

Words

Typing Procedure

On a separate sheet of paper, type the following words at least two times, concentrating on the correct spelling and pronunciation.

Shorthand Procedure

On a separate sheet of paper, type the following words once, concentrating on the correct spelling and pronunciation. Then write the shorthand outline for each word on the lines to the right or on your shorthand machine. Cover the printed words with a sheet of paper and transcribe from the shorthand outlines one time on your typewriter.

stay / supersedeas / injunction / suppress /   _____

conclusion of fact / conclusion of law / enjoin /   _____

damages / compensatory damages / award / redress /   _____

nunc pro tunc / status quo /   _____

Sentences

Type each of the following sentences one time. Concentrate on the correct spelling and pronunciation of each underlined legal term.

Write the correct shorthand outlines for the following sentences on the lines to the right or on your shorthand machine. Cover the printed material with a sheet of paper and transcribe from your shorthand outlines one time on the typewriter.

These sentences will be used for practice dictation on the cassettes.

To <u>stay</u> a proceeding is a delay or a stopping of a legal proceeding by the court. <u>Supersedeas</u> is the Latin name for a writ issued by a judge to stay a legal proceeding. A writ issued by a court commanding a person to do or not to do some act is an <u>injunction</u>. To <u>suppress</u> something is to hold it back or to stop it. A <u>conclusion of fact</u> is an assumption or conclusion based on the facts in a case; whereas, a <u>conclusion of law</u> is an assumption or conclusion arrived at by applying the law to the facts as presented in a case. <u>Enjoin</u> means to require or forbid an act to be or not to be done. Therefore, a writ of injunction enjoins a person to perform or not to perform some act. An amount of money awarded by a court to one who was injured by another is <u>damages</u>. Damages awarded which are equal to and no more than the amount of actual loss are called <u>compensatory damages</u>. <u>Award</u> means to grant, give, or to decide by law. <u>Redress</u> is the correcting of a wrong or to provide satisfaction or relief for one who has been injured by another. The awarding of compensatory damages by a jury is redress for the plaintiff. <u>Nunc pro tunc</u> is a Latin term meaning "now for then." Nunc pro tunc applies to a decision or order of the court which is retroactive. The Latin term referring to the way things are or their existing state at a given time is <u>status quo</u>. The status quo would refer to the way things were preceding a cause of action.

Directions: This dictation emphasizes and reinforces the legal terms and definitions you have studied. Listen carefully to the pronunciation of each of the legal terms. Unless otherwise directed, use a 70-space line and double spacing. Correct all errors. Follow one of the procedures below.

Typing Procedure

Using the cassette from Lesson 10, Part A, transcribe the dictation directly at your typewriter.

Shorthand Procedure

Using the cassette from Lesson 10, Part A, take the dictation using your shorthand system and then transcribe on the typewriter from your shorthand notes.

When you have finished transcribing Part A of the practice dictation, check your transcript with the printed copy. If you made any mistakes in the transcription, you should practice those words several times before going on.

Part B | Terminology and Definitions

Directions: Study the terms, pronunciations, and definitions until you are thoroughly familiar with them. In order to complete this lesson successfully, you must understand the meaning and usage of all the legal terms presented. If you are using shorthand, write your shorthand outline in the space provided or on your shorthand machine for each legal term.

LEGAL TERM	PRONUNCIATION	DEFINITION	SHORTHAND OUTLINE
1. appeal	ə-'pēl	To request an appellate court to review a case which was tried in a lower court.	_____
2. appellant	ə-'pel-ənt	One who appeals a decision or verdict.	_____
3. respondent	ri-'spän-dənt	The party who must contend against an appeal.	_____
4. review	ri-'vyü	An examination by an appellate court of a case that was tried in a lower court.	_____
5. brief	brēf	A statement filed with an appellate court which gives the facts and points of law on which the appeal is based.	_____
6. abrogate	'ab-rə-gāt	To abolish or do away with something, such as an order issued by a lower court.	_____
7. reverse	ri-'vərs	To repeal or change to the opposite.	_____
8. certiorari	sər-shə-'rar-ē	Latin. An order or writ of review or inquiry used in an appellate proceeding.	_____

9. remittitur	ri-'mit-ə-tər	Latin. The sending back of a case by the appellate court to a lower court. Also, the plaintiff returning damages awarded in a case which were in excess of what the plaintiff requested.	_____
10. error coram vobis	'er-ər 'kō-ram 'vō-bis	Latin. A writ issued by an appellate court to a lower court which states that an error was made in the proceedings "before you."	_____
11. error coram nobis	'er-ər 'kō-ram 'nō-bis	Latin. A writ issued by an appellate court stating that an error was committed in the proceeding "before us."	_____
12. mandamus	man-'dā-məs	Latin. A writ issued by a higher court to a lower court commanding that a certain thing be done.	_____
13. rehearing	rē-'hir-iŋ	A retrial of a case in the court which heard it the first time in an effort to correct an error or omission.	_____
14. trial de novo	trīl dē 'nō-vō	A new trial of a case conducted by an appellate court as though there had been no other trial.	_____

Turn to page 108 and complete Quiz No. 2 before continuing this lesson.

Typing Legal Terms

Directions: Unless otherwise instructed, use a 70-space line and double spacing. Correct all errors. Follow one of the procedures below.

Words

Typing Procedure

On a separate sheet of paper, type the following words at least two times, concentrating on the correct spelling and pronunciation.

Shorthand Procedure

On a separate sheet of paper, type the following words once, concentrating on the correct spelling and pronunciation. Then write the shorthand outline for each word on the lines to the right or on your shorthand machine. Cover the printed words with a sheet of paper and transcribe from the shorthand outlines one time on your typewriter.

appeal / appellant / respondent / review / brief / _____

abrogate / reverse / certiorari / remittitur / _____

error coram vobis / error coram nobis / mandamus / _____

rehearing / trial de novo / _____

Lesson 10, Part B

Sentences

Typing Procedure

Type each of the following sentences one time. Concentrate on the correct spelling and pronunciation of each underlined legal term.

Shorthand Procedure

Write the correct shorthand outlines for the following sentences on the lines to the right or on your shorthand machine. Cover the printed material with a sheet of paper and transcribe from your shorthand outlines one time on the typewriter.

These sentences will be used for practice dictation on the cassettes.

An underline appeal is a request to an appellate court to review a case which was tried in a lower court. The party who appeals a decision or a verdict is called the appellant. The respondent is the party who must contend against an appeal. The appellate court will review or re-examine the case based upon the information filed in the brief by the appellant's counsel. The appeals court may abrogate or abolish an order by a lower court. An appeals court may reverse a judgment, sentence, or decree of a lower court, or the appeals court may order a new trial. Certiorari is an order or writ of review or inquiry used in an appellate proceeding. Remittitur means a remission or surrender. Remittitur is involved in cases that are sent back by an appellate court to a lower court. Remittitur also refers to the plaintiff returning damages awarded which were in excess of what the plaintiff requested. This is usually done upon an order by the court. An error coram vobis is a writ of error issued by an appellate court that an error was made in the proceedings "before you." An error coram nobis is a writ issued by an appellate court stating that an error was committed in the proceedings "before us." A mandamus is a writ issued by a higher court to a lower court commanding that a certain thing be done such as a rehearing or retrial of the issues. If a new trial is held in an appellate court, it is called a trial de novo.

Directions: This dictation emphasizes and reinforces the legal terms and definitions you have studied. Listen carefully to the pronunciation of each of the legal terms. Unless otherwise directed, use a 70-space line and double spacing. Correct all errors. Follow one of the procedures below.

Typing Procedure

Using the cassette from Lesson 10, Part B, transcribe the dictation directly at your typewriter.

Shorthand Procedure

Using the cassette from Lesson 10, Part B, take the dictation using your shorthand system and then transcribe on the typewriter from your shorthand notes.

When you have finished transcribing Part B of the practice dictation, check your transcript with the printed copy. If you have made any mistakes in the transcription, you should practice those words several times before going on to Evaluation 5.

Check List

	PART A, DATE	PART B, DATE	SUBMITTTED TO INSTRUCTOR	
			YES	NO
Terminology and Definitions	_____	_____	_____	_____
*Typing Legal Terms	_____	_____	_____	_____
Words	_____	_____	_____	_____
Sentences	_____	_____	_____	_____
*Transcribing from Dictation	_____	_____	_____	_____
Quiz No. 1	_____	_____	_____	_____
Quiz No. 2	_____	_____	_____	_____

When you have successfully completed all the exercises in this lesson and submitted to your instructor those called for, you are ready to proceed with Evaluation 5.

*If you are using a shorthand system, turn in to your instructor your shorthand notes along with your transcript.

Quiz No. 1

Terminology and Definition Recall

Directions: In the Answers column write the letter from Column I that represents the word or phrase that best matches each item in Column II. After you have completed this quiz, check your answers with the key on page 334. Unless otherwise directed, turn in this quiz to your instructor upon completion of this lesson.

COLUMN I	COLUMN II	ANSWERS
A. award	1. "Now for then." A decision or order of the court which is retroactive.	1. _____
B. compensatory damages	2. To grant or to give. To decide or settle by law.	2. _____
C. conclusion of fact	3. To require or forbid an act to be or not to be done.	3. _____
D. conclusion of law	4. An assumption or conclusion based on the facts in a case.	4. _____
E. damages	5. An amount of money awarded by a court to one who was injured by another.	5. _____
F. enjoin	6. A delay or stopping of a legal proceeding by the court.	6. _____
G. injunction	7. A writ issued by a judge commanding a person not to do some act.	7. _____
H. nunc pro tunc	8. The way things are or their existing state at a given time.	8. _____
I. redress	9. To correct a wrong. To provide satisfaction or relief for one who has been injured by another.	9. _____
J. reward	10. An assumption or conclusion arrived at by applying the law to the facts as presented in a case.	10. _____
K. status quo	11. A writ issued by a judge to stay a legal proceeding.	11. _____
L. stay	12. To hold or stop something.	12. _____
M. supersedeas	13. Damages which are equal to and no more than the amount of the actual loss.	13. _____
N. suppress		

Turn back to page 100 and continue with this lesson.

Quiz No. 2

Terminology and Definition Recall

Directions: In the Answers column at the right of each statement, write the letter that represents the word, or group of words, that correctly completes the statement. After you have completed this quiz, check your answers with the key on page 334. Unless otherwise directed, turn in this quiz to your instructor upon completion of this lesson.

ANSWERS

1. The party who must contend against an appeal is the (a) respondent, (b) appellant, (c) remittitur...   1. _____

2. An order or writ of review or inquiry used in an appellate proceeding is (a) certiorari, (b) mandamus, (c) trial de novo...........................   2. _____

3. A writ issued by an appellate court stating that an error was committed in the proceeding "before us" is a/an (a) error coram vobis, (b) error coram nobis, (c) trial de novo..   3. _____

4. A new trial of a case conducted by an appellate court as though there had been no other trial is a/an (a) abrogate, (b) rehearing, (c) trial de novo..........   4. _____

5. To abolish or do away with something such as an order issued by a lower court is to (a) abrogate, (b) reverse, (c) review ....   5. _____

6. To repeal or change to the opposite is to (a) abrogate, (b) reverse, (c) appeal   6. _____

7. A writ issued by a higher court to a lower court commanding that a certain thing be done is a (a) respondent, (b) mandamus, (c) brief.....................   7. _____

8. A writ issued by an appellate court to a lower court which states that an error was made in the proceedings "before you" is a/an (a) error coram vobis, (b) error coram nobis, (c) trial de novo.......................................   8. _____

9. An examination by an appellate court of a case that was tried in a lower court is a/an (a) error coram vobis, (b) rehearing, (c) review ....   9. _____

10. The request for an appellate court to review a case which was tried in a lower court is called a/an (a) certiorari, (b) appeal, (c) review....................   10. _____

11. A statement filed with an appellate court which gives the facts and points of law on which the appeal is based is a/an (a) mandamus, (b) brief, (c) appeal....   11. _____

12. The sending back of a case by the appellate court to a lower court or the plaintiff returning damages awarded in a case which were in excess of what the plaintiff requested is called (a) reverse, (b) remittitur, (c) error coram nobis ....   12. _____

13. A retrial of a case in the court which heard it the first time in an effort to correct an error or omission is a (a) remittitur, (b) review, (c) rehearing ....   13. _____

14. One who appeals a decision or verdict is a/an (a) appellant, (b) respondent, (c) certiorari..   14. _____

Turn back to page 103 and continue with this lesson.

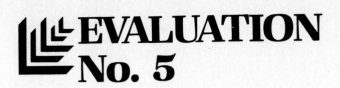# EVALUATION No. 5

SCORING RECORD

	Perfect Score	Student's Score
Section A	50	
Section B	20	
Section C	30	
Total	100	

SECTION A

Directions: This dictation/transcription evaluation will test your spelling and transcription ability on the legal terms that you studied in the two preceding lessons. Use a 5-space paragraph indention, a 70-space line and double spacing unless otherwise instructed. Correct all errors. Follow one of the procedures below.

Typing Procedure

Using the cassette from Evaluation 5, transcribe the dictation directly at your typewriter.

Shorthand Procedure

Using the cassette from Evaluation 5, take the dictation using your shorthand system and then transcribe on the typewriter from your shorthand notes.

SECTIONS B AND C ARE AVAILABLE FROM YOUR INSTRUCTOR.

"One must so use one's own rights as not to infringe upon the rights of another."

—Legal Maxim

LESSON 11

To Wit: Civil Actions

A civil action involves a violation of an individual's legal rights. It includes all the fields of law that govern relationships between individuals or institutions. Therefore, this lesson will cover terms that deal with civil law in general, and the more specialized areas of civil law will be presented in separate lessons. When you have completed these exercises you will be able to pronounce, define, spell, and transcribe the civil law terms that are included.

Part A	Terminology and Definitions

Directions: Study the terms, pronunciations, and definitions until you are thoroughly familiar with them. In order to complete this lesson successfully, you must understand the meaning and usage of all the legal terms presented. If you are using shorthand, write your shorthand outline in the space provided or on your shorthand machine for each legal term.

	LEGAL TERM	PRONUNCIATION	DEFINITION	SHORTHAND OUTLINE
1.	civil law	'sɪv-əl lō	Law which deals with the private rights of individuals.	_____
2.	actio civilis	'ak-shē-ō si-'vil-əs	Latin. A civil action.	_____
3.	actio in personam	'ak-shē-ō in pər-'son-am	Latin. A civil action directed against a specific person.	_____
4.	ex delicto	eks di-'likt-ō	Latin. A cause of action based on a civil wrong or tort.	_____
5.	tort	tȯrt	A civil wrong, other than a breach of contract, for which one has the right to bring a suit for recovery in a civil court.	_____
6.	willful tort	'wil-fəl tȯrt	A tort which was committed intentionally and maliciously.	_____

7.	tortious activity	'tor-shəs ak-'tiv-ət-ē	A wrongful or devious act.	_____
8.	tortfeasor	'tort-fē-zər	One who commits a tortious activity.	_____
9.	replevin	ri-'plev-ən	An action to recover personal property which another is illegally possessing.	_____
10.	allegation	al-i-'gā-shən	A statement of the facts made in a pleading which one intends to prove.	_____
11.	grievance	'grē-vəns	A cause or basis for a complaint.	_____
12.	intent	in-'tent	The purpose which one has for doing a certain thing.	_____

Turn to page 119 and complete Quiz No. 1 before continuing this lesson.

Typing Legal Terms

Directions: Unless otherwise instructed, use a 70-space line and double spacing. Correct all errors. Follow one of the procedures below.

Words

Typing Procedure

On a separate sheet of paper, type the following words at least two times, concentrating on the correct spelling and pronunciation.

Shorthand Procedure

On a separate sheet of paper, type the following words once, concentrating on the correct spelling and pronunciation. Then write the shorthand outline for each word on the lines to the right or on your shorthand machine. Cover the printed words with a sheet of paper and transcribe from the shorthand outlines one time on your typewriter.

civil law / actio civilis / actio in personam /

ex delicto / tort / willful tort / tortious activity /

tortfeasor / replevin / allegation / grievance /

intent /

_____

_____

_____

_____

Sentences

Typing Procedure

Type each of the following sentences one time. Concentrate on the correct spelling and pronunciation of each underlined legal term.

Shorthand Procedure

Write the correct shorthand outlines for the following sentences on the lines to the right or on your shorthand machine. Cover the printed material with a sheet of paper and transcribe from your shorthand outlines one time on the typewriter.

These sentences will be used for practice dictation on the cassettes.

Civil law is the law which deals with the private rights of individuals. Actio civilis means a civil action. An actio civilis is every action other than a criminal action. A civil action directed against a specific person is expressed in Latin as actio in personam. A tort is a civil wrong, other than a breach of contract, for which one has the right to bring a suit for recovery in a civil court. One who commits a tort is a tortfeasor. A willful tort is committed by a tortfeasor when the tortfeasor intentionally and maliciously injures another. A tortious activity is a wrongful or devious act. Ex delicto is a cause of action based on a civil wrong or tort. An action ex delicto would be an action based upon a tort. Replevin is an action to recover personal property which another is illegally possessing. A replevin may be filed against a tortfeasor who takes another's property illegally. An allegation is a statement of the facts made in a pleading which one intends to prove. A grievance is a cause or basis for a complaint. A grievance may become the basis for an allegation in a civil action. Intent is the purpose which one has for doing a certain thing. Intent is an element in the commission of a willful tort. One committing a tortious activity has an intent of harming another and is liable to become the defendant in an actio civilis.

Transcribing from Dictation

Directions: This dictation emphasizes and reinforces the legal terms and definitions you have studied. Listen carefully to the pronunciation of each of the legal terms. Unless otherwise directed, use a 70-space line and double spacing. Correct all errors. Follow one of the procedures below.

Typing Procedure

Using the cassette from Lesson 11, Part A, transcribe the dictation directly at your typewriter.

Shorthand Procedure

Using the cassette from Lesson 11, Part A, take the dictation using your shorthand system and then transcribe on the typewriter from your shorthand notes.

When you have finished transcribing Part A of the practice dictation, check your transcript with the printed copy. If you made any mistakes in the transcription, you should practice those words several times before going on.

Part B | Terminology and Definitions

Directions: Study the terms, pronunciations, and definitions until you are thoroughly familiar with them. In order to complete this lesson successfully, you must understand the meaning and usage of all the legal terms presented. If you are using shorthand, write your shorthand outline in the space provided or on your shorthand machine for each legal term.

LEGAL TERM	PRONUNCIATION	DEFINITION	SHORTHAND OUTLINE
1. right	rīt	Something that a person is legally entitled to.	_____
2. duty	'düt-ē	An obligation which one person has to another.	_____
3. due care or diligence	dü ker or 'dil-ə-zhans	As much care and attention as is required by the circumstances. The care that a reasonable person would have used in the same situation.	_____
4. damnum absque injuria	'dam-nəm 'abs-kwē 'inj-re-ə	Latin. "Loss without injury." A loss which cannot be recovered in a court of law.	_____
5. actio in rem	'ak-shē-ō in rem	Latin. An action for or against a thing rather than against a specific person.	_____
6. in forma pauperis	in for-ma 'po-pə-rəs	Latin. Permission granted by the court to a pauper or poor person to bring a suit without paying the court costs.	_____
7. negligence	'neg-li-jəns	The want of due care or diligence. The failure to do something or the doing of something which an ordinary, reasonable person would or would not do.	_____
8. comparative negligence	kəm-'par-ət-iv 'neg-li-jəns	A comparison of the negligence of the plaintiff and defendant. In some states, the plaintiff is permitted recovery when the plaintiff's negligence is less than that of the defendant. The amount of recovery may be decreased proportionately to the amount or degree of negligence.	_____
9. contributory negligence	kən-'trib-yə-tōr-ē 'neg-li-jəns	The negligence of the plaintiff which, together with the negligence of the defendant, caused the injury. In cases of contributory negligence, the plaintiff is not permitted to recover damages from the defendant.	_____

10. culpable   'kəl-pə-bəl   Failure to act with due care. The person   _____
    negligence 'neg-li-jəns   who commits culpable negligence is at fault
                               or blamable for injuries or damages.

11. imputation of   im-pyə-'tā-shən   A negligent act committed by one person   _____
    negligence   əv 'neg-li-jəns   but chargeable to another person who is re-
                                      sponsible for that person's acts. Thus, an
                                      employer may be held responsible for the
                                      negligence of an employee.

12. liability   lī-ə-'bil-ət-ē   Duty, obligation, or responsibility.   _____

13. absolute   'ab-sə-lüt   Liability without fault. Even though one   _____
    liability   lī-ə-'bil-ət-ē   exercises due care, the nature of the activ-
                                  ity which is being done may constitute a
                                  risk and harm to others in which case, one
                                  would be liable for any injury and damages
                                  to another even though no negligence was
                                  involved.

Turn to page 120 and complete Quiz No. 2 before continuing this lesson.

Typing Legal Terms

Directions: Unless otherwise instructed, use a 70-space line and double spacing. Correct all errors. Follow one of the procedures below.

Words

Typing Procedure

On a separate sheet of paper, type the following words at least two times, concentrating on the correct spelling and pronunciation.

Shorthand Procedure

On a separate sheet of paper, type the following words once, concentrating on the correct spelling and pronunciation. Then write the shorthand outline for each word on the lines to the right or on your shorthand machine. Cover the printed words with a sheet of paper and transcribe from the shorthand outlines one time on your typewriter.

right / duty / due care or diligence / damnum absque   _____
injuria / actio in rem / in forma pauperis /   _____
negligence / comparative negligence / contributory   _____
negligence / culpable negligence / imputation of   _____
negligence / liability / absolute liability   _____

Sentences

Typing Procedure

Type each of the following sentences one time. Concentrate on the correct spelling and pronunciation of each underlined legal term.

Shorthand Procedure

Write the correct shorthand outlines for the following sentences on the lines to the right or on your shorthand machine. Cover the printed material with a sheet of paper and transcribe from your shorthand outlines one time on the typewriter.

These sentences will be used for practice dictation on the cassettes.

A right is that which a person is entitled to. A duty is an obligation which one person has to another. Right and duty are reciprocal terms when used within their legal meanings. Thus, if one person has a right, then another person has a duty. Due care or diligence means as much care and attention as is required by the circumstances. A loss which cannot be recovered in a court of law is expressed in Latin as damnum absque injuria. Actio in rem is an action for the recovery of something another is possessing. In forma pauperis describes permission granted by the court to a pauper or a poor person to bring a suit without paying the court costs. The want of due care or diligence is negligence. If one fails to do something or does something that an ordinary, reasonable person would or would not do, that person may be charged with negligence. In law, negligence may be more specifically defined as contributory, comparative, and culpable. Contributory negligence means that the complaining party contributed to the cause of the injury. Comparative negligence involves negligence on the part of both parties but permits a recovery if the plaintiff's negligence is considerably less than that of the defendant. Culpable negligence is the failure to act with due care and could result in a criminal action in addition to a civil action. Imputation of negligence is negligence attributed to a person but actually committed by another person for whom one may be

responsible. Liability is a duty, obligation, or responsibility. Absolute liability is liability without
fault. Absolute liability applies to situations where
one is doing a legal, but very risky, act and another
is injured as a result of the act even though there
was no negligence involved.

Transcribing from Dictation

Directions: This dictation emphasizes and reinforces the legal terms and definitions you have studied. Listen carefully to the pronunciation of each of the legal terms. Unless otherwise directed, use a 70-space line and double spacing. Correct all errors. Follow one of the procedures below.

Typing Procedure

Using the cassette from Lesson 11, Part B, transcribe the dictation directly at your typewriter.

Shorthand Procedure

Using the cassette from Lesson 11, Part B, take the dictation using your shorthand system and then transcribe on the typewriter from your shorthand notes.

When you have finished transcribing Part B of the practice dictation, check your transcript with the printed copy. If you have made any mistakes in the transcription, you should practice those words several times before going on to Lesson 12.

Check List

	PART A, DATE	PART B, DATE	SUBMITTED TO INSTRUCTOR	
			YES	NO
Terminology and Definitions	_____	_____	_____	_____
*Typing Legal Terms	_____	_____	_____	_____
Words	_____	_____	_____	_____
Sentences	_____	_____	_____	_____
*Transcribing from Dictation	_____	_____	_____	_____
Quiz No. 1	_____	_____	_____	_____
Quiz No. 2	_____	_____	_____	_____

When you have successfully completed all the exercises in this lesson, and submitted to your instructor those called for, you are ready to proceed with Lesson 12.

*If you are using a shorthand system, turn in to your instructor your shorthand notes along with your transcript.

Quiz No. 1

Terminology and Definition Recall

Directions: In the Answers column write the legal term that is most representative of the corresponding statement. After you have completed this quiz, check your answers with the key on page 334. Unless otherwise directed, turn in this quiz to your instructor upon completion of this lesson.

ANSWERS

1. A wrongful or devious act is referred to as a/an _____ activity.

   1. _____

2. A statement of the facts made in a pleading which one intends to prove is the _____.

   2. _____

3. The purpose which one has for doing a certain thing is referred to as _____.

   3. _____

4. An action to recover personal property which another is illegally possessing is known as _____.

   4. _____

5. A tort which was committed intentionally and maliciously is a/an _____.

   5. _____

6. A cause of action based on a civil wrong or tort expressed in Latin is _____.

   6. _____

7. A cause or basis for a complaint is a/an _____.

   7. _____

8. One who commits a tortious activity is known as a/an _____.

   8. _____

9. The Latin term for a civil action is _____.

   9. _____

10. A civil wrong, other than a breach of contract, for which one has the right to bring a suit for recovery in a civil court is a/an _____.

    10. _____

11. Law which deals with the private rights of individuals is called _____.

    11. _____

12. A Latin term which means a civil action directed against a specific person is _____.

    12. _____

Turn back to page 112 and continue with this lesson.

Quiz No. 2

Terminology and Definition Recall

Directions: In the Answers column at the right of each statement, write the letter that represents the word, or group of words, that correctly completes the statement. After you have completed this quiz, check your answers with the key on page 334. Unless otherwise directed, turn in this quiz to your instructor upon completion of this lesson.

1. The care that a reasonable person would have used in the same situation or as much care and attention as is required by the circumstances is referred to as (a) right, (b) duty, (c) due care or diligence .... 1. _____

2. A liability without fault is referred to as (a) in forma pauperis, (b) absolute liability, (c) imputation of negligence .... 2. _____

3. Something that a person is legally entitled to is a (a) right, (d) duty, (c) liability 3. _____

4. An action for or against a thing rather than against a specific person is a/an (a) damnum absque injuria, (b) actio in rem, (c) in forma pauperis............. 4. _____

5. Permission granted by the court to a pauper or poor person to bring a suit without paying the court costs is expressed in Latin as (a) damnum absque injuria, (b) in forma pauperis, (c) actio in rem.. 5. _____

6. A comparison of the negligence of the plantiff and defendant is (a) contributory negligence, (b) culpable negligence, (c) comparative negligence .... 6. _____

7. A loss which cannot be recovered in a court of law is referred to in Latin as a/an (a) in forma pauperis, (b) actio in rem, (c) damnum absque injuria .... 7. _____

8. A duty, obligation, or responsibility is a (a) liability, (b) right, (c) duty ...... 8. _____

9. The negligence of the plaintiff which, together with the negligence of the defendant, caused the injury is (a) contributory negligence, (b) culpable negligence, (c) comparative negligence.................................. 9. _____

10. A negligent act committed by one person but chargeable to another who is responsible for that person's acts is (a) liability, (b) absolute liability, (c) imputation of negligence.. 10. _____

11. Failure to act with due care is (a) contributory negligence, (b) culpable negligence, (c) comparative negligence.................................. 11. _____

12. The failure to do something or the doing of something which an ordinary, reasonable person would or would not do is (a) negligence, (b) liability, (c) due care or diligence.. 12. _____

13. An obligation which one person has to another is a/an (a) right, (b) duty, (c) actio in rem .... 13. _____

Turn back to page 115 and continue with this lesson.

Lesson 11, Quiz No. 2

"No one should suffer by the act of another."

—Legal Maxim

LESSON 12

To Wit: Civil Actions

This lesson continues the study of some of the general terms involved in civil law or civil actions. A knowledge and understanding of this terminology will assist you in applying the terms to various civil actions and procedures. Upon completion of these exercises, you will be able to spell, pronounce, define, and transcribe the legal words presented herein.

| Part A | Terminology and Definitions |

Directions: Study the terms, pronunciations, and definitions until you are thoroughly familiar with them. In order to complete this lesson successfully, you must understand the meaning and usage of all the legal terms presented. If you are using shorthand, write your shorthand outline in the space provided or on your shorthand machine for each legal term.

LEGAL TERM	PRONUNCIATION	DEFINITION	SHORTHAND OUTLINE
1. proximate cause	'präk-sə-mət koz	The actual cause of an injury. Also referred to as the efficient cause.	_____
2. intervening cause	int-ər-'vēn-iŋ koz	A cause of injury which occurs after the negligent act of another and which could not have been expected to occur. One is not liable for an injury resulting from an intervening cause.	_____
3. misfeasance	mis-'fēz-ns	Improperly doing a legal act.	_____
4. nonfeasance	nän-'fēz-ns	Failure to do an act which one has a duty to perform.	_____
5. doctrine of last clear chance	'däk-trən əv last klir chans	A plaintiff who was contributorily negligent may recover for injuries if the defendant had a last clear chance to avoid the injury.	_____
6. tangible damages	'tan-jə-bəl 'dam-ijs	Damages which are real or actual. An essential element of torts.	_____

7.	punitive or exemplary damages	'pyü-nət-iv or ig-'zem-plə-rē 'dam-ijs	Damages over and above the amount of the actual loss which are awarded for mental anguish or the feelings of the one injured to serve as a punishment for the defendant or to set an example for others.	_____
8.	nominal damages	'näm-ən-l 'dam-ijs	A small amount of damages awarded in cases where an injury has occurred but tangible damages cannot be determined.	_____
9.	mental anguish	'ment-l 'aŋ-gwish	Suffering caused from emotional distress. In some states, damages may be awarded for mental anguish caused by an accident or injury.	_____
10.	trespasser	'tres-pəs-ər	One who unlawfully enters or goes upon another's property.	_____
11.	attractive nuisance doctrine	ə-'trak-tiv 'nüs-ens 'däk-trən	The doctrine applies to situations where something is on one's property that will attract young children and that person has a duty to exercise due care to prevent injury to them.	_____
12.	licensee	līs-n'sē	One who is on the premises of another for one's own advantage and without any enticement from the owner. A salesperson would be a licensee.	_____
13.	invitee	in-və-'tē	One who is upon the premises of another by express or implied invitation of the owner and whose purpose in being there is an advantage to the owner.	_____

Turn to page 129 and complete Quiz No. 1 before continuing this lesson.

Typing Legal Terms

Directions: Unless otherwise instructed, use a 70-space line and double spacing. Correct all errors. Follow one of the procedures below.

Words

Typing Procedure

On a separate sheet of paper, type the following words at least two times, concentrating on the correct spelling and pronunciation.

Shorthand Procedure

On a separate sheet of paper, type the following words once, concentrating on the correct spelling and pronunciation. Then write the shorthand outline for each word on the lines to the right or on your shorthand machine. Cover the printed words with a sheet of paper and transcribe from the shorthand outlines one time on your typewriter.

proximate cause / intervening cause / misfeasance /

nonfeasance / doctrine of last clear chance /

tangible damages / punitive or exemplary damages /

nominal damages / mental anguish / trespasser /

attractive nuisance doctrine / licensee / invitee /

Sentences

Typing Procedure

Type each of the following sentences one time. Concentrate on the correct spelling and pronunciation of each underlined legal term.

Shorthand Procedure

Write the correct shorthand outlines for the following sentences on the lines to the right or on your shorthand machine. Cover the printed material with a sheet of paper and transcribe from your shorthand outlines one time on the typewriter.

These sentences will be used for practice dictation on the cassettes.

Proximate cause is the actual cause of an injury. A proximate cause is also referred to as an efficient cause. An intervening cause is a cause of injury which occurs after the negligent act and which could not have been expected to occur. One is not liable for an injury resulting from an intervening cause. If a person is accused of misfeasance, the person did a lawful act improperly; but, if one is accused of nonfeasance, then the person failed to do an act which that person had a duty to perform. The doctrine of last clear chance makes a person liable if there was a last clear chance to avoid injuring or damaging another. Several types of damages may be awarded in a civil action. Tangible damages are an essential element of torts. Damages which are real or actual are tangible damages. Punitive or exemplary damages are damages over and above the amount of the actual loss that are awarded for mental anguish or the feelings of the one injured to serve as a punishment for the defendant or to set an example for others. Nominal damages are a small amount of damages awarded in cases where an injury has occurred but tangible damages cannot be determined. <u>Mental anguish</u> is suffering caused from emotional distress. In some states, damages may be awarded for mental anguish caused by an accident or injury. The <u>attractive nuisance doctrine</u> applies to situations where something is on one's property which will attract young children and that person has a duty to exercise due care to prevent an injury to them. A <u>trespasser</u>, <u>licensee</u>, and <u>invitee</u> are classifications of persons who enter or use another's premises. A trespasser is one who unlawfully enters or goes upon another's property; a licensee is there legally but for the licensee's own advantage; and the invitee is there for a reason which is of advantage to the owner.

Transcribing from Dictation

Directions: This dictation emphasizes and reinforces the legal terms and definitions you have studied. Listen carefully to the pronunciation of each of the legal terms. Unless otherwise directed, use a 70-space line and double spacing. Correct all errors. Follow one of the procedures below.

Typing Procedure

Using the cassette from Lesson 12, Part A, transcribe the dictation directly at your typewriter.

Shorthand Procedure

Using the cassette from Lesson 12, Part A, take the dictation using your shorthand system and then transcribe on the typewriter from your shorthand notes.

When you have finished transcribing Part A of the practice dictation, check your transcript with the printed copy. If you made any mistakes in the transcription, you should practice those words several times before going on.

Part B | Terminology and Definitions

Directions: Study the terms, pronunciations, and definitions until you are thoroughly familiar with them. In order to complete this lesson successfully, you must understand the meaning and usage of all the legal terms presented. If you are using shorthand, write your shorthand outline in the space provided or on your shorthand machine for each legal term.

LEGAL TERM	PRONUNCIATION	DEFINITION	SHORTHAND OUTLINE
1. assumption of risk	ə-'səm-shən əv risk	If one voluntarily takes a chance and is injured as a result thereof, then that person is not considered to be injured in the eyes of the law.	_____
2. foreseeability of injury	fōr-'sē-ə-bil-ət-ē əv 'inj-rē	The capability of seeing and knowing that an injury may result from certain acts or omissions.	_____
3. knowledge of the peril	'näl-ij əv thə 'per-əl	When one has knowledge of something that may cause injury to another and fails to do something about it. An element which is essential to prove negligence.	_____
4. probable consequences	'präb-ə-bəl 'kän-sə-kwens-əs	A result which is most likely to follow a particular cause.	_____
5. ordinary, reasonable person	'ȯrd-n-er-ē 'rēz-nə-bəl 'pərs-n	A normal, average person who has good judgment in everyday affairs.	_____
6. act or omission	akt ȯr ō-'mish-ən	The doing or the failure to do something. The test is applied to determine whether a tort has been committed.	_____
7. constructive notice	kən-'strək-tiv 'nōt-əs	Knowledge that one should have because the condition has existed for such a period of time that the person would have known had due care been exercised.	_____
8. wanton, reckless, and intentional	'wȯnt-n 'rek-ləs ən in-'tench-nəl	Willful misconduct which constitutes culpable negligence. Acts done with indifference and disregard of the consequences to others.	_____
9. implied or imputed knowledge	im-'plīd ȯr im-'pyüt-əd 'näl-ij	Knowledge which a person should have had or is responsible for having. Usually applies to an employer-employee relationship or an agency.	_____
10. Good Samaritan Statute	güd sə-'mar-ət-n 'stach-üt	If one sees another in serious danger and tries to help the person, the one who gives assistance cannot be charged with contributory negligence. This doctrine varies from state to state.	_____
11. sudden emergency doctrine	'sən-n i-'mər-jən-sē 'däk-trən	The degree of care required of a person in an emergency situation is less than would be required if the person had time to think before acting.	_____

| 12. sovereign immunity | 'säv-rən im-'yü-nət-ē | Protection from tort prosecution which is given to governmental units and officials in connection with the performance of their official duties. | _____ |
| 13. res ipsa loquitur | rēz 'ip-sa 'lō-kwə-tər | Latin. "The thing speaks for itself." A presumption that the thing that happened does not normally happen unless there is negligence involved. It is a rebuttable presumption that may be proven otherwise by the facts. | _____ |

Turn to page 130 and complete Quiz No. 2 before continuing this lesson.

Typing Legal Terms

Directions: Unless otherwise instructed, use a 70-space line and double spacing. Correct all errors. Follow one of the procedures below.

Words

Typing Procedure

On a separate sheet of paper, type the following words at least two times, concentrating on the correct spelling and pronunciation.

Shorthand Procedure

On a separate sheet of paper, type the following words once, concentrating on the correct spelling and pronunciation. Then write the shorthand outline for each word on the lines to the right or on your shorthand machine. Cover the printed words with a sheet of paper and transcribe from the shorthand outlines one time on your typewriter.

assumption of risk / foreseeability of injury /

knowledge of the peril / probable consequences /

ordinary, reasonable person / act or omission /

constructive notice / wanton, reckless, and

intentional / implied or imputed knowledge / Good

Samaritan Statute / sudden emergency doctrine /

sovereign immunity / res ipsa loquitur /

Sentences

Typing Procedure

Type each of the following sentences one time. Concentrate on the correct spelling and pronunciation of each underlined legal term.

Shorthand Procedure

Write the correct shorthand outlines for the following sentences on the lines to the right or on your shorthand machine. Cover the printed material with a sheet of paper and transcribe from your shorthand outlines one time on the typewriter.

These sentences will be used for practice dictation on the cassettes.

Assumption of risk means if one voluntarily takes a chance and is injured as a result thereof, then that person is not considered to be injured in the eyes of the law. Knowledge of the peril exists whenever one has the capability of seeing or knowing that an injury may result from certain acts or omissions. Foreseeability of injury is the ability to see or know in advance the probable consequences of an act or omission. An ordinary, reasonable person is one who is normal, average, and has good judgment in everyday affairs. If a person could have discovered a fact by exercising due care, the person is said to have had constructive notice of the fact. Wanton, reckless, and intentional describe an act done with indifference and disregard of the consequences to others. Implied or imputed knowledge is knowledge which a person should have had or is responsible for having. Implied or imputed knowledge usually applies to an employer-employee relationship or an agency. Under the sudden emergency doctrine, the degree of care required of a person in an emergency situation is less than that required if the person had time to think before acting. The Good Samaritan Statute protects one from contributory negligence if assistance is given to someone who is in danger provided a certain degree of care is used. Sovereign immunity is protection from tort prosecution which is given to governmental units and officials in connection with the performance of their official duties. Res ipsa loquitur is a Latin phrase meaning "the thing speaks for itself."

Directions: This dictation emphasizes and reinforces the legal terms and definitions you have studied. Listen carefully to the pronunciation of each of the legal terms. Unless otherwise directed, use a 70-space line and double spacing. Correct all errors. Follow one of the procedures below.

Typing Procedure

Using the cassette from Lesson 12, Part B, transcribe the dictation directly at your typewriter.

Shorthand Procedure

Using the cassette from Lesson 12, Part B, take the dictation using your shorthand system and then transcribe on the typewriter from your shorthand notes.

When you have finished transcribing Part B of the practice dictation, check your transcript with the printed copy. If you have made any mistakes in the transcription, you should practice those words several times before going on to Evaluation 6.

Check List

I have completed the following for Lesson 12:

	PART A, DATE	PART B, DATE	SUBMITTED TO INSTRUCTOR YES	NO
Terminology and Definitions	_____	_____	_____	_____
*Typing Legal Terms	_____	_____	_____	_____
Words	_____	_____	_____	_____
Sentences	_____	_____	_____	_____
*Transcribing from Dictation	_____	_____	_____	_____
Quiz No. 1	_____	_____	_____	_____
Quiz No. 2	_____	_____	_____	_____

When you have successfully completed all the exercises in this lesson and submitted to your instructor those called for, you are ready to proceed with Evaluation 6.

*If you are using a shorthand system, turn in to your instructor your shorthand notes along with your transcript.

Quiz No. 1

Terminology and Definition Recall

Directions: In the Answers column write the legal term that is most representative of the corresponding statement. After you have completed this quiz, check your answers with the key on page 334. Unless otherwise directed, turn in this quiz to your instructor upon completion of this lesson.

ANSWERS

1. A plaintiff who was contributorily negligent may recover for injuries if the defendant had an opportunity just before the injury occurred to prevent it under the doctrine of _____.

1. _____

2. One who is on the premises of another for one's own advantage and without any enticement from the owner is a/an _____.

2. _____

3. A doctrine which applies to a situation where something is on one's property which will attract young children and which requires that person to exercise due care to prevent injury to them is the _____ doctrine.

3. _____

4. A cause of injury which occurs after the negligent act of another and which could not have been expected to occur is a/an _____ cause.

4. _____

5. A small amount of damages awarded in cases where an injury has occurred but tangible damages cannot be determined are _____ damages.

5. _____

6. Damages which are awarded over and above the amount of the actual loss for mental anguish or the feelings of the one injured to serve as a punishment for the defendant or to set an example for others are referred to as (a) _____ or (b) _____ damages.

6(a). _____
6(b). _____

7. Damages which are real or actual and which are an essential element of torts are _____ damages.

7. _____

8. One who is upon the premises of another by express or implied invitation of the owner and whose purpose in being there is an advantage to the owner is a/an _____.

8. _____

9. Suffering which is caused from emotional distress is referred to as _____.

9. _____

10. One who unlawfully enters or goes upon another's property is a/an _____.

10. _____

11. The failure to do an act which one has a duty to perform is referred to as _____.

11. _____

12. The improper doing of a legal act is called _____.

12. _____

13. The actual cause of an injury or the efficient cause is the _____.

13. _____

Turn back to page 122 and continue with this lesson.

Quiz No. 2

Terminology and Definition Recall

Directions: In the Answers column write the letter from Column I that represents the word or phrase that best matches each item in Column II. After you have completed this quiz, check your answers with the key on page 334. Unless otherwise directed, turn in this quiz to your instructor upon completion of this lesson.

COLUMN I	COLUMN II	ANSWERS
A. act or omission	**1.** A normal, average, person who has good judgment in everyday affairs.	1. _____
B. assumption of risk		
C. constructive notice	**2.** A doctrine which states that the degree of care required of a person in an emergency situation is less than would be required if the person had time to think before acting.	2. _____
D. foreseeability of injury		
E. Good Samaritan Statute	**3.** A doctrine which states that if one sees another in serious danger and tries to help the person, the one giving assistance cannot be charged with contributory negligence.	3. _____
F. implied or imputed knowledge		
G. knowledge of the peril	**4.** A situation where one voluntarily takes a chance and is injured as a result thereof, and, in the eyes of the law, that person is not considered to be injured.	4. _____
H. ordinary, reasonable person		
I. probable consequences	**5.** Willful misconduct which constitutes culpable negligence. Acts done with indifference and disregard of the consequences to others.	5. _____
J. res ipsa loquitur		
K. res judicata	**6.** When one has knowledge of something that may cause injury to another and fails to do anything about it.	6. _____
L. sovereign immunity		
M. sudden emergency doctrine	**7.** Knowledge that one should have because the condition has existed for such a period of time that the person would have known if due care had been exercised.	7. _____
N. wanton, reckless, and intentional		
	8. The capability of seeing or knowing that an injury may result from certain acts or omissions.	8. _____
	9. The doing or the failure to do something. The test applied to determine whether a tort has been committed.	9. _____
	10. Protection from tort prosecution which is given to governmental units and officials in connection with the performance of their official duties.	10. _____
	11. A presumption that the thing which happened does not normally happen unless there is negligence involved.	11. _____
	12. A result which is most likely to follow a particular cause.	12. _____

Turn back to page 126 and continue with this lesson.

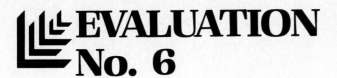 **EVALUATION No. 6**

Student _____

Class _____ Date _____

SCORING RECORD

	Perfect Score	Student's Score
Section A	50	
Section B	20	
Section C	30	
Total	100	

SECTION A

Directions: This dictation/transcription evaluation will test your spelling and transcription ability on the legal terms that you studied in the two preceding lessons. Use a 5-space paragraph indention, a 70-space line and double spacing unless otherwise instructed. Correct all errors. Follow one of the procedures below.

Typing Procedure

Using the cassette from Evaluation 6, transcribe the dictation directly at your typewriter.

Shorthand Procedure

Using the cassette from Evaluation 6, take the dictation using your shorthand system and then transcribe on the typewriter from your shorthand notes.

SECTIONS B AND C ARE AVAILABLE FROM YOUR INSTRUCTOR.

"An act does not make guilty unless there be a guilty intent."

—Legal Maxim

LESSON 13

To Wit: Criminal Law

Criminal law deals with crimes committed in violation of a law. A crime is a public wrong and is prosecuted by the state or "the people." This lesson contains some of the basic terminology involved in criminal procedures. You should be able to spell, pronounce, define, and transcribe the terms presented when you have completed these exercises.

| Part A | Terminology and Definitions |

Directions: Study the terms, pronunciations, and definitions until you are thoroughly familiar with them. In order to complete this lesson successfully, you must understand the meaning and usage of all the legal terms presented. If you are using shorthand, write your shorthand outline in the space provided or on your shorthand machine for each legal term.

LEGAL TERM	PRONUNCIATION	DEFINITION	SHORTHAND OUTLINE
1. grand jury	grand ′jur-ē	A jury which makes inquiries into criminal cases and, when the evidence indicates that a crime has been committed, issues indictments.	_____
2. indictment	in-′dīt-mənt	A written accusation issued by a grand jury charging that there is evidence that a crime has been committed and that the person so charged should be brought to trial.	_____
3. crime	krīm	An illegal act which is punishable in a court of law.	_____
4. corpus delicti	′kor-pəs di-′lik-tī	Latin. "The body of a crime." The material evidence that indicates a crime has been committed.	_____
5. felony	′fel-ə-nē	A crime of a serious nature which is punishable by imprisonment or death.	_____

6.	misdemeanor	mis-di-'mē-nər	Any crime that is not a felony. Usually punishable by fine or a short jail sentence.	_____
7.	warrant	'wȯr-ənt	A written order giving the authority to arrest a person or to search or seize property.	_____
8.	arrest	ə-'rest	The act of taking a person into legal custody to answer to a criminal or civil charge.	_____
9.	habeas corpus	'hā-bē-əs 'kȯr-pəs	Latin. A writ requiring someone holding a person to bring that person into court to determine if the person is being held justly or legally.	_____
10.	extradition	ek-strə-'dish-ən	The delivery of a person from one state to another for trial or punishment.	_____
11.	preliminary examination	pri-'lim-ə-ner-ē ig-zam-ə-'nā-shən	A hearing conducted by a judge to determine if there is enough evidence to hold a person accused of a crime for trial.	_____
12.	information	in-fər-'mā-shən	A written accusation issued by a prosecuting attorney charging a person with a crime.	_____
13.	offense	ə-'fens	A wrongdoing which is punishable by fine or imprisonment.	_____
14.	arraignment	ə-'rān-mənt	To bring a person before a court of law to hear the charges in the indictment or information and to enter a plea of guilty or not guilty.	_____

Turn to page 141 and complete Quiz No. 1 before continuing this lesson.

Typing Legal Terms

Directions: Unless otherwise instructed, use a 70-space line and double spacing. Correct all errors. Follow one of the procedures below.

Words

Typing Procedure

On a separate sheet of paper, type the following words at least two times, concentrating on the correct spelling and pronunciation.

Shorthand Procedure

On a separate sheet of paper, type the following words once, concentrating on the correct spelling and pronunciation. Then write the shorthand outline for each word on the lines to the right or on your shorthand machine. Cover the printed words with a sheet of paper and transcribe from the shorthand outlines one time on your typewriter.

grand jury / indictment / crime / corpus delicti /

felony / misdemeanor / warrant / arrest / habeas

corpus / extradition / preliminary examination /

information / offense / arraignment /

_____

_____

_____

_____

Sentences

Typing Procedure

Type each of the following sentences one time. Concentrate on the correct spelling and pronunciation of each underlined legal term.

Shorthand Procedure

Write the correct shorthand outlines for the following sentences on the lines to the right or on your shorthand machine. Cover the printed material with a sheet of paper and transcribe from your shorthand outlines one time on the typewriter.

These sentences will be used for practice dictation on the cassettes.

A grand jury is a jury which makes inquiries into criminal cases and, when the evidence indicates that a crime has been committed, issues indictments. An indictment is a written accusation issued by a grand jury charging that there is evidence that a crime has been committed and that the person so charged should be brought to trial. A crime is an illegal act which is punishable in a court of law. An indictment issued by a grand jury is based on the corpus delicti. Corpus delicti means "the body of a crime" or the material evidence that indicates a crime has been committed. A crime is classified as a felony or a misdemeanor. A felony is a crime of a serious nature which is punishable by imprisonment or death. A misdemeanor is any crime that is not a felony and is usually punishable by fine or a short jail sentence. When a person has been charged with the commission of a crime, a warrant is issued requiring the arrest of that person. When a person is arrested, the person is taken into custody and held to answer the charge made against that person. A writ of habeas corpus requires someone holding a person to bring that person to court. If a person charged with a crime is arrested in a state other than the one in which the crime was committed, the person may be returned _____

to the state in which the crime was committed by _____

the process of extradition. A preliminary examina- _____

tion is a hearing conducted by a judge to determine _____

if there is enough evidence to hold for trial the per- _____

son accused of a crime. An information is a written _____

accusation issued by a prosecuting attorney charg- _____

ing a person with committing a criminal offense. At _____

the arraignment, the prisoner is brought before the _____

court to hear the reading of the indictment or the _____

information and to enter a plea of guilty or not _____

guilty. _____

Transcribing from Dictation

Directions: This dictation emphasizes and reinforces the legal terms and definitions you have studied. Listen carefully to the pronunciation of each of the legal terms. Unless otherwise directed, use a 70-space line and double spacing. Correct all errors. Follow one of the procedures below.

Typing Procedure

Using the cassette from Lesson 13, Part A, transcribe the dictation directly at your typewriter.

Shorthand Procedure

Using the cassette from Lesson 13, Part A, take the dictation using your shorthand system and then transcribe on the typewriter from your shorthand notes.

When you have finished transcribing Part A of the practice dictation, check your transcript with the printed copy. If you made any mistakes in the transcription, you should practice those words several times before going on.

Part B | Terminology and Definitions

Directions: Study the terms, pronunciations, and definitions until you are thoroughly familiar with them. In order to complete this lesson successfully, you must understand the meaning and usage of all the legal terms presented. If you are using shorthand, write your shorthand outline in the space provided or on your shorthand machine for each legal term.

LEGAL TERM	PRONUNCIATION	DEFINITION	SHORTHAND OUTLINE
1. plea	plē	An answer made by a defendant at the arraignment for a criminal offense.	_____

2. confession	kən-ˈfesh-ən	A statement made voluntarily by a person admitting that the person committed a crime.	_____
3. admission	əd-ˈmish-ən	A statement which confirms that certain facts in a case are true. It is not a confession of guilt.	_____
4. nolo contendere	ˈnō-lō kən-ˈten-də-rē	Latin. "I do not wish to contend." The plea of a defendant in a criminal action that means the punishment will be accepted but guilt will not be admitted.	_____
5. defense	di-ˈfens	The defendant's denial to an accusation. The contesting of a lawsuit.	_____
6. insanity	in-ˈsan-ət-ē	A state of unsound mind in which a person does not know right from wrong and is, therefore, not responsible for any acts committed.	_____
7. Durham Rule	ˈdər-əm rül	A rule applied in some states which does not hold a person responsible for an act if it was done as the result of mental disease or defect.	_____
8. M'Naghten Rule	mə-nät-ən rül	A rule applied in some states that if a person does not have the mental capacity to know right from wrong, that person is not criminally responsible.	_____
9. non compos mentis	nän ˈkäm-pəs ˈmənt-əs	Latin. "Not of sound mind." Indicates that one is mentally unable to control one's own actions or to handle one's own affairs. Insanity.	_____
10. criminal intent	ˈkrim-ən-l in-ˈtent	The plan or design to commit a crime.	_____
11. sine qua non	sin-i kwä nan	Latin. Something that is essential.	_____
12. scienter	sī-ˈen-tər	Latin. Knowingly, intent or knowledge.	_____
13. irresistible impulse	ir-i-ˈzis-tə-bəl ˈim-pəls	An uncontrollable urge to commit a crime due to insanity or a mental defect or disease.	_____

Turn to page 142 and complete Quiz No. 2 before continuing this lesson.

Typing Legal Terms

Directions: Unless otherwise instructed, use a 70-space line and double spacing. Correct all errors. Follow one of the procedures below.

Words

Typing Procedure

On a separate sheet of paper, type the following words at least two times, concentrating on the correct spelling and pronunciation.

plea / confession / admission / nolo contendere /

defense / insanity / Durham Rule / M'Naghten Rule /

non compos mentis / criminal intent / sine qua non /

scienter / irresistible impulse /

Shorthand Procedure

On a separate sheet of paper, type the following words once, concentrating on the correct spelling and pronunciation. Then write the shorthand outline for each word on the lines to the right or on your shorthand machine. Cover the printed words with a sheet of paper and transcribe from the shorthand outlines one time on your typewriter.

_____

_____

_____

_____

Sentences

Typing Procedure

Type each of the following sentences one time. Concentrate on the correct spelling and pronunciation of each underlined legal term.

Shorthand Procedure

Write the correct shorthand outlines for the following sentences on the lines to the right or on your shorthand machine. Cover the printed material with a sheet of paper and transcribe from your shorthand outlines one time on the typewriter.

These sentences will be used for practice dictation on the cassettes.

A <u>plea</u> is an answer made by a defendant at the arraignment. A <u>confession</u> is a statement made voluntarily by a person admitting that the person committed a crime. An <u>admission</u> is a statement which confirms that certain facts in a case are true, but it is not a confession of guilt. <u>Nolo contendere</u> is a Latin term meaning "I do not wish to contend." Nolo contendere is a plea of a defendant in a criminal action that means the punishment will be accepted but guilt will not be admitted. A <u>defense</u> is the defendant's denial to an accusation or the contesting of a lawsuit. As a defense in criminal law, <u>insanity</u> is a state of unsound mind in which a person does not know right from wrong and is, therefore, not responsible for any acts committed. The Latin term <u>non compos mentis</u> means "not of

_____

_____

_____

_____

_____

_____

_____

_____

_____

_____

_____

_____

_____

_____

_____

_____

_____

sound mind." The Durham Rule and the M'Naghten Rule are sometimes applied to a defendant who pleads non compos mentis. The Durham Rule is applied in some states as an irresistible impulse test. An irresistible impulse is an uncontrollable urge to commit a crime due to insanity or a mental defect or disease. The M'Naghten Rule is a right-wrong test of criminal responsibility—did the person have sufficient understanding to know right from wrong? A criminal intent is the plan or design to commit a crime. Criminal intent is a sine qua non—an essential element—for one to be guilty of a crime. Scienter means "knowingly" and when used in a pleading, it means that the defendant was aware of what was being done.

Transcribing from Dictation

Directions: This dictation emphasizes and reinforces the legal terms and definitions you have studied. Listen carefully to the pronunciation of each of the legal terms. Unless otherwise directed, use a 70-space line and double spacing. Correct all errors. Follow one of the procedures below.

Typing Procedure

Using the cassette from Lesson 13, Part B, transcribe the dictation directly at your typewriter.

Shorthand Procedure

Using the cassette from Lesson 13, Part B, take the dictation using your shorthand system and then transcribe on the typewriter from your shorthand notes.

When you have finished transcribing Part B of the practice dictation, check your transcript with the printed copy. If you have made any mistakes in the transcription, you should practice those words several times before going on to Lesson 14.

Check List

	PART A, DATE	PART B, DATE	SUBMITTED TO INSTRUCTOR	
			YES	NO
Terminology and Definitions	_____	_____	_____	_____
*Typing Legal Terms	_____	_____	_____	_____
Words	_____	_____	_____	_____
Sentences	_____	_____	_____	_____
*Transcribing from Dictation	_____	_____	_____	_____
Quiz No. 1	_____	_____	_____	_____
Quiz No. 2	_____	_____	_____	_____

When you have successfully completed all the exercises in this lesson and submitted to your instructor those called for, you are ready to proceed with Lesson 14.

*If you are using a shorthand system, turn in to your instructor your shorthand notes along with your transcript.

Quiz No. 1

Terminology and Definition Recall

Directions: In the Answers column write the legal term that is most representative of the corresponding statement. After you have completed this quiz, check your answers with the key on page 335. Unless otherwise directed, turn in this quiz to your instructor upon completion of this lesson.

ANSWERS

1. A crime of a serious nature which is punishable by imprisonment or death is a/an _____.

1. _____

2. A written accusation issued by a prosecuting attorney charging a person with a crime is a/an _____.

2. _____

3. A wrongdoing which is punishable by fine or imprisonment is a/an _____.

3. _____

4. A writ requiring someone holding a person to bring that person into court to determine if the person is being held justly or legally is a writ of _____.

4. _____

5. An illegal act which is punishable in a court of law is a/an _____.

5. _____

6. A written order giving the authority to arrest a person or to search or seize property is a/an _____.

6. _____

7. The delivery of a person from one state to another for trial or punishment is a/an _____.

7. _____

8. A written accusation issued by a grand jury charging that there is evidence that a crime has been committed and that the person so charged should be brought to trial is a/an _____.

8. _____

9. A jury which makes inquiries into criminal cases and, when the evidence indicates that a crime has been committed, issues indictments is a/an _____.

9. _____

10. The act of taking a person into legal custody to answer to a criminal charge is a/an _____.

10. _____

11. The process of bringing a person before a court of law to hear the charges in the indictment or information and to enter a plea of guilty or not guilty is the _____.

11. _____

12. The body of a crime or the material evidence that indicates a crime has been committed is expressed in Latin as _____.

12. _____

13. Any crime that is not a felony and which is usually punishable by fine or short jail sentence is called a/an _____.

13. _____

14. A hearing conducted by a judge to determine if there is enough evidence to hold for trial a person accused of a crime is the _____.

14. _____

Turn back to page 134 and continue with this lesson.

Quiz No. 2

Terminology and Definition Recall

Directions: In the Answers column at the right of each statement, write the letter that represents the word, or group of words, that correctly completes the statement. After you have completed this quiz, check your answers with the key on page 335. Unless otherwise directed, turn in this quiz to your instructor upon completion of this lesson.

ANSWERS

1. The plan or design to commit a crime is a/an (a) irresistible impulse, (b) criminal intent, (c) defense. . . . .

1. _____

2. A statement made voluntarily by a person admitting that the person committed a crime is a/an (a) admission, (b) confession, (c) plea. . . . .

2. _____

3. Something that is essential is (a) non compos mentis, (b) scienter, (c) sine qua non. . . . .

3. _____

4. A Latin term which indicates that one is mentally unable to control one's own actions or to handle one's own affairs is (a) non compos mentis, (b) nolo contendere, (c) sine qua non. . . . .

4. _____

5. A rule applied in some states which does not hold a person responsible for an act if it was done as the result of mental disease or defect is the (a) criminal intent, (b) M'Naghten Rule, (c) Durham Rule. . . . .

5. _____

6. The plea of a defendant in a criminal action that means the punishment will be accepted but guilt will not be admitted is (a) nolo contendere, (b) non compos mentis, (c) sine qua non. . . . .

6. _____

7. An answer made by a defendant at the arraignment for a criminal offense is a/an (a) confession, (b) plea, (c) admission. . . . .

7. _____

8. A statement which confirms that certain facts in a case are true is a/an (a) admission, (b) plea, (c) scienter. . . . .

8. _____

9. A state of unsound mind in which a person does not know right from wrong and is, therefore, not responsible for any acts committed is (a) insanity, (b) defense, (c) confession. . . . .

9. _____

10. A rule applied in some states that if a person does not have the mental capacity to know right from wrong, that person is not criminally responsible is the (a) Durham Rule, (b) irresistible impulse test, (c) M'Naghten Rule. . . . .

10. _____

11. An uncontrollable urge to commit a crime due to insanity or a mental defect or disease is a/an (a) scienter, (b) irresistible impulse, (c) criminal intent. . . . . .

11. _____

12. A Latin term which means "knowingly" or intent and knowledge is (a) scienter, (b) sine qua non, (c) nolo contendere. . . . .

12. _____

13. The defendant's denial to an accusation or the contesting of a lawsuit is the (a) defense, (b) admission, (c) plea. . . . .

13. _____

Turn back to page 137 and continue with this lesson.

"One who spares the guilty threatens the innocent."
—Legal Maxim

LESSON 14

To Wit: Criminal Law

This lesson continues the study of some of the basic terms which are applicable to the field of criminal law. When you have successfully completed these exercises, you will be able to spell, define, pronounce, and transcribe the legal terms presented which pertain to criminal law.

| Part A | Terminology and Definitions |

Directions: Study the terms, pronunciations, and definitions until you are thoroughly familiar with them. In order to complete this lesson successfully, you must understand the meaning and usage of all the legal terms presented. If you are using shorthand, write your shorthand outline in the space provided or on your shorthand machine for each legal term.

	LEGAL TERM	PRONUNCIATION	DEFINITION	SHORTHAND OUTLINE
1.	principal	'prin-sə-pəl	One who actually commits the crime or who actually or constructively aids and abets in its commission.	_____
2.	accomplice	ə-'käm-pləs	One who knowingly assists a principal in the commission of a crime.	_____
3.	accessory	ik-'ses-ə-rē	One who aids the principal in the commission of a crime but is not present when the crime is actually committed. An accessory before the fact knowingly takes steps to effect the crime; whereas, an accessory after the fact knowingly assists in concealing the crime and/or the offender.	_____
4.	aid and abet	ād ən ə-'bet	To assist in a criminal act by giving encouragement or support to its commission.	_____

5.	reasonable doubt	'rēz-nə-bəl daut	Doubt which is logical, credible, or plausible. It is not an imaginary or fictitious doubt which one can have about anything. In a criminal case, proof must be "beyond a reasonable doubt" not "beyond all doubt."	_____
6.	conviction	kən-'vik-shən	The outcome of a criminal trial whereby one is found guilty of the charges that were made.	_____
7.	imprisonment	im-'priz-ən-mənt	The act of placing a person in a prison or place of confinement.	_____
8.	incarcerate	in-'kär-sə-rāt	To imprison in a jail or penitentiary as a result of due legal process.	_____
9.	bail	bāl	Security placed with the court in order to obtain release for one being held in jail until the time of the trial.	_____
10.	sentence	'sent-ens	The punishment given by the court to one convicted of a crime.	_____
11.	reprieve	ri-'prēv	A delay or postponement of punishment.	_____
12.	pardon	'pärd-n	Releases one who has committed a crime from the punishment required by law. A pardon may be absolute or conditional.	_____
13.	parole	pə-'rōl	The release of one from prison before the end of the sentence. A parole is conditional in that if one violates the terms of the parole, the remainder of the sentence must be served.	_____

Turn to page 151 and complete Quiz No. 1 before continuing this lesson.

Typing Legal Terms

Directions: Unless otherwise instructed, use a 70-space line and double spacing. Correct all errors. Follow one of the procedures below.

Words

Typing Procedure

On a separate sheet of paper, type the following words at least two times, concentrating on the correct spelling and pronunciation.

Shorthand Procedure

On a separate sheet of paper, type the following words once, concentrating on the correct spelling and pronunciation. Then write the shorthand outline for each word on the lines to the right or on your shorthand machine. Cover the printed words with a sheet of paper and transcribe from the shorthand outlines one time on your typewriter.

principal / accomplice / accessory / aid and abet / reasonable doubt / conviction / imprisonment / incarcerate / bail / sentence / reprieve / pardon / parole /

_____
_____
_____
_____

Sentences

Typing Procedure

Type each of the following sentences one time. Concentrate on the correct spelling and pronunciation of each underlined legal term.

Shorthand Procedure

Write the correct shorthand outlines for the following sentences on the lines to the right or on your shorthand machine. Cover the printed material with a sheet of paper and transcribe from your shorthand outlines one time on the typewriter.

These sentences will be used for practice dictation on the cassettes.

The parties to a crime may be a underline{principal}, an underline{accomplice}, and an underline{accessory}. One who actually commits the crime or who aids and abets in its commission is a principal. An accomplice is one who knowingly assists the principal in the commission of a crime. An accessory is one who aids the principal in the commission of a crime but is not present when the crime is actually committed. To underline{aid and abet} is to assist in a criminal act by giving encouragement or support to its commission. underline{Reasonable doubt} is a doubt which is logical, credible, or plausible. Reasonable doubt is not an imaginary or fictitious doubt. A underline{conviction} is the outcome of a criminal trial whereby one is found guilty of the charges that were made. Proof beyond a reasonable doubt is required in a criminal case for conviction. When one is convicted of a criminal offense, the underline{sentence} may be underline{imprisonment} in a jail or penitentiary. underline{Incarcerate} also means to imprison. A defendant may be released on underline{bail} which means that security is placed with the court in order to obtain release for one being held in jail until the time of the trial. underline{Reprieve}, underline{pardon}, and underline{parole} all relate to the prisoner serving a lesser sentence than that given at the end of the trial. A reprieve is a _____

delay or postponement of punishment. A pardon _____

releases one who has committed a crime from the _____

punishment required by law. A parole is a _____

conditional release of a person from prison before _____

the end of the sentence. _____

Transcribing from Dictation

Directions: This dictation emphasizes and reinforces the legal terms and definitions you have studied. Listen carefully to the pronunciation of each of the legal terms. Unless otherwise directed, use a 70-space line and double spacing. Correct all errors. Follow one of the procedures below.

Typing Procedure

Using the cassette from Lesson 14, Part A, transcribe the dictation directly at your typewriter.

Shorthand Procedure

Using the cassette from Lesson 14, Part A, take the dictation using your shorthand system and then transcribe on the typewriter from your shorthand notes.

When you have finished transcribing Part A of the practice dictation, check your transcript with the printed copy. If you made any mistakes in the transcription, you should practice those words several times before going on.

Part B — Terminology and Definitions

Directions: Study the terms, pronunciations, and definitions until you are thoroughly familiar with them. In order to complete this lesson successfully, you must understand the meaning and usage of all the legal terms presented. If you are using shorthand, write your shorthand outline in the space provided or on your shorthand machine for each legal term.

	LEGAL TERM	PRONUNCIATION	DEFINITION	SHORTHAND OUTLINE
1.	mala in se (plural, malum in se)	'ma-lə in se / 'ma-ləm in se	Latin. A wrong which is bad in itself. Wrongs which violate the morals of society such as murder, arson, rape, and robbery.	_____
2.	mala prohibita (plural, malum prohibitum)	'ma-lə prō-'hib-ə-tə / 'ma-ləm prō-'hib-ə-təm	Latin. A wrong which is bad because it is prohibited by law.	_____
3.	murder	'mərd-ər	The intentional killing of another human being with malice aforethought.	_____
4.	homicide	'häm-ə-sīd	The killing of a human being by another whether intentional or unintentional.	_____

5. malice aforethought	'mal-əs ə-'for-thot	The deliberate planning and intention to kill or seriously injure another person. An essential element which distinguishes murder from other types of homicide.	_____
6. manslaughter	'man-slot-ər	A killing of another human being which is unlawful and done without malice aforethought. Manslaughter may be voluntary or involuntary. Voluntary manslaughter is a killing done in a heat of passion or on a provoked sudden impulse. Involuntary manslaughter is usually the result of negligence.	_____
7. larceny	'lärs-nē	Illegally taking and carrying away personal property belonging to another with no intention of returning the property to the owner. The value of the goods stolen determines whether it is petit larceny or grand larceny.	_____
8. robbery	'räb-ə-rē	A felony which is committed by one taking the property from the person or in the presence of the person by the use of force or violence and with no intention of returning the property to the owner.	_____
9. animus furandi	'an-ə-məs 'fyur-an-dī	Latin. The intent to steal the property of another and to permanently deprive the owner of said property. An essential element of a larceny.	_____
10. assault and battery	ə-'solt ən 'bat-ə-rē	Assault is an actual threat to inflict bodily harm upon another, and battery is the putting of the threat into effect. Usually, the two terms are used together in a charge because a battery is assumed, in law, to be preceded by an assault.	_____
11. utter and publish	'ət-ər ən 'pəb-lish	The offering of a forged instrument with the intent to defraud.	_____
12. forgery	'forj-ə-rē	The alteration of anything in writing with the intention of defrauding another.	_____
13. break and enter	brāk ən 'ent-ər	Forcible and unlawful entry such as into a building, car, or boat with the intent to commit a crime therein. A burglary. Sometimes called a "B & E."	_____
14. constructive breaking	kən-'strək-tiv 'brāk-iŋ	A breaking and entering which is accomplished by fraud, threats, or trickery.	_____

Turn to page 152 and complete Quiz No. 2 before continuing this lesson.

Lesson 14, Part B

Typing Legal Terms

Directions: Unless otherwise instructed, use a 70-space line and double spacing. Correct all errors. Follow one of the procedures below.

Words

Typing Procedure

On a separate sheet of paper, type the following words at least two times, concentrating on the correct spelling and pronunciation.

Shorthand Procedure

On a separate sheet of paper, type the following words once, concentrating on the correct spelling and pronunciation. Then write the shorthand outline for each word on the lines to the right or on your shorthand machine. Cover the printed words with a sheet of paper and transcribe from the shorthand outlines one time on your typewriter.

mala in se / malum in se / mala prohibita / malum

prohibitum / murder / homicide / malice aforethought /

manslaughter / larceny / robbery / animus furandi /

assault and battery / utter and publish / forgery /

break and enter / constructive breaking /

Sentences

Typing Procedure

Type each of the following sentences one time. Concentrate on the correct spelling and pronunciation of each underlined legal term.

Shorthand Procedure

Write the correct shorthand outlines for the following sentences on the lines to the right or on your shorthand machine. Cover the printed material with a sheet of paper and transcribe from your shorthand outlines one time on the typewriter.

These sentences will be used for practice dictation on the cassettes.

Malum in se are wrongs which are bad in themselves. Malum prohibitum are wrongs which are bad because they are prohibited by law. An act such as murder is mala in se (bad in itself); whereas, double parking would be mala prohibita (bad because prohibited by law). Homicide is the killing of a human being by another whether intentional or unintentional. Homicide is a necessary ingredient of the crimes of murder and manslaughter. Murder is the intentional killing of another human being with malice aforethought which is the deliberate planning and intention to kill or seriously injure another person. Manslaughter is the killing of another human being which is unlawful and done without malice aforethought. Larceny and robbery both are felonies which involve the taking of another's personal property unlawfully. An essential element of larceny is <u>animus furandi</u>, the intent to steal the property of another and to permanently deprive the owner of said property. <u>Assault and battery</u> are two terms that are often combined. Assault is the threat to inflict bodily harm upon another; whereas, battery is the putting of the threat into effect. <u>Forgery</u> is the alteration of anything in writing with the intent to defraud. Thus, one might forge a signature on a check. The offering of a forged check for payment is to <u>utter and publish</u>. Forcible and unlawful entry into a building with the intent to commit a crime therein is to <u>break and enter</u>. Breaking and entering is commonly referred to as a "B & E." If a burglar gains entry into a house by fraud, threats, or trickery, it is referred to as <u>constructive breaking</u>.

Transcribing from Dictation

Directions: This dictation emphasizes and reinforces the legal terms and definitions you have studied. Listen carefully to the pronunciation of each of the legal terms. Unless otherwise directed, use a 70-space line and double spacing. Correct all errors. Follow one of the procedures below.

Typing Procedure

Using the cassette from Lesson 14, Part B, transcribe the dictation directly at your typewriter.

Shorthand Procedure

Using the cassette from Lesson 14, Part B, take the dictation using your shorthand system and then transcribe on the typewriter from your shorthand notes.

When you have finished transcribing Part B of the practice dictation, check your transcript with the printed copy. If you have made any mistakes in the transcription, you should practice those words several times before going on to Evaluation 7.

Check List

	PART A, DATE	PART B, DATE	SUBMITTED TO INSTRUCTOR	
			YES	NO
Terminology and Definitions	_____	_____	_____	_____
*Typing Legal Terms	_____	_____	_____	_____
Words	_____	_____	_____	_____
Sentences	_____	_____	_____	_____
*Transcribing from Dictation	_____	_____	_____	_____
Quiz No. 1	_____	_____	_____	_____
Quiz No. 2	_____	_____	_____	_____

When you have successfully completed all the exercises in this lesson and submitted to your instructor those called for, you are ready to proceed with Evaluation 7.

*If you are using a shorthand system, turn in to your instructor your shorthand notes along with your transcript.

Quiz No. 1

Terminology and Definition Recall

Directions: In the Answers column write the legal term that is most representative of the corresponding statement. After you have completed this quiz, check your answers with the key on page 335. Unless otherwise directed, turn in this quiz to your instructor upon completion of this lesson.

ANSWERS

1. An absolute or conditional release of one who has committed a crime from the punishment required by law is a/an _____.

   1. _____

2. A delay or postponement of punishment is referred to as a/an _____.

   2. _____

3. The release of one from prison before the end of the sentence on the condition that if that person violates the terms of the release, the remainder of the sentence must be served is known as a/an _____.

   3. _____

4. Security placed with the court in order to obtain release for one being held in jail until the time of the trial is called _____.

   4. _____

5. The punishment given by the court to one convicted of a crime is the _____.

   5. _____

6. To imprison in a jail or penitentiary as a result of due legal process is to _____.

   6. _____

7. Doubt which is logical, credible, or plausible is _____ doubt.

   7. _____

8. The act of placing a person in a prison or other place of confinement is a/an _____.

   8. _____

9. The outcome of a criminal trial whereby one is found guilty of the charges that were made is a/an _____.

   9. _____

10. One who knowingly assists a principal in the commission of a crime is a/an _____.

    10. _____

11. One who aids the principal in the commission of a crime but is not present when the crime is actually committed is a/an _____.

    11. _____

12. To assist in a criminal act by giving encouragement or support to its commission is to _____.

    12. _____

13. One who actually commits the crime or who actually or constructively aids and abets in its commission is a/an _____.

    13. _____

Turn back to page 144 and continue with this lesson.

Quiz No. 2

Terminology and Definition Recall

Directions: In the Answers column write the letter from Column I that represents the word or phrase that best matches each item in Column II. After you have completed this quiz, check your answers with the key on page 335. Unless otherwise directed, turn in this quiz to your instructor upon completion of this lesson.

COLUMN I	COLUMN II	ANSWERS
A. amicus curiae	1. A killing of another human being which is unlawful and done without malice aforethought.	1. _____
B. animus furandi	2. The killing of a human being by another whether intentional or unintentional.	2. _____
C. assault and battery	3. The intentional killing of another human being with malice aforethought.	3. _____
D. break and enter	4. The deliberate planning and intention to kill or seriously injure another person.	4. _____
E. constructive breaking	5. Illegally taking and carrying away personal property belonging to another with no intention of returning the property to the owner.	5. _____
F. forgery	6. A wrong which is bad because it is prohibited by law.	6. _____
G. homicide	7. A wrong which is bad in itself.	7. _____
H. larceny	8. An actual threat to inflict bodily harm upon another and the putting of the threat into effect.	8. _____
I. mala in se	9. A felony which is committed by one taking the property from the person or in the presence of the person by the use of force or violence and with no intention of returning the property to the owner.	9. _____
J. mala prohibita	10. The alteration of anything in writing with the intention of defrauding another.	10. _____
K. malice aforethought	11. A breaking and entering which is accomplished by fraud, threats, or trickery.	11. _____
L. manslaughter	12. The offering of a forged instrument with the intent to defraud.	12. _____
M. murder	13. Forcible and unlawful entry such as into a building, car, or boat with the intent to commit a crime therein.	13. _____
N. robbery	14. A Latin term meaning the intent to steal the property of another and to permanently deprive the owner of said property.	14. _____
O. utter and publish		

Turn back to page 148 and continue with this lesson.

 # EVALUATION No. 7

Student_____

Class_____Date_____

SCORING RECORD

	Perfect Score	Student's Score
Section A	50	
Section B	20	
Section C	30	
Total	100	

SECTION A

Directions: This dictation/transcription evaluation will test your spelling and transcription ability on the legal terms that you studied in the two preceding lessons. Use a 5-space paragraph indention, a 70-space line and double spacing unless otherwise instructed. Correct all errors. Follow one of the procedures below.

Typing Procedure

Using the cassette from Evaluation 7, transcribe the dictation directly at your typewriter.

Shorthand Procedure

Using the cassette from Evaluation 7, take the dictation using your shorthand system and then transcribe on the typewriter from your shorthand notes.

SECTIONS B AND C ARE AVAILABLE FROM YOUR INSTRUCTOR.

"Every testament is perfected by death."

—Legal Maxim

LESSON 15

To Wit: Probate

When a person dies, that person's property must be distributed through probate procedures. State laws regarding probate procedures will vary considerably. However, the terminology and definitions in this lesson are standard in most jurisdictions. When you have satisfactorily completed the following exercises, you will be able to correctly spell, define, pronounce, and transcribe the terms which are related to probate procedures.

Part A	Terminology and Definitions

Directions: Study the terms, pronunciations, and definitions until you are thoroughly familiar with them. In order to complete this lesson successfully, you must understand the meaning and usage of all the legal terms presented. If you are using shorthand, write your shorthand outline in the space provided or on your shorthand machine for each legal term.

	LEGAL TERM	PRONUNCIATION	DEFINITION	SHORTHAND OUTLINE
1.	probate	'pro-bāt	The official proving of a will as being valid or genuine.	_____
2.	petition for probate	pə-'tish-ən fər 'pro-bāt	A written application to a court having jurisdiction over probate matters requesting that a will be admitted to probate.	_____
3.	will	wil	A legal document which expresses how one wants property disposed of upon that person's death.	_____
4.	codicil	'käd-ə-səl	Something that is added to a will which changes or modifies it in some way.	_____
5.	formal will	'for-məl wil	A will which conforms to the state laws.	_____
6.	nuncupative will	'nən-kyu-pāt-iv wil	A will made in anticipation of immediate death which is stated orally before other persons and later put in written form.	_____

7.	holographic will	hō-lə-'graf-ik wil	A will which is in the handwriting of the one making the will.	_____
8.	testate	'tes-tāt	A person who dies leaving a legal and valid will. If one dies leaving a will, that person is said to die testate.	_____
9.	testator (male); testatrix (female)	'tes-tāt-ər 'tes-tā-triks	A person who makes a will, or one who dies that has made a will.	_____
10.	intestate	in-'tes-tāt	One who dies without a will. If one dies without a will, then that person is said to have died intestate.	_____
11.	attestation clause	a-tes-'tā-shən klȯz	The clause at the end of a will by which witnesses verify or certify that the will was properly executed.	_____
12.	animus testandi	'an-ə-məs tes-'tan-dī	Latin. The intention to make a will. Essential to a valid will.	_____
13.	testamentary capacity	tes-tə-'ment-ə-rē kə-'pas-ət-ē	The mental ability and capacity required by law to be sufficient for one to make a valid will.	_____

Turn to page 163 and complete Quiz No. 1 before continuing this lesson.

Typing Legal Terms

Directions: Unless otherwise instructed, use a 70-space line and double spacing. Correct all errors. Follow one of the procedures below.

Words

Typing Procedure

On a separate sheet of paper, type the following words at least two times, concentrating on the correct spelling and pronunciation.

Shorthand Procedure

On a separate sheet of paper, type the following words once, concentrating on the correct spelling and pronunciation. Then write the shorthand outline for each word on the lines to the right or on your shorthand machine. Cover the printed words with a sheet of paper and transcribe from the shorthand outlines one time on your typewriter.

probate / petition for probate / will / codicil / _____

formal will / nuncupative will / holographic will / _____

testate / testator / testatrix / intestate / attestation _____

clause / animus testandi / testamentary capacity / _____

Sentences

Type each of the following sentences one time. Concentrate on the correct spelling and pronunciation of each underlined legal term.

Write the correct shorthand outlines for the following sentences on the lines to the right or on your shorthand machine. Cover the printed material with a sheet of paper and transcribe from your shorthand outlines one time on the typewriter.

These sentences will be used for practice dictation on the cassettes.

Probate is the official proving of a will as being valid or genuine. A will is a legal document which expresses how one wants property disposed of upon that person's death. A written application to a probate court requesting that a will be admitted to probate is a petition for probate. A will may be added to or changed by a codicil. There are basically three types of wills—formal, nuncupative, and holographic. A formal will is one which conforms to the state laws. A will made in anticipation of immediate death which is stated orally by the testator or testatrix before other persons and later put in written form is a nuncupative will. A holographic will is one that is in the handwriting of the testator or testatrix. A testator or testatrix is a person who makes a will, or one who dies who has made a will. If one dies leaving a will, then the person dies testate. However, if one dies without a will, that person is said to have died intestate. An attestation clause is a clause at the end of a will by which witnesses verify or certify that the will was properly executed. Animus testandi is essential to the making of a will. Animus testandi means the intention to make a will. Additionally, for a will to be valid, the testator or testatrix must have testamentary capacity. Testamentary capacity is the mental ability and capacity required by law to be sufficient for one to make a valid will. Wills are also referred to as the last will and testament.

Directions: This dictation emphasizes and reinforces the legal terms and definitions you have studied. Listen carefully to the pronunciation of each of the legal terms. Unless otherwise directed, use a 70-space line and double spacing. Correct all errors. Follow one of the procedures below.

Typing Procedure

Using the cassette from Lesson 15, Part A, transcribe the dictation directly at your typewriter.

Shorthand Procedure

Using the cassette from Lesson 15, Part A, take the dictation using your shorthand system and then transcribe on the typewriter from your shorthand notes.

When you have finished transcribing Part A of the practice dictation, check your transcript with the printed copy. If you made any mistakes in the transcription, you should practice those words several times before going on.

Part B | Terminology and Definitions

Directions: Study the terms, pronunciations, and definitions until you are thoroughly familiar with them. In order to complete this lesson successfully, you must understand the meaning and usage of all the legal terms presented. If you are using shorthand, write your shorthand outline in the space provided or on your shorthand machine for each legal term.

LEGAL TERM	PRONUNCIATION	DEFINITION	SHORTHAND OUTLINE
1. publication	'pəb-lə-ka-shən	The formal declaration made by a testator or testatrix at the time a will is signed stating that it is that person's last will and testament.	_____
2. estate	is-'tāt	Property of any kind which one owns and can dispose of in a will.	_____
3. executor (male); executrix (female)	ig-'zek-ət-ər ig-'zek-ə-triks	A person named by a testator or testatrix to carry out the directions as stated in the will.	_____
4. administrator (male); administratrix (female)	əd-'min-ə-strāt-ər əd-min-ə-strā-triks	A person who is appointed by the court to administer or take charge of an estate.	_____
5. administrator or administratrix cum testamento annexo	əd-'min-ə-strāt-ər or əd-'min-ə-strā-triks kum tes-tə-'men-tō ə-'neks-ō	Latin. "With the will annexed." A person appointed by the court to administer a will in which the executors named are incapable or unable to administer the will.	_____

6.	residuary estate	ri-ʹzij-ə-wer-ē is-ʹtāt	The estate remaining after debts, expenses, and specific bequests have been settled.	_____
7.	creditor's claim	ʹkred-ət-ərs klām	A written request for the payment of a bill from the estate of the deceased.	_____
8.	bequest	bi-ʹkwest	Something which is given to another by will. Usually money or personal property.	_____
9.	bequeath	bi-ʹkwēth	The giving of something, such as personal property or money, to another by will. A legacy.	_____
10.	devise	di-ʹvīz	A bequest, or to bequeath.	_____
11.	abatement	ə-ʹbāt-mənt	A decrease in the legacies because there is not enough money in the estate to pay the full amount. The legacies are usually decreased proportionately.	_____
12.	chattel	ʹchat-l	Any article of personal property. Does not include real estate.	_____
13.	hereditaments	her-ə-ʹdit-ə-mənts	Any kind of property that may be inherited.	_____

Turn to page 164 and complete Quiz No. 2 before continuing this lesson.

Typing Legal Terms

Directions: Unless otherwise instructed, use a 70-space line and double spacing. Correct all errors. Follow one of the procedures below.

Words

Typing Procedure

On a separate sheet of paper, type the following words at least two times, concentrating on the correct spelling and pronunciation.

Shorthand Procedure

On a separate sheet of paper, type the following words once, concentrating on the correct spelling and pronunciation. Then write the shorthand outline for each word on the lines to the right or on your shorthand machine. Cover the printed words with a sheet of paper and transcribe from the shorthand outlines one time on your typewriter.

publication / estate / executor / executrix / _____

administrator / administratrix / administrator or _____

administratrix cum testamento annexo / residuary _____

estate / creditor's claim / bequest / bequeath / _____

devise / abatement / chattel / hereditaments / _____

Sentences

Typing Procedure

Type each of the following sentences one time. Concentrate on the correct spelling and pronunciation of each underlined legal term.

Shorthand Procedure

Write the correct shorthand outlines for the following sentences on the lines to the right or on your shorthand machine. Cover the printed material with a sheet of paper and transcribe from your shorthand outlines one time on the typewriter.

These sentences will be used for practice dictation on the cassettes.

Publication is the formal declaration made by a testator or testatrix at the time of signing a will that it is that person's last will and testament. An estate is property of any kind which one owns and can dispose of in a will. An executor or executrix is a person named by a testator or testatrix to carry out the directions as stated in the will after the testator's or testatrix's death. If a person dies intestate, the court will appoint an administrator or an administratrix to administer or take charge of the estate. If a testator or testatrix does not name an executor or executrix in a will, or the persons named are incapable or unable to administer the will, the court will appoint an administrator or administratrix cum testamento annexo, often abbreviated administrator cta or administratrix cta. After all debts and expenses of a will have been settled, the remainder is called the residuary estate. A written request for the payment of a bill from the estate of a deceased person is a creditor's claim. Bequest and bequeath are used in relation to personal property disposed of by a will. A bequest is money or personal property given to another by will, and bequeath is the giving of something, such as personal property or money, to another by will. Devise is a bequest, or it may also be used to mean to bequeath. If the assets of an estate are not sufficient to pay the legacies in full, abatement results. Abatement is a proportional decrease of the legacies. Things or

property which may be inherited are referred to as
<u>hereditaments</u>. Hereditaments include <u>chattels</u>
and real estate. A chattel is any article of personal
property, but does not include real estate.

_____

_____

_____

_____

Directions: This dictation emphasizes and reinforces the legal terms and definitions you have studied. Listen carefully to the pronunciation of each of the legal terms. Unless otherwise directed, use a 70-space line and double spacing. Correct all errors. Follow one of the procedures below.

Typing Procedure

Using the cassette from Lesson 15, Part B, transcribe the dictation directly at your typewriter.

Shorthand Procedure

Using the cassette from Lesson 15, Part B, take the dictation using your shorthand system and then transcribe on the typewriter from your shorthand notes.

When you have finished transcribing Part B of the practice dictation, check your transcript with the printed copy. If you have made any mistakes in the transcription, you should practice those words several times before going on to Lesson 16.

Check List

	PART A, DATE	PART B, DATE	SUBMITTED TO INSTRUCTOR YES	NO
Terminology and Definitions	_____	_____	_____	_____
*Typing Legal Terms	_____	_____	_____	_____
Words	_____	_____	_____	_____
Sentences	_____	_____	_____	_____
*Transcribing from Dictation	_____	_____	_____	_____
Quiz No. 1	_____	_____	_____	_____
Quiz No. 2	_____	_____	_____	_____

When you have successfully completed all the exercises in this lesson and submitted to your instructor those called for, you are ready to proceed with Lesson 16.

*If you are using a shorthand system, turn in to your instructor your shorthand notes along with your transcript.

Quiz No. 1

Terminology and Definition Recall

Directions: In the Answers column write the legal term that is most representative of the corresponding statement. After you have completed this quiz, check your answers with the key on page 335. Unless otherwise directed, turn in this quiz to your instructor upon completion of this lesson.

ANSWERS

1. A will made in anticipation of immediate death which is made orally before other persons and later put in written form is a/an _____ will.

   1. _____

2. The mental ability and capacity required by law to be sufficient for one to make a valid will is referred to as _____.

   2. _____

3. A person who dies leaving a legal and valid will is said to have died _____.

   3. _____

4. A legal document which expresses what a person wants done with property upon that person's death is a/an _____.

   4. _____

5. The clause at the end of a will by which witnesses verify or certify that the will was properly executed is the _____ clause.

   5. _____

6. A will which conforms to the state laws is a/an _____ will.

   6. _____

7. One who dies without a will is said to have died _____.

   7. _____

8. The official proving of a will as being valid or genuine is referred to as _____.

   8. _____

9. A will which is in the handwriting of the one making the will is a/an _____ will.

   9. _____

10. Something that is added to a will which changes or modifies it in some way is called a/an _____.

    10. _____

11. A person who makes a will or one who dies that has made a will is referred to as a/an _____.

    11. _____

12. A written application to a court having jurisdiction over probate matters requesting that a will be admitted to probate is a/an _____.

    12. _____

13. The intention to make a will is expressed in Latin as _____.

    13. _____

Turn back to page 156 and continue with this lesson.

Quiz No. 2

Terminology and Definition Recall

Directions: In the Answers column write the letter from Column I that represents the word or phrase that best matches each item in Column II. After you have completed this quiz, check your answers with the key on page 335. Unless otherwise directed, turn in this quiz to your instructor upon completion of this lesson.

COLUMN I	COLUMN II	ANSWERS
A. abatement	**1.** A person named by a testator or testatrix in a will to carry out the directions as stated in the will.	1. _____
B. administrator or administratrix	**2.** A written request for the payment of a bill from the estate of the deceased.	2. _____
C. administrator or administratrix cum testemento annexo	**3.** A Latin term meaning "with the will annexed" and used to indicate a person appointed by the court to administer a will in which the executors named are incapable or unable to administer the will.	3. _____
D. bequeath		
E. bequest	**4.** Something which is given to another by will. Usually money or personal property.	4. _____
F. chattel		
G. creditor's claim	**5.** The estate remaining after debts, expenses, and specific bequests have been settled.	5. _____
H. devise		
I. estate	**6.** A proportional decrease in the legacies because there is not enough money in the estate to pay the full amount.	6. _____
J. executor or executrix		
K. hereditaments	**7.** The giving of something such as personal property or money to another by will.	7. _____
L. publication		
M. residuary estate	**8.** Property of any kind which one owns and can dispose of in a will.	8. _____
N. testator or testatrix		
	9. A person who is appointed by the court to administer or take charge of an estate.	9. _____
	10. Any article of personal property.	10. _____
	11. The formal declaration made by a testator or testatrix at the time of signing a will that it is that person's last will and testament.	11. _____
	12. Any kind of property that may be inherited.	12. _____
	13. A bequest, or to bequeath.	13. _____

Turn back to page 159 and continue with this lesson.

LESSON 16

To Wit: Probate

This lesson continues the study of some of the basic terms which are applicable to probate procedures. When you have successfully completed the following exercises, you will be able to spell, define, pronounce, and transcribe the legal terms presented.

Part A	Terminology and Definitions

Directions: Study the terms, pronunciations, and definitions until you are thoroughly familiar with them. In order to complete this lesson successfully, you must understand the meaning and usage of all the legal terms presented. If you are using shorthand, write your shorthand outline in the space provided or on your shorthand machine for each legal term.

	LEGAL TERM	PRONUNCIATION	DEFINITION	SHORTHAND OUTLINE
1.	citation	sī-'tā-shən	A summons issued which requires the person to appear in court or risk losing a right to something. In probate matters, that right may be the right to inherit.	_____
2.	cy pres doctrine	sē prā 'däk-trən	French. "As near as possible." The court will endeavor to carry out the testator's or testatrix's general intention as near as may be possible.	_____
3.	per stirpes	pər 'stir-pās	Latin. A method of dividing an estate. If an estate is to be divided between two persons and one has died leaving three heirs, then one half of the estate is given to the surviving person and the other half is divided among the heirs of the deceased person.	_____
4.	precatory words	'prek-ə-tōr-ē wərds	Words in a will which express a desire on the part of the testator or testatrix but are not binding upon the court.	_____

5. escheat	is-'chēt	A reversion of property to the state if there is no individual competent to inherit it.	_____
6. ademption	ə-'dem-shən	The revoking, recalling, or voiding a legacy. This can occur when a testator or testatrix disposes of property that is included in the will prior to the testator's or testatrix's death, thus voiding that part of the will.	_____
7. beneficiary	ben-ə-'fish-ē-er-ē	Anyone who is to receive benefit from a will.	_____
8. cestui que trust	'ses-twē kē trəst	French. "A beneficiary of a trust." The one who receives benefits from a trust.	_____
9. heir	ar	A person who has a right by law to inherit the property of another.	_____
10. pretermitted heir	prēt-ər-'mit-təd ar	A legal heir who is unintentionally omitted in the will by the testator or testatrix.	_____
11. succession	sək-'sesh-ən	The right to an inheritance. The taking over of property that has been inherited.	_____
12. legacy	'leg-ə-sē	A bequest. Usually money or personal property given to another by a will.	_____
13. trust	trəst	Property which is placed in the care of one person for the benefit of another.	_____

Turn to page 173 and complete Quiz No. 1 before continuing this lesson.

Typing Legal Terms

Directions: Unless otherwise instructed, use a 70-space line and double spacing. Correct all errors. Follow one of the procedures below.

Words

Typing Procedure

On a separate sheet of paper, type the following words at least two times, concentrating on the correct spelling and pronunciation.

Shorthand Procedure

On a separate sheet of paper, type the following words once, concentrating on the correct spelling and pronunciation. Then write the shorthand outline for each word on the lines to the right or on your shorthand machine. Cover the printed words with a sheet of paper and transcribe from the shorthand outlines one time on your typewriter.

citation / cy pres doctrine / per stirpes / precatory   _____

words / escheat / ademption / beneficiary / cestui   _____

que trust / heir / pretermitted heir / succession /   _____

legacy / trust /   _____

Sentences

Typing Procedure

Type each of the following sentences one time. Concentrate on the correct spelling and pronunciation of each underlined legal term.

Shorthand Procedure

Write the correct shorthand outlines for the following sentences on the lines to the right or on your shorthand machine. Cover the printed material with a sheet of paper and transcribe from your shorthand outlines one time on the typewriter.

These sentences will be used for practice dictation on the cassettes.

A citation issued in probate matters requires a person to appear in court or risk losing a right to inherit something. The cy pres doctrine calls for the court to endeavor to carry out the testator's or testatrix's general intention as near as possible. If an estate is divided per stirpes, it is divided by representation or family groups rather than by individuals. Precatory words in a will express a desire or a wish rather than a command. Precatory words may not be legally binding. Escheat is a reversion of property to the state if there is no individual competent to inherit it. Ademption involves the revoking, recalling, or voiding a legacy. Ademption occurs when a testator or testatrix disposes of property named in the will prior to death. Property disposed of by ademption makes it impossible to carry out the terms of the will. A beneficiary is one who is to receive benefit from a will. The person to whom a policy of insurance is payable is also a beneficiary. The beneficiary of a trust is also known as a cestui que trust. An heir is a person who has a right by law to inherit the property of another. A pretermitted heir is one who is unintentionally omitted in the will by a testator or testatrix. Succession involves the transferring of property according to law to heirs when the person dies intestate. A legacy is a bequest, usually money or personal property, given to another by a will. A trust exists when real or personal property is held by one party for the benefit and use by a beneficiary or a cestui que trust.

Directions: This dictation emphasizes and reinforces the legal terms and definitions you have studied. Listen carefully to the pronunciation of each of the legal terms. Unless otherwise directed, use a 70-space line and double spacing. Correct all errors. Follow one of the procedures below.

Typing Procedure

Using the cassette from Lesson 16, Part A, transcribe the dictation directly at your typewriter.

Shorthand Procedure

Using the cassette from Lesson 16, Part A, take the dictation using your shorthand system and then transcribe on the typewriter from your shorthand notes.

When you have finished transcribing Part A of the practice dictation, check your transcript with the printed copy. If you made any mistakes in the transcription, you should practice these words several times before going on.

Part B — Terminology and Definitions

Directions: Study the terms, pronunciations, and definitions until you are thoroughly familiar with them. In order to complete this lesson successfully, you must understand the meaning and usage of all the legal terms presented. If you are using shorthand, write your shorthand outline in the space provided or on your shorthand machine for each legal term.

	LEGAL TERM	PRONUNCIATION	DEFINITION	SHORTHAND OUTLINE
1.	trust estate	trəst is-′tāt	Property which is held in trust for the benefit of another.	_____
2.	curtesy	kərt-ə-sē	An estate which a husband or a wife has a right to upon the death of one or the other.	_____
3.	reversion	ri-′vər-zhən	The future interest of the heirs of a testator or testatrix in property left to another for a specified period of time, at which time the property would revert back to the heirs of the testator or testatrix.	_____
4.	guardian	′gärd-ē-ən	A person who is legally responsible for the care of a minor and /or the minor's estate.	_____
5.	guardian ad litem	′gärd-ē-ən ad ′līt-əm	Latin. A person designated by the court to conduct litigation on behalf of a minor.	_____
6.	ward	wȯrd	A person who has a legal guardian.	_____
7.	conservatorship	kən-′sər-vət-ər-ship	Created by law to care for the property of an incompetent person or a minor.	_____

8.	conservator	kən-ˈsər-vət-ər	One who is in charge of a conservatorship and manages the property of an incompetent person or a minor.	_____
9.	ambulatory instrument	ˈam-byə-lə-tōr-ē ˈin-strə-mənt	One that can be changed. A will is an ambulatory instrument because it can be changed during the lifetime of the testator or testatrix.	_____
10.	indefeasible	in-di-ˈfē-zə-bəl	Something which cannot be voided, annuled, or revoked. A right to an estate which cannot be defeated is said to be "indefeasible."	_____
11.	revocation	rev-ə-ˈkā-shən	A voiding of a will by a testator or a testatrix.	_____
12.	animus revocandi	ˈan-ə-məs rev-ə-ˈkan-dī	Latin. "The intent to revoke."	_____

Turn to page 174 and complete Quiz No. 2 before continuing this lesson.

Typing Legal Terms

Directions: Unless otherwise instructed, use a 70-space line and double spacing. Correct all errors. Follow one of the procedures below.

Words

Typing Procedure

On a separate sheet of paper, type the following words at least two times, concentrating on the correct spelling and pronunciation.

Shorthand Procedure

On a separate sheet of paper, type the following words once, concentrating on the correct spelling and pronunciation. Then write the shorthand outline for each word on the lines to the right or on your shorthand machine. Cover the printed words with a sheet of paper and transcribe from the shorthand outlines one time on your typewriter.

trust estate / curtesy / reversion / guardian / _____

guardian ad litem / ward / conservatorship / _____

conservator / ambulatory instrument / indefeasible / _____

revocation / animus revocandi / _____

Sentences

Typing Procedure

Type each of the following sentences one time. Concentrate on the correct spelling and pronunciation of each underlined legal term.

Shorthand Procedure

Write the correct shorthand outlines for the following sentences on the lines to the right or on your shorthand machine. Cover the printed material with a sheet of paper and transcribe from your shorthand outlines one time on the typewriter.

These sentences will be used for practice dictation on the cassettes.

A trust estate is property which is held in trust for the benefit of another. Curtesy is an estate which a husband or wife has a right to upon the death of one or the other. Reversion is the future interest of the heirs of a testator or testatrix in property left to another for a specified period of time, at which time the property would revert back to the heirs of the testator or testatrix. A guardian is legally responsible for the care of a minor and/or the minor's estate. A guardian ad litem is a person designated by the court to conduct litigation on behalf of a minor. However, a guardian ad litem has no responsibility for the minor personally or for the property which belongs to the minor. A person or an infant who has a legal guardian is called a ward. If one is incompetent and cannot care for one's property, a conservatorship may be created by law to manage the property of that person. The person who manages a conservatorship is called the conservator. An ambulatory instrument is one that can be changed. A will is an ambulatory instrument because it can be changed during the lifetime of the testator or testatrix. An estate which cannot be defeated, revoked, or made void is indefeasible. Revocation is the voiding of a will by the testator or testatrix. "The intent to revoke" is expressed in Latin as animus revocandi. Animus revocandi is an element that must be present for a will to be revoked.

Transcribing from Dictation

Directions: This dictation emphasizes and reinforces the legal terms and definitions you have studied. Listen carefully to the pronunciation of each of the legal terms. Unless otherwise directed, use a 70-space line and double spacing. Correct all errors. Follow one of the procedures below.

Typing Procedure

Using the cassette from Lesson 16, Part B, transcribe the dictation directly at your typewriter.

Shorthand Procedure

Using the cassette from Lesson 16, Part B, take the dictation using your shorthand system and then transcribe on the typewriter from your shorthand notes.

When you have finished transcribing Part B of the practice dictation, check your transcript with the printed copy. If you have made any mistakes in the transcription, you should practice those words several times before going on to Evaluation 8.

Check List

	PART A, DATE	PART B, DATE	SUBMITTED TO INSTRUCTOR	
			YES	NO
Terminology and Definitions	_____	_____	____	____
*Typing Legal Terms	_____	_____	____	____
Words	_____	_____	____	____
Sentences	_____	_____	____	____
*Transcribing from Dictation	_____	_____	____	____
Quiz No. 1	_____	_____	____	____
Quiz No. 2	_____	_____	____	____

When you have successfully completed all the exercises in this lesson and submitted to your instructor those called for, you are ready to proceed with Evaluation 8.

*If you are using a shorthand system, turn in to your instructor your shorthand notes along with your transcript.

Quiz No. 1

Terminology and Definition Recall

Directions: In the Answers column write the legal term that is most representative of the corresponding statement. After you have completed this quiz, check your answers with the key on page 336. Unless otherwise directed, turn in this quiz to your instructor upon completion of this lesson.

ANSWERS

1. A doctrine which indicates that the court will endeavor to carry out the testator's or testatrix's general intention as near as may be is the _____.

    1. _____

2. A beneficiary of a trust or the one who receives benefits from a trust is expressed in French as _____.

    2. _____

3. A method of dividing an estate is _____.

    3. _____

4. A reversion of property to the state if there is no individual competent to inherit it is known as _____.

    4. _____

5. The right to an inheritance or the taking over of property that has been inherited is called _____.

    5. _____

6. The revoking, recalling, or voiding a legacy is referred to as _____.

    6. _____

7. A summons issued which requires the person to appear in court or risk losing a right to something, which, in probate matters, may be the right to inherit is a/an _____.

    7. _____

8. A bequest which is usually money or personal property given to another by a will is a/an _____.

    8. _____

9. Words in a will which express a desire on the part of the testator or testatrix but which are not binding upon the courts are called _____.

    9. _____

10. Anyone who is to receive benefit from a will is known as a/an _____.

    10. _____

11. A legal heir who is unintentionally omitted in the will by the testator or testatrix is a/an _____.

    11. _____

12. A person who has a right by law to inherit the property of another is known as a/an _____.

    12. _____

13. Property which is placed in the care of one person for the benefit of another person is known as a/an _____.

    13. _____

Turn back to page 166 and continue with this lesson.

Quiz No. 2

Terminology and Definition Recall

Directions: In the Answers column at the right of each statement, write the letter that represents the word, or group of words, that correctly completes the statement. After you have completed this quiz, check your answers with the key on page 336. Unless otherwise directed, turn in this quiz to your instructor upon completion of this lesson.

ANSWERS

1. A person who has a legal guardian is a (a) conservator, (b) curtesy, (c) ward.   1. _____

2. A husband's or wife's right to the estate of a deceased spouse is (a) trust estate, (b) curtesy, (c) conservatorship. . . . .   2. _____

3. The intent to revoke as expressed in Latin is (a) ad litem, (b) animus revocandi, (c) indefeasible. . . . .   3. _____

4. A person who is legally responsible for the care of a minor and/or the minor's estate is a (a) ward, (b) guardian ad litem, (c) guardian. . . . .   4. _____

5. Something which cannot be voided, annulled, or revoked is said to be (a) indefeasible, (b) animus revocandi, (c) reversion. . . . .   5. _____

6. An instrument that can be changed, such as a will which can be changed during the lifetime of the testator or testatrix, is a/an (a) ambulatory instrument, (b) trust estate, (c) conservatorship. . . . .   6. _____

7. Property which is held in trust for the benefit of another is a (a) conservatorship, (b) curtesy, (c) trust estate. . . . .   7. _____

8. One who is in charge of a conservatorship and manages the property of an incompetent person or a minor is a (a) trust estate, (b) conservator, (c) guardian.   8. _____

9. A person designated by the court to conduct litigation on behalf of a minor is a/an (a) animus revocandi, (b) guardian ad litem, (c) ward. . . . .   9. _____

10. A trust created by the court for the care of the property of an incompetent person or a minor is a/an (a) conservatorship, (b) ward, (c) ambulatory instrument. . .   10. _____

11. The future interest of the heirs in property left to another for a specified period of time at which time the property would revert back to the heirs is (a) reversion, (b) curtesy, (c) revocation. . . . .   11. _____

12. A voiding of a will by a testator or testatrix is (a) reversion, (b) revocation, (c) indefeasible. . . . .   12. _____

Turn back to page 169 and continue with this lesson.

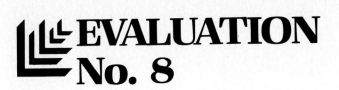 **EVALUATION No. 8**

SCORING RECORD

	Perfect Score	Student's Score
Section A	50	
Section B	20	
Section C	30	
Total	100	

SECTION A

Directions: This dictation/transcription evaluation will test your spelling and transcription ability on the legal terms that you studied in the two preceding lessons. Use a 5-space paragraph indention, a 70-space line and double spacing unless otherwise instructed. Correct all errors. Follow one of the procedures below.

Typing Procedure

Using the cassette from Evaluation 8, transcribe the dictation directly at your typewriter.

Shorthand Procedure

Using the cassette from Evaluation 8, take the dictation using your shorthand system and then transcribe on the typewriter from your shorthand notes.

SECTIONS B AND C ARE AVAILABLE FROM YOUR INSTRUCTOR.

"One who possesses land, possesses also that which is above it."

—Legal Maxim

LESSON 17

To Wit: Real Property

The area of law dealing with property governs the ownership and transfer of lands, tenements, and hereditaments. Many of the terms dealing with hereditaments (that which can be inherited) were covered in the lessons on probate. Also terms involving leases are included in the lessons on contracts. Therefore, this lesson will include those terms that basically apply to the ownership and transfer of real property not involved in leases or probate. Upon successful completion of these exercises, you will be able to spell, pronounce, define, and transcribe the basic real estate terms presented herein.

Part A	Terminology and Definitions

Directions: Study the terms, pronunciations, and definitions until you are thoroughly familiar with them. In order to complete this lesson successfully, you must understand the meaning and usage of all the legal terms presented. If you are using shorthand, write your shorthand outline in the space provided or on your shorthand machine for each legal term.

LEGAL TERM	PRONUNCIATION	DEFINITION	SHORTHAND OUTLINE
1. real property	rēl ′präp-ərt-ē	Land including everything which is built or growing on the land, such as buildings and trees.	_____
2. realty	′rēl-tē	Real property.	_____
3. premises	′prem-ə-səz	Generally means land which has a building on it.	_____
4. title	′tit-l	The ownership of real property. Also, the proof of the right to ownership in land or real property.	_____
5. deed	dēd	A document or instrument which is used to convey the title to real property from one person to another.	_____

6. warranty deed	'wȯr-ənt-ē dēd	A deed which guarantees that the one transferring real property has a good and complete title to said property.	_____
7. habendum clause	'ha-ben-dəm klȯz	A clause in a deed which clarifies the amount of ownership in the real property being transferred.	_____
8. quitclaim deed	'kwit-klām dēd	A deed which conveys only the person's interest in the property if any such interest exists. It does not warrant or guarantee the title but it does give up any right or interest one might have in the property.	_____
9. fee simple	fē 'sim-pəl	An absolute and unconditional ownership in land.	_____
10. defeasible title	di-'fē-zə-bəl 'tit-l	A title which could be voided or made invalid.	_____
11. defective title	di-'fek-tiv 'tit-l	A title that is deficient or incomplete in some aspect which is required by law.	_____
12. seisin (also seizin)	'sēz-n	Actual possession of real property with the intention of claiming title to said property.	_____

Turn to page 185 and complete Quiz No. 1 before continuing this lesson.

Typing Legal Terms

Directions: Unless otherwise instructed, use a 70-space line and double spacing. Correct all errors. Follow one of the procedures below.

Words

Typing Procedure

On a separate sheet of paper, type the following words at least two times, concentrating on the correct spelling and pronunciation.

Shorthand Procedure

On a separate sheet of paper, type the following words once, concentrating on the correct spelling and pronunciation. Then write the shorthand outline for each word on the lines to the right or on your shorthand machine. Cover the printed words with a sheet of paper and transcribe from the shorthand outlines one time on your typewriter.

real property / realty / premises / title / deed / _____

warranty deed / habendum clause / quitclaim deed / _____

fee simple / defeasible title / defective title / _____

seisin / _____

Sentences

Typing Procedure

Type each of the following sentences one time. Concentrate on the correct spelling and pronunciation of each underlined legal term.

Shorthand Procedure

Write the correct shorthand outlines for the following sentences on the lines to the right or on your shorthand machine. Cover the printed material with a sheet of paper and transcribe from your shorthand outlines one time on the typewriter.

These sentences will be used for practice dictation on the cassettes.

Real property consists of land and everything which is built or growing on the land, such as buildings and trees. Realty is another term for real property. Premises generally means land which has a building on it. Title is the ownership of real property. Title may also be the proof of the right to ownership in land or real property. A deed is a document or instrument which is used to convey the title to real property from one person to another. A warranty deed guarantees that the one transferring real property has a good and complete title to said property. The habendum clause in a deed clarifies the amount of ownership in the real property which is being transferred. A quitclaim deed conveys only the person's interest in the property if any such interest exists. A quitclaim deed does not warrant or guarantee the title, but it does give up any right or interest one might have in the property. A fee simple is an absolute and unconditional ownership in land. A defeasible title is one that is presently valid but could be voided or made invalid. A defective title is deficient or incomplete in some aspect which is required by law. Seisin is the actual possession of real property with the intention of claiming title to said property.

Directions: This dictation emphasizes and reinforces the legal terms and definitions you have studied. Listen carefully to the pronunciation of each of the legal terms. Unless otherwise directed, use a 70-space line and double spacing. Correct all errors. Follow one of the procedures below.

Typing Procedure

Using the cassette from Lesson 17, Part A, transcribe the dictation directly at your typewriter.

Shorthand Procedure

Using the cassette from Lesson 17, Part A, take the dictation using your shorthand system and then transcribe on the typewriter from your shorthand notes.

When you have finished transcribing Part A of the practice dictation, check your transcript with the printed copy. If you made any mistakes in the transcription, you should practice those words several times before going on.

Part B — Terminology and Definitions

Directions: Study the terms, pronunciations, and definitions until you are thoroughly familiar with them. In order to complete this lesson successfully, you must understand the meaning and usage of all the legal terms presented. If you are using shorthand, write your shorthand outline in the space provided or on your shorthand machine for each legal term.

LEGAL TERM	PRONUNCIATION	DEFINITION	SHORTHAND OUTLINE
1. abstract	′ab-strakt	A history of the title to realty which includes previous owners and any liens or encumbrances which may affect the title to the land.	_____
2. land description	land di-′skrip-shən	Describes or identifies a specific parcel of land which may be the subject of a conveyance.	_____
3. plat	plat	A map or a plot which shows how a certain piece of land is divided into lots.	_____
4. metes and bounds	mēts ən bäunds	A measurement of land which indicates the boundary lines, points, and angles.	_____
5. servitude	′sər-və-tüd	A right which the owner of property has in an adjoining property, such as the owner of an adjoining property could not construct something on the property that would detract from or infringe on the neighbors' rightful use or enjoyment of their property.	_____

180

6. easement	´ēz-mənt	A right to use the land of another for a specified purpose. For example, a utility company may have a right to cross the property with electric wires and water or gas lines.	_____
7. homestead	´hōm-sted	A dwelling place and the land surrounding it which is occupied by a family and protected by law from the claims of creditors.	_____
8. tenancy in common	´ten-ən-sē in ´käm-ən	Where two or more persons own the same land or property together with each being entitled to a distinct and specified share.	_____
9. joint tenancy	´joint ´ten-ən-sē	Title to land held by two or more persons who have the same interest in the land with undivided possession. In case of death of one of the owners, the other owner or owners have full ownership of the property.	_____
10. tenancy by the entirety	´ten-ən-sē bī thē in-´tī-rət-ē	A husband and wife who own land together with full ownership going to the survivor if one dies.	_____
11. freehold	´frē-hōld	A right of ownership to land for life.	_____
12. convey	kən-´vā	To transfer the title to property from one person to another.	_____
13. conveyance	kən-´vā-əns	The instrument by which the title to property is transferred from one person to another.	_____

Turn to page 186 and complete Quiz No. 2 before continuing this lesson.

Typing Legal Terms

Directions: Unless otherwise instructed, use a 70-space line and double spacing. Correct all errors. Follow one of the procedures below.

Words

Typing Procedure

On a separate sheet of paper, type the following words at least two times, concentrating on the correct spelling and pronunciation.

Shorthand Procedure

On a separate sheet of paper, type the following words once, concentrating on the correct spelling and pronunciation. Then write the shorthand outline for each word on the lines to the right or on your shorthand machine. Cover the printed words with a sheet of paper and transcribe from the shorthand outlines one time on your typewriter.

abstract / land description / plat / metes and bounds / servitude / easement / homestead / tenancy in common / joint tenancy / tenancy by the entirety / freehold / convey / conveyance /

_____

_____

_____

_____

Sentences

Typing Procedure

Type each of the following sentences one time. Concentrate on the correct spelling and pronunciation of each underlined legal term.

Shorthand Procedure

Write the correct shorthand outlines for the following sentences on the lines to the right or on your shorthand machine. Cover the printed material with a sheet of paper and transcribe from your shorthand outlines one time on the typewriter.

These sentences will be used for practice dictation on the cassettes.

An underline{abstract} is a condensed history of the title to land, consisting of a summary of all the conveyances, liens, or encumbrances, which may affect the title to the land. A land description identifies or describes a specific parcel of land which may be the subject of a conveyance. A map or plot that shows how a certain piece of land is divided into lots and which is usually drawn to a scale is a plat. Metes and bounds indicate the boundary lines, points, and angles of a parcel of land. Servitude is a right which the owner of property has in an adjoining property; for instance, something cannot be constructed on a property if it will interfere with the adjoining property. An easement is a right to use the land of another for a specified purpose. A homestead is a dwelling place and the land surrounding it which is occupied by a family and protected by law from the claims of creditors. When two or more persons own the same land or property together with each being entitled to a distinct and specified share, the ownership is a tenancy in common. Joint tenancy exists when two or more persons have the same interest in the land with undivided possession. Tenancy by the entirety refers to a husband and wife who own land together with full ownership going to the survivor if one or the other dies. A <u>freehold</u> is a right of ownership to land for life. To <u>convey</u> the title to property is to transfer the title from one person to another. A <u>conveyance</u> is the instrument by which the title to property is transferred from one person to another.

_____

Transcribing from Dictation

Directions: This dictation emphasizes and reinforces the legal terms and definitions you have studied. Listen carefully to the pronunciation of each of the legal terms. Unless otherwise directed, use a 70-space line and double spacing. Correct all errors. Follow one of the procedures below.

Typing Procedure

Using the cassette from Lesson 17, Part B, transcribe the dictation directly at your typewriter.

Shorthand Procedure

Using the cassette from Lesson 17, Part B, take the dictation using your shorthand system and then transcribe on the typewriter from your shorthand notes.

When you have finished transcribing Part B of the practice dictation, check your transcript with the printed copy. If you have made any mistakes in the transcription, you should practice those words several times before going on to Lesson 18.

Check List

	PART A, DATE	PART B, DATE	SUBMITTED TO INSTRUCTOR	
			YES	NO
Terminology and Definitions	_____	_____	_____	_____
*Typing Legal Terms	_____	_____	_____	_____
Words	_____	_____	_____	_____
Sentences	_____	_____	_____	_____
*Transcribing from Dictation	_____	_____	_____	_____
Quiz No. 1	_____	_____	_____	_____
Quiz No. 2	_____	_____	_____	_____

When you have successfully completed all the exercises in this lesson and submitted to your instructor those called for, you are ready to proceed with Lesson 18.

*If you are using a shorthand system, turn in to your instructor your shorthand notes along with your transcript.

Quiz No. 1

Terminology and Definition Recall

Directions: In the Answers column write the legal term that is most representative of the corresponding statement. After you have completed this quiz, check your answers with the key on page 336. Unless otherwise directed, turn in your quiz to your instructor upon completion of this lesson.

ANSWERS

1. A deed which guarantees that the one transferring real property has a good and complete title to said property is a/an _____ deed.

   1. _____

2. Land including everything which is built or growing on the land is referred to as _____ property.

   2. _____

3. A term which generally means land which has a building on it is _____.

   3. _____

4. Another word meaning real property is _____.

   4. _____

5. A clause in a deed which clarifies the amount of ownership in the real property being transferred is the _____ clause.

   5. _____

6. A deed which conveys only the person's interest in the property if any such interest exists is a/an _____ deed.

   6. _____

7. An absolute and unconditional ownership in land is referred to as _____.

   7. _____

8. Actual possession of real property with the intention of claiming title to said property is called _____.

   8. _____

9. The ownershp of real property or the proof of the right of ownership in land or real property is a/an _____.

   9. _____

10. A title which could be voided or made invalid is a/an _____.

    10. _____

11. A title that is deficient or incomplete in some aspect which is required by law is a/an _____.

    11. _____

12. A document or instrument which is used to convey the title to real property from one person to another is a/an _____.

    12. _____

Turn back to page 178 and continue with this lesson.

Quiz No. 2

Terminology and Definition Recall

Directions: In the Answers column write the letter from Column I that represents the word or phrase that best matches each item in Column II. After you have completed this quiz, check your answers with the key on page 336. Unless otherwise directed, turn in this quiz to your instructor upon completion of this lesson.

COLUMN I	COLUMN II	ANSWERS
A. abstract	**1.** Describes or identifies a specific parcel of land which may be the subject of a conveyance.	**1.** _____
B. convey	**2.** To transfer the title to property from one person to another.	**2.** _____
C. conveyance		
D. easement	**3.** A history of the title to realty which includes previous owners and any liens or encumbrances which may affect the title to the land.	**3.** _____
E. freehold		
F. homestead	**4.** A right to use the land of another for a specified purpose.	**4.** _____
G. joint ownership		
H. joint tenancy	**5.** A measurement of land which indicates the boundary lines, points, and angles.	**5.** _____
I. land description		
J. metes and bounds	**6.** The instrument by which the title to property is transferred from one person to another.	**6.** _____
K. plat		
L. servitude	**7.** A husband and wife who own land together with full ownership going to the survivor if one dies.	**7.** _____
M. tenancy in common		
N. tenancy by the entirety	**8.** Where two or more persons own the same land or property together with each being entitled to a distinct and specified share.	**8.** _____
	9. A right which the owner of property has in an adjoining property.	**9.** _____
	10. A right of ownership to land for life.	**10.** _____
	11. Title to land held by two or more persons who have the same interest in the land with undivided possession.	**11.** _____
	12. A dwelling place and the land surrounding it which is occupied by a family and protected by law from the claims of creditors.	**12.** _____
	13. A map or a plot which shows how a certain piece of land is divided into lots.	**13.** _____

Turn back to page 181 and continue with this lesson.

"Everything built on the soil belongs to the soil."
—Legal Maxim

LESSON 18

To Wit: Real Property

Additional terms which are applicable to the ownership and transfer of real property are given in this lesson. When you have successfully completed these exercises, you will be able to spell, define, pronounce, and transcribe the legal terms presented herein.

	Part A	Terminology and Definitions

Directions: Study the terms, pronunciations, and definitions until you are thoroughly familiar with them. In order to complete this lesson successfully, you must understand the meaning and usage of all the legal terms presented. If you are using shorthand, write your shorthand outline in the space provided or on your shorthand machine for each legal term.

	LEGAL TERM	PRONUNCIATION	DEFINITION	SHORTHAND OUTLINE
1.	fixture	'fiks-chər	Chattel or personal property which is attached to land or a building.	_____
2.	appurtenance	ə-'pərt-nəns	Something which is permanently attached to land.	_____
3.	possession	pə-'zesh-ən	The control or ownership of property for one's own use.	_____
4.	domain	dō-'mān	The ownership of real property.	_____
5.	eminent domain	'em-ə-nənt dō-'mān	The right or the power of the government to purchase private property for public use.	_____
6.	public domain	'pəb-lik dō-'mān	Property which is owned by the government.	_____
7.	condemnation	kän-dem-'na-shən	The forced sale of private property to the government for public use.	_____

Lesson 18, Part A

8. ejectment	i-'jek-mənt	An action for the recovery of land which was unlawfully taken away.	_____
9. adverse possession	ad-'vərs pə-'zesh-ən	The possession of another's land for a certain period of time after which the one in possession claims title to the land.	_____
10. prescription	pri-'skrip-shən	The right or title to the use of another's property.	_____
11. prescriptive rights	prī-'skrip-tiv rīts	Rights acquired by prescription.	_____
12. reversionary interest	ri-'vər-zhə-ner-ē 'in-trəst	The future interest which one has in property that is presently in the possession of another. For example, the owner of property which is rented to another has a reversionary interest in the property.	_____
13. riparian owner	rə-'per-ē-ən 'ō-nər	One who owns property which adjoins a waterway and who has the right to use the waterway.	_____

Turn to page 195 and complete Quiz No. 1 before continuing this lesson.

Turn to page 195 and complete Quiz No. 1 before continuing this lesson.

┌─────────────────────────────────┐
│   │
│   │
└─────────────────────────────────┘

Typing Legal Terms

Directions: Unless otherwise instructed, use a 70-space line and double spacing. Correct all errors. Follow one of the procedures below.

Words

Typing Procedure

On a separate sheet of paper, type the following words at least two times, concentrating on the correct spelling and pronunciation.

Shorthand Procedure

On a separate sheet of paper, type the following words once, concentrating on the correct spelling and pronunciation. Then write the shorthand outline for each word on the lines to the right or on your shorthand machine. Cover the printed words with a sheet of paper and transcribe from the shorthand outlines one time on your typewriter.

fixture / appurtenance / possession / domain /   _____

eminent domain / public domain / condemnation /   _____

ejectment / adverse possession / prescription /   _____

prescriptive rights / reversionary interest /   _____

riparian owner /   _____

Sentences

Type each of the following sentences one time. Concentrate on the correct spelling and pronunciation of each underlined legal term.

Write the correct shorthand outlines for the following sentences on the lines to the right or on your shorthand machine. Cover the printed material with a sheet of paper and transcribe from your shorthand outlines one time on the typewriter.

These sentences will be used for practice dictation on the cassettes.

A fixture is a chattel or personal property which is attached to land or a building. An appurtenance is something which is permanently attached to land. Fixtures may, in some cases, be removed from realty but an appurtenance cannot be removed. Possession is the control or ownership of property for one's own use. Domain is the ownership of real property. Domain also refers to the real estate which is owned. Eminent domain is the right or the power of the government to purchase private property for public use such as the building of a highway. Public domain is property which is owned by the government. If a private owner refuses to sell property for public use, the government may take the property by condemnation. In a condemnation proceeding, the owner is paid just compensation for the forced sale of the property. Ejectment is an action for the recovery of land which was unlawfully taken away. Ejectment has been modified in many states and may include the eviction of a tenant, such as an enforcement of a sale contract for land, etc. Adverse possession is the possession of another's land for a certain period of time after which the one in possession claims title to the land. Prescription is the right or title to the use of another's property. Rights acquired by prescription are called prescriptive rights. A reversionary interest is a future interest which one has in property that is presently

in the possession of another. One who owns property adjoining a waterway and has a right to use the
waterway is a <u>riparian owner</u>.

_____

_____

_____

Transcribing from Dictation

Directions: This dictation emphasizes and reinforces the legal terms and definitions you have studied. Listen carefully to the pronunciation of each of the legal terms. Unless otherwise directed, use a 70-space line and double spacing. Correct all errors. Follow one of the procedures below.

Typing Procedure

Using the cassette from Lesson 18, Part A, transcribe the dictation directly at your typewriter.

Shorthand Procedure

Using the cassette from Lesson 18, Part A, take the dictation using your shorthand system and then transcribe on the typewriter from your shorthand notes.

When you have finished transcribing Part A of the practice dictation, check your transcript with the printed copy. If you made any mistakes in the transcription, you should practice those words several times before going on.

Part B Terminology and Definitions

Directions: Study the terms, pronunciations, and definitions until you are thoroughly familiar with them. In order to complete this lesson successfully, you must understand the meaning and usage of all the legal terms presented. If you are using shorthand, write your shorthand outline in the space provided or on your shorthand machine for each legal term.

LEGAL TERM	PRONUNCIATION	DEFINITION	SHORTHAND OUTLINE
1. mortgage	ʹmȯr-gij	The pledging of property as security for a loan. In some states, a mortgage is a lien on the property, and, in others, it is a conditional conveyance of land.	_____
2. hypothecate	hip-ʹäth-ə-kāt	To mortgage property without conveying the title or possession.	_____
3. land contract	land ʹkän-trakt	A contract for the purchase of real property whereby the purchaser makes only a small down payment and the title to the property remains in the seller's name until the payments are made in full.	_____
4. lien	lēn	A legal claim on property for the payment of a debt such as a mortgage.	_____
5. encumbrance	in-ʹkəm-brəns	A lien.	_____

6. escrow	'es-krō	Something which is delivered to a third party to be held by that party until certain conditions are met. Thus, a mortgagee may collect money and hold it in escrow for the payment of future taxes or insurance.	_____
7. foreclosure	fōr-'klō-zhər	Taking away the rights a mortgagor has in the property which is mortgaged. Usually occurs when payments are not made or some other condition of the mortgage is not met.	_____
8. collateral	kə-'lat-ə-rəl	Some security pledged in addition to the personal obligation of the borrower to insure repayment of a loan.	_____
9. acceleration clause	ik-sel-ə-'rā-shən klȯz	A clause in a contract which requires immediate payment of the balance of the contract in the event that certain terms or conditions are not met, such as the failure to make payments when due.	_____
10. release	ri-'lēs	The giving up of a right or claim against another person. Thus, a release of a lien means that it has been paid in full.	_____
11. recording	ri-'kȯrd-iŋ	The filing of a lien, mortgage, title, or other documents in the public records.	_____
12. assessment	ə-'ses-mənt	The valuation or appraisal of property for the purpose of taxation.	_____
13. ad valorem	ad-və-'lȯr-əm	Latin. Taxes which are based upon the value of the thing being taxed.	_____

Turn to page 196 and complete Quiz No. 2 before continuing this lesson.

Typing Legal Terms

Directions: Unless otherwise instructed, use a 70-space line and double spacing. Correct all errors. Follow one of the procedures below.

Words

Typing Procedure

On a separate sheet of paper, type the following words at least two times, concentrating on the correct spelling and pronunciation.

Shorthand Procedure

On a separate sheet of paper, type the following words once, concentrating on the correct spelling and pronunciation. Then write the shorthand outline for each word on the lines to the right or on your shorthand machine. Cover the printed words with a sheet of paper and transcribe from the shorthand outlines one time on your typewriter.

mortgage / hypothecate / land contract / lien /
encumbrance / escrow / foreclosure / collateral /
acceleration clause / release / recording /
assessment / ad valorem /

_____

_____

_____

_____

Sentences

Typing Procedure

Type each of the following sentences one time.
Concentrate on the correct spelling and pronunciation of each underlined legal term.

Shorthand Procedure

Write the correct shorthand outlines for the following sentences on the lines to the right or on your
shorthand machine. Cover the printed material with
a sheet of paper and transcribe from your shorthand
outlines one time on the typewriter.

These sentences will be used for practice dictation on the cassettes.

A mortgage is the pledging of property as security
for a loan. In some states, a mortgage is a lien on
the property, and, in others, it is a conditional conveyance of land. To hypothecate is to mortgage
property. If property is purchased on land contract,
the purchaser makes only a small down payment
and the title of the property remains in the seller's
name until the balance is paid in full. A lien is a
legal claim or encumbrance upon property. When
something is delivered to a third party to be held by
that party until certain conditions are met, it is in
escrow. Thus, a mortgagee may collect money and
hold it in escrow for the payment of future taxes
or insurance. A foreclosure is the taking away the
rights that a mortgagor has in the property which is
mortgaged. A foreclosure usually occurs when
payments are not made or some other condition of
the mortgage is not met. Collateral is some security
pledged in addition to the personal obligation of the
borrower to insure repayment of a loan. An acceleration clause in a contract requires immediate
payment of the balance of the contract in the event
that certain terms or conditions are not met. A release is the giving up of a right or claim against
another person. A release of a lien means that it

Lesson 18, Part B

has been paid in full. <u>Recording</u> is the filing of a lien, mortgage, title, or other documents in the public records. An <u>assessment</u> is the valuation or appraisal of property for the purpose of taxation. <u>Ad valorem</u> refers to taxes which are based upon the value of the thing being taxed.

_____

_____

_____

_____

_____

_____

Transcribing from Dictation

Directions: This dictation emphasizes and reinforces the legal terms and definitions you have studied. Listen carefully to the pronunciation of each of the legal terms. Unless otherwise directed, use a 70-space line and double spacing. Correct all errors. Follow one of the procedures below.

Typing Procedure

Using the cassette from Lesson 18, Part B, transcribe the dictation directly at your typewriter.

Shorthand Procedure

Using the cassette from Lesson 18, Part B, take the dictation using your shorthand system and then transcribe on the typewriter from your shorthand notes.

When you have finished transcribing Part B of the practice dictation, check your transcript with the printed copy. If you have made any mistakes in the transcription, you should practice those words several times before going on to Evaluation 9.

Check List

	PART A, DATE	PART B, DATE	SUBMITTED TO INSTRUCTOR	
			YES	NO
Terminology and Definitions	_____	_____	_____	_____
*Typing Legal Terms	_____	_____	_____	_____
Words	_____	_____	_____	_____
Sentences	_____	_____	_____	_____
*Transcribing from Dictation	_____	_____	_____	_____
Quiz No. 1	_____	_____	_____	_____
Quiz No. 2	_____	_____	_____	_____

When you have successfully completed all the exercises in this lesson and submitted to your instructor those called for, you are ready to proceed with Evaluation 9.

*If you are using a shorthand system, turn in to your instructor your shorthand notes along with your transcript.

Quiz No. 1

Terminology and Definition Recall

Directions: In the Answers column at the right of each statement, write the letter that represents the word, or group of words, that correctly completes the statement. After you have completed this quiz, check your answers with the key on page 336. Unless otherwise directed, turn in this quiz to your instructor upon completion of this lesson.

ANSWERS

1. Rights acquired by the right or title to use another's property are referred to as (a) prescriptive rights, (b) reversionary interest, (c) possession. . . . .   1. _____

2. The control or ownership of property for one's own use is called (a) reversionary interest, (b) riparian owner, (c) possession. . . . .   2. _____

3. Property which is owned by the government is (a) public domain, (b) domain, (c) eminent domain. . . . .   3. _____

4. The ownership of real property is (a) domain, (b) eminent domain, (c) public domain. . . . .   4. _____

5. The future interest which one has in property that is presently in the possession of another is known as (a) reversionary interest, (b) prescriptive right, (c) appurtenance. . . . .   5. _____

6. One who owns property which adjoins a waterway is a/an (a) ejectment, (b) adverse possession, (c) riparian owner. . . . .   6. _____

7. The forced sale of private property to the government for public use is (a) condemnation, (b) ejectment, (c) adverse possession. . . . .   7. _____

8. An action for the recovery of land which was unlawfully taken away is (a) condemnation, (b) possession, (c) ejectment. . . . .   8. _____

9. The right or title to the use of another's property is known as (a) adverse possession, (b) prescription, (c) riparian ownership. . . . .   9. _____

10. The right or the power of the government to purchase private property for public use is known as (a) eminent domain, (b) public domain, (c) prescriptive rights.   10. _____

11. Something which is permanently attached to land is a/an (a) fixture, (b) appurtenance, (c) prescription. . . . .   11. _____

12. The possession of another's land for a certain period of time after which the one in possession claims title to the land is referred to as (a) prescription, (b) reversionary interest, (c) adverse possession. . . . .   12. _____

13. A chattel or personal property which is attached to land or a building is a/an (a) fixture, (b) appurtenance, (c) domain. . . . .   13. _____

Turn back to page 188 and continue with this lesson.

Quiz No. 2

Terminology and Definition Recall

Directions: In the Answers column write the legal term that is most representative of the corresponding statement. After you have completed this quiz, check your answers with the key on page 336. Unless otherwise directed, turn in this quiz to your instructor upon completion of this lesson.

ANSWERS

1. Some security pledged in addition to the personal obligation of the borrower to insure repayment of a loan is called _____.

   1. _____

2. The taking away the rights a mortgagor has in the property which is mortgaged is known as a/an _____.

   2. _____

3. A lien is also referred to as a/an _____.

   3. _____

4. Something which is delivered to the third party to be held by that party until certain conditions are met is in _____.

   4. _____

5. Taxes which are based upon the value of the thing being taxed are referred to as _____.

   5. _____

6. To mortgage property without conveying the title or possession to the property is to _____.

   6. _____

7. The giving up of a right or claim against another is a/an _____.

   7. _____

8. A contract for the purchase of real property whereby the purchaser makes only a small down payment and the title to the property remains in the seller's name until the payments are made in full is a/an _____.

   8. _____

9. The pledging of property as security for a loan is to _____ the property.

   9. _____

10. A clause in a contract which requires immediate payment of the balance of the contract in the event certain terms or conditions are not met is a/an _____.

    10. _____

11. The filing of a lien, mortgage, title, or other documents in the public records is referred to as _____ the document.

    11. _____

12. A legal claim on property for the payment of a debt such as a mortgage is a/an _____.

    12. _____

13. The valuation or appraisal of property for the purpose of taxation is a/an _____.

    13. _____

Turn back to page 191 and continue with this lesson.

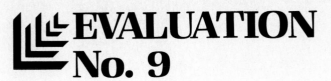 **EVALUATION No. 9**

Student_____

Class_____Date_____

SCORING RECORD

	Perfect Score	Student's Score
Section A	50	
Section B	20	
Section C	30	
Total	100	

SECTION A

Directions: This dictation/transcription evaluation will test your spelling and transcription ability on the legal terms that you studied in the two preceding lessons. Use a 5-space paragraph indention, a 70-space line and double spacing unless otherwise instructed. Correct all errors. Follow one of the procedures below.

Typing Procedure

Using the cassette from Evaluation 9, transcribe the dictation directly at your typewriter.

Shorthand Procedure

Using the cassette from Evaluation 9, take the dictation using your shorthand system and then transcribe on the typewriter from your shorthand notes.

SECTIONS B AND C ARE AVAILABLE FROM YOUR INSTRUCTOR.

"Equal knowledge on both sides makes the position of the contracting parties the same."

—Legal Maxim

LESSON 19

To Wit: Contracts

Contract law involves agreements between persons. Contracts must consist of persons competent to contract, a proper legal subject matter, an offer, an acceptance, and sufficient and legal consideration to be legally binding. Every person has the right to make a contract regardless of the wisdom or desirability of the provisions. The terminology presented deals with that which is involved in legally binding contracts. When you complete this lesson successfully, you will have a knowledge of some of the broad terminology of contract law.

	Part A	Terminology and Definitions

Directions: Study the terms, pronunciations, and definitions until you are thoroughly familiar with them. In order to complete this lesson successfully, you must understand the meaning and usage of all the legal terms presented. If you are using shorthand, write your shorthand outline in the space provided or on your shorthand machine for each legal term.

LEGAL TERM	PRONUNCIATION	DEFINITION	SHORTHAND OUTLINE
1. contract	'kän-trakt	An agreement whereby two or more persons promise to do or not to do certain things.	_____
2. ex contractu	eks 'kän-trak-tü	Latin. Emerging or coming from a contract.	_____
3. contract law	'kän-trakt lȯ	Law which governs agreements made between individuals.	_____
4. parol evidence rule	'par-əl 'ev-əd-əns rül	Once a contract is made in writing, it cannot be changed or altered by oral or parol evidence unless there was a mistake or fraud involved.	_____
5. offer	'ȯf-ər	A proposal by one person to make an agreement or a contract with another person. One of the essential elements of a contract.	_____

| 6. acceptance | ik-'sep-təns | An agreement to an offer received from another. An essential element of a contract. | _____ |

| 7. counteroffer | 'kaünt-ər-ȯf-ər | Changes made in an offer received from another. A counteroffer must be accepted by the one who made the original offer. | _____ |

| 8. option | 'äp-shən | An agreement whereby a person has the right to buy, sell, or lease certain property within a specified time. Thus, if one has an option on land, he or she has the right to buy it within a certain period of time. | _____ |

| 9. binder | 'bīn-dər | Money or security given with an offer to insure the intentions of the person making the offer. Also refers to a temporary insurance agreement which provides coverage for property until a formal policy is issued. | _____ |

| 10. lex loci contractus | leks 'lō-sī 'kän-trak-təs | Latin. The law of the place where a contract is made. | _____ |

| 11. surety | 'shu̇r-ət-ē | A person who agrees to be responsible for the debt of another in the event the other person fails to pay the debt. | _____ |

| 12. bailment | 'bāl-mənt | The delivery of personal property by the owner to another person for a specific purpose and period of time after which the property is to be returned to the owner. An example would be the delivery of an article for repair. | _____ |

| 13. caveat emptor | 'kav-ē-ät 'em-tər | Latin. "Let the buyer beware." A legal maxim which means that a person is responsible for examining an article before purchasing it and the article is bought at that person's own risk. | _____ |

Turn to page 207 and complete Quiz No. 1 before continuing this lesson.

Typing Legal Terms

Directions: Unless otherwise instructed, use a 70-space line and double spacing. Correct all errors. Follow one of the procedures below.

Words

Typing Procedure

On a separate sheet of paper, type the following words at least two times, concentrating on the correct spelling and pronunciation.

contract / ex contractu / contract law / parol

evidence rule / offer / acceptance / counteroffer /

option / binder / lex loci contractus / surety /

bailment / caveat emptor /

Shorthand Procedure

On a separate sheet of paper, type the following words once, concentrating on the correct spelling and pronunciation. Then write the shorthand outline for each word on the lines to the right or on your shorthand machine. Cover the printed words with a sheet of paper and transcribe from the shorthand outlines one time on your typewriter.

_____

_____

_____

_____

Sentences

Typing Procedure

Type each of the following sentences one time. Concentrate on the correct spelling and pronunciation of each underlined legal term.

Shorthand Procedure

Write the correct shorthand outlines for the following sentences on the lines to the right or on your shorthand machine. Cover the printed material with a sheet of paper and transcribe from your shorthand outlines one time on the typewriter.

These sentences will be used for practice dictation on the cassettes.

A contract is an agreement whereby two or more persons promise to do or not to do certain things. Ex contractu means emerging or coming from a contract. Contract law governs agreements made between individuals. Once a contract is made in writing, it cannot be changed by oral or parol evidence unless there was a mistake or fraud involved. An offer is a proposal by one person to make a contract with another person. An acceptance is an agreement to an offer received by another. Offer and acceptance are two of the essential elements of a contract. If a party makes changes in an offer received from another party, it is then a counteroffer. An option is a continuing offer. If one has an option on a property, that person has the right to buy, sell, or lease it within a specified time. A binder is money or security presented with an offer to insure the intentions of the person making the offer. Lex loci contractus is a Latin term which means the law of the place where a contract is made. A surety is a person who agrees to be responsible for the debt of another in the event the other person fails to pay the debt. Bailment is the delivery of personal property by the owner to another person for a specific purpose and period of time after which the property is to be returned to the owner. An example of a bailment would be the delivery of an article for repair. Caveat emptor is Latin for "let the buyer beware." Caveat emptor is a legal maxim that a person is responsible for examining an article before purchasing it, and the purchase is made at that person's own risk.

Transcribing from Dictation

Directions: This dictation emphasizes and reinforces the legal terms and definitions you have studied. Listen carefully to the pronunciation of each of the legal terms. Unless otherwise directed, use a 70-space line and double spacing. Correct all errors. Follow one of the procedures below.

Typing Procedure

Using the cassette from Lesson 19, Part A, transcribe the dictation directly at your typewriter.

Shorthand Procedure

Using the cassette from Lesson 19, Part A, take the dictation using your shorthand system and then transcribe on the typewriter from your shorthand notes.

When you have finished transcribing Part A of the practice dictation, check your transcript with the printed copy. If you made any mistakes in the transcription, you should practice those words several times before going on.

Part B — Terminology and Definitions

Directions: Study the terms, pronunciations, and definitions until you are thoroughly familiar with them. In order to complete this lesson successfully, you must understand the meaning and usage of all the legal terms presented. If you are using shorthand, write your shorthand outline in the space provided or on your shorthand machine for each legal term.

LEGAL TERM	PRONUNCIATION	DEFINITION	SHORTHAND OUTLINE
1. condition	kən-'dish-ən	A provision in a contract pertaining to a future event which, if it occurs, would change the agreement.	————
2. consideration	kən-sid-ə-'rā-shən	The main reason for making a contract. An essential element of a contract.	————
3. pro tanto	prō 'tan-tō	Latin. "As far as it goes." One may recover on a contract which was not completely fulfilled for the value of one's partial performance or pro tanto.	————
4. quid pro quo	kwid prō kwō	Latin. "Something for something." The consideration in a contract.	————
5. nudum pactum	'nū-dəm 'pakt-əm	Latin. An agreement made without any consideration other than a promise.	————
6. quantum meruit	'kwänt-əm me-'rủit	Latin. "As much as one deserves." One may recover the reasonable value of one's performance on a contract.	————
7. competent parties	'käm-pət-ənt 'pärt-ēs	Persons who are legally qualified to make a contract. An essential element of a contract.	————
8. mutual obligations	'myüch-wəl äb-lə-'gā-shəns	A promise for a promise. Both parties to a legally binding contract must agree to do or not to do something.	————
9. performance	pə-'for-məns	The fulfillment of the terms of a contract.	————
10. assignable	ə-'sī-nə-bəl	That which may be assigned or transferred.	————
11. assignment	ə-'sīn-mənt	A transfer of the title of property from one person to another.	————
12. subrogation	səb-rō-'gā-shən	The standing in the place of the one who made the contract. A right of recovery granted to one for whose benefit a contract was made but who was not actually a party to the contract.	————
13. accord and satisfaction	ə-'kord ən sat-əs-'fak-shən	An accord is the agreement between two persons whereby one agrees to accept an amount less than the full amount in satisfaction of the debt. Accord and satisfaction is when the agreement is made and the debt has been paid.	————

14. assumpsit   ə-'səm-sət   Latin. "A person promised." A written or oral promise made by one person to another. _____

Turn to page 208 and complete Quiz No. 2 before continuing this lesson.

Typing Legal Terms

Directions: Unless otherwise instructed, use a 70-space line and double spacing. Correct all errors. Follow one of the procedures below.

Words

Typing Procedure

On a separate sheet of paper, type the following words at least two times, concentrating on the correct spelling and pronunciation.

Shorthand Procedure

On a separate sheet of paper, type the following words once, concentrating on the correct spelling and pronunciation. Then write the shorthand outline for each word on the lines to the right or on your shorthand machine. Cover the printed words with a sheet of paper and transcribe from the shorthand outlines one time on your typewriter.

condition / consideration / pro tanto / quid pro quo / _____

nudum pactum / quantum meruit / competent _____

parties / mutual obligations / performance / _____

assignable / assignment / subrogation / accord and _____

satisfaction / assumpsit / _____

Sentences

Typing Procedure

Type each of the following sentences one time. Concentrate on the correct spelling and pronunciation of each underlined legal term.

Shorthand Procedure

Write the correct shorthand outlines for the following sentences on the lines to the right or on your shorthand machine. Cover the printed material with a sheet of paper and transcribe from your shorthand outlines one time on the typewriter.

These sentences will be used for practice dictation on the cassettes.

A <u>condition</u> is a provision in a contract which pertains to a future event which, if it occurs, would change the agreement. <u>Consideration</u> is the main reason for making a contract. Consideration is an essential element of a contract. <u>Pro tanto</u> means "as far as it goes." <u>Quid pro quo</u> means "something for something." Quid pro quo is the consideration in a contract. An agreement made without any consideration other than a promise is a <u>nudum pactum</u>. <u>Quantum meruit</u> refers to the amount one may recover for the reasonable value of that person's performance on a contract. <u>Competent parties</u> are persons who are legally qualified to make a contract. Competent parties are an essential element of a contract. <u>Mutual obligations</u> consist of a promise for a promise. <u>Performance</u> refers to the fulfillment of the terms of a contract. A contract which is <u>assignable</u> is one that may be transferred to another party. An <u>assignment</u> of a contract is the transfer or making over to another the title of any property or interest in a contract. If one person is substituted in the place of the one who made the contract, it is called <u>subrogation</u>. When an agreement between two parties is made and the debt has been paid, it is called <u>accord and satisfaction</u>. <u>Assumpsit</u> is a Latin term meaning "a person promised." An assumpsit may be either a written or oral promise made by one person to another.

Transcribing from Dictation

Directions: This dictation emphasizes and reinforces the legal terms and definitions you have studied. Listen carefully to the pronunciation of each of the legal terms. Unless otherwise directed, use a 70-space line and double spacing. Correct all errors. Follow one of the procedures below.

Typing Procedure

Using the cassette from Lesson 19, Part B, transcribe the dictation directly at your typewriter.

Shorthand Procedure

Using the cassette from Lesson 19, Part B, take the dictation using your shorthand system and then transcribe on the typewriter from your shorthand notes.

When you have finished transcribing Part B of the practice dictation, check your transcript with the printed copy. If you have made any mistakes in the transcription, you should practice those words several times before going on to Lesson 20.

Check List

	PART A, DATE	PART B, DATE	SUBMITTED TO INSTRUCTOR	
			YES	NO
Terminology and Definitions	_____	_____	_____	_____
*Typing Legal Terms	_____	_____	_____	_____
Words	_____	_____	_____	_____
Sentences	_____	_____	_____	_____
*Transcribing from Dictation	_____	_____	_____	_____
Quiz No. 1	_____	_____	_____	_____
Quiz No. 2	_____	_____	_____	_____

When you have successfully completed all the exercises in this lesson and submitted to your instructor those called for, you are ready to proceed with Lesson 20.

*If you are using a shorthand system, turn in to your instructor your shorthand notes along with your transcript.

Quiz No. 1

Terminology and Definition Recall

Directions: In the Answers column write the legal term that is most representative of the corresponding statement. After you have completed this quiz, check your answers with the key on page 337. Unless otherwise directed, turn in this quiz to your instructor upon completion of this lesson.

ANSWERS

1. An agreement whereby a person has the right to buy, sell, or lease certain property within a specified time is a/an _____.

1. _____

2. A legal maxim which means that a person is responsible for examining an article before purchasing it, and the article is bought at that person's own risk is expressed in Latin as _____.

2. _____

3. An agreement whereby two or more persons promise to do or not to do certain things is a/an _____.

3. _____

4. A proposal of one person to make an agreement or a contract with another person is a/an _____.

4. _____

5. An agreement to an offer received from another is called a/an _____.

5. _____

6. When changes are made in an offer received from another, the offer is then referred to as a/an _____.

6. _____

7. A Latin term which means emerging or coming from a contract is _____.

7. _____

8. The delivery of personal property by the owner to another person for a specific purpose and period of time after which the property is to be returned to the owner is referred to as _____.

8. _____

9. Once a contract is made in writing, unless there was mistake or fraud involved, it cannot be changed or altered by _____.

9. _____

10. Law which governs agreements made between individuals is called _____.

10. _____

11. Money or security given with an offer to insure the intentions of the person making the offer is called a/an _____.

11. _____

12. A person who agrees to be responsible for the debt of another in the event the other person fails to pay the debt is known as a/an _____.

12. _____

Turn back to page 200 and continue with this lesson.

Quiz No. 2

Terminology and Definition Recall

Directions: In the Answers column at the right of each statement, write the letter that represents the word, or group of words, that correctly completes the statement. After you have completed this quiz, check your answers with the key on page 337. Unless otherwise directed, turn in this quiz to your instructor upon completion of this lesson.

ANSWERS

1. Persons who are legally qualified to make a contract are said to be (a) assumpsit, (b) competent, (c) quantum meruit. . . . .

1. _____

2. The main reason for making a contract is the (a) condition, (b) consideration, (c) subrogation. . . . .

2. _____

3. A situation in which one may recover "as much as one deserves" or the reasonable value of the performance on a contract is expressed in Latin as (a) quantum meruit, (b) pro tanto, (c) nudum pactum. . . . .

3. _____

4. A Latin phrase meaning "as far as it goes" which applies to the recovery on a contract which was not completely fulfilled for the value of the partial performance is (a) pro tanto, (b) quid pro quo, (c) quantum meruit. . . . .

4. _____

5. A transfer to the title of property from one person to another is a/an (a) assignment, (b) performance, (c) quid pro quo. . . . .

5. _____

6. A written or oral promise made by one person to another is (a) quid pro quo, (b) assumpsit, (c) nudum pactum. . . . .

6. _____

7. The fulfillment of the terms of a contract is referred to as the (a) consideration, (b) assumpsit, (c) performance. . . . .

7. _____

8. A provision in a contract pertaining to a future event which, if it occurs, would change the agreement is a/an (a) condition, (b) performance, (c) accord and satisfaction. . . . .

8. _____

9. When the agreement is made and the debt has been paid, it is called (a) pro tanto, (b) accord and satisfaction, (c) mutual obligation. . . . .

9. _____

10. That which may be assigned or transferred is said to be (a) subrogation, (b) assignable, (c) performance. . . . .

10. _____

11. The standing in the place of the one who made the contract, or a right of recovery granted to one for whose benefit a contract was made but who was not actually a party to the contract is referred to as (a) assumpsit, (b) mutual obligations, (c) subrogation. . . . .

11. _____

12. A promise for a promise, or when both parties to a legally binding contract must agree to do or not to do something, is called (a) conditions, (b) accord and satisfaction, (c) mutual obligations. . . . .

12. _____

13. An agreement made without any consideration other than a promise is a/an (a) nudum pactum, (b) quantum meruit, (c) assumpsit. . . . .

13. _____

Turn back to page 204 and continue with this lesson.

"Whatsoever it is certain a person ought to do, the law will suppose the person to have promised to do."

—Legal Maxim

LESSON 20

To Wit: Contracts and Leases

Legal terms which relate to contracts and leases are presented in the following exercises. Leases, which are a form of contract, involve the relationship between landlords and tenants. When you satisfactorily complete this lesson, you should have a knowledge and understanding of the terminology involving contracts and leases.

| Part A | Terminology and Definitions |

Directions: Study the terms, pronunciations, and definitions until you are thoroughly familiar with them. In order to complete this lesson successfully, you must understand the meaning and usage of all the legal terms presented. If you are using shorthand, write your shorthand outline in the space provided or on your shorthand machine for each legal term.

LEGAL TERM	PRONUNCIATION	DEFINITION	SHORTHAND OUTLINE
1. implied contract	im-'plīd 'kän-trakt	An agreement which arises from the actions or legal duties of the parties rather than from an actual contract. Implied contracts may be implied in fact or implied in law.	_____
2. implied in fact	im-'plīd in fakt	An implied contract which is created by the actions of the parties.	_____
3. implied in law	im-'plīd in ló	An implied contract which is based on obligations created by law.	_____
4. express contract	ik-'spres 'kän-trakt	An actual agreement, not implied, which may be oral or written.	_____
5. bilateral contract	bī-'lat-ə-rəl 'kän-trakt	A contract which involves mutual obligations for both sides of the contract.	_____

6. unilateral contract	yü-ni-'lat-ə-rəl 'kän-trakt	A contract in which a promise or obligation exists only on one side. A unilateral contract is not enforceable until the specified act has been performed.	_____
7. default	di-'fȯlt	To fail to fulfill a legal duty.	_____
8. rescind	ri-'sind	To cancel or void a contract and to treat it as though no contract had ever been made.	_____
9. vitiate	'vish-ē-āt	To destroy the legality of a contract.	_____
10. inchoate	in-'kō-ət	Incomplete. Relates to valid contracts or instruments which are required by law to be recorded but have not been and are, therefore, called incomplete or inchoate instruments.	_____
11. breach of contract	brēch əv 'kän-trakt	Failure to fulfill the terms of a contract.	_____
12. privity of contract	'priv-ət-ē əv 'kän-trakt	The relationship of the parties to a contract. It is an essential element to recovery on a contract since only parties directly involved or with privity of contract have a right to sue.	_____
13. escalator clause	'es-kə-lāt-ər klȯz	A clause in a contract which states that if costs increase or decrease, the payments may increase or decrease proportionately.	_____

Turn to page 217 and complete Quiz No. 1 before continuing this lesson.

Typing Legal Terms

Directions: Unless otherwise instructed, use a 70-space line and double spacing. Correct all errors. Follow one of the procedures below.

Words

Typing Procedure

On a separate sheet of paper, type the following words at least two times, concentrating on the correct spelling and pronunciation.

Shorthand Procedure

On a separate sheet of paper, type the following words once, concentrating on the correct spelling and pronunciation. Then write the shorthand outline for each word on the lines to the right or on your shorthand machine. Cover the printed words with a sheet of paper and transcribe from the shorthand outlines one time on your typewriter.

implied contract / implied in fact / implied in law / express contract / bilateral contract / unilateral contract / default / rescind / vitiate / inchoate / breach of contract / privity of contract / escalator clause /

_____
_____
_____
_____
_____

Sentences

Typing Procedure

Type each of the following sentences one time. Concentrate on the correct spelling and pronunciation of each underlined legal term.

Shorthand Procedure

Write the correct shorthand outlines for the following sentences on the lines to the right or on your shorthand machine. Cover the printed material with a sheet of paper and transcribe from your shorthand outlines one time on the typewriter.

These sentences will be used for practice dictation on the cassettes.

An implied contract is an agreement which arises from the actions or legal duties of the parties rather than from an actual contract. Implied contracts may be implied in fact or implied in law. A contract implied in fact is created by the actions of the parties. A contract implied in law is based on obligations created by law. An express contract is an actual agreement, not implied, which may be oral or written. A bilateral contract involves mutual obligations for both parties of the contract. A unilateral contract is one in which a promise or obligation exists only on one side. A unilateral contract is not enforceable until the specified act has been performed. To fail to fulfill a legal duty is to default. If one defaults on a contract, that person did not fulfill the terms of the agreement. To rescind a contract is to cancel or void it and to treat it as though no contract had ever been made. To vitiate a contract is to legally destroy it. Fraud will vitiate a contract. An inchoate contract is a valid contract or instrument that is required by law to be recorded but has not been. A breach of contract involves the failure to fulfill the terms of a contract. Privity of contract refers to the relationship of the parties to a contract. It is an essential element to _____

recovery on a contract since only parties directly _____

involved or with privity of contract have a right to _____

sue. Some contracts or leases contain an <u>escalator</u> _____

<u>clause</u> which states that if costs increase or _____

decrease, the payment may increase or decrease _____

proportionately.

_____

Transcribing from Dictation

Directions: This dictation emphasizes and reinforces the legal terms and definitions you have studied. Listen carefully to the pronunciation of each of the legal terms. Unless otherwise directed, use a 70-space line and double spacing. Correct all errors. Follow one of the procedures below.

Typing Procedure

Using the cassette from Lesson 20, Part A, transcribe the dictation directly at your typewriter.

Shorthand Procedure

Using the cassette from Lesson 20, Part A, take the dictation using your shorthand system and then transcribe on the typewriter from your shorthand notes.

When you have finished transcribing Part A of the practice dictation, check your transcript with the printed copy. If you made any mistakes in the transcription, you should practice those words several times before going on.

Part B | Terminology and Definitions

Directions: Study the terms, pronunciations, and definitions until you are thoroughly familiar with them. In order to complete this lesson successfully, you must understand the meaning and usage of all the legal terms presented. If you are using shorthand, write your shorthand outline in the space provided or on your shorthand machine for each legal term.

LEGAL TERM	PRONUNCIATION	DEFINITION	SHORTHAND OUTLINE
1. lease	lēs	An agreement whereby a tenant or person has possession of property belonging to a landlord for a specified period of time. A landlord-tenant relationship.	_____
2. lessee	le-'sē	One who leases the property of another and has possession of said property.	_____
3. lessor	'les-or	The one who owns the property which is leased.	_____

4.	landlord	'lan-lȯrd	The owner of leased property. Another name for a lessor.	_____
5.	tenant	'ten-ənt	One who leases property from a landlord. A lessee.	_____
6.	demise	di-'mīz	A lease. When used in a lease, it means that the lessee shall have full use and enjoyment of the leased premises.	_____
7.	demised premises	di-'mīzd 'prem-ə-səz	Land and buildings which are leased.	_____
8.	habitation	hab-ə-'tā-shən	The occupying of leased premises as a residence.	_____
9.	sublease	'səb-'lēs	One whereby the lessee lets another person occupy the leased premises either for a shorter period of time than for which the premises are leased or until the lease expires.	_____
10.	notice to quit	'nōt-əs tü kwit	A written notice to the tenant from the landlord which states that the tenant is to vacate the premises by a specified time if certain conditions are not met.	_____
11.	eviction	i-'vik-shən	The legal removal of a tenant from leased property.	_____
12.	inure	in-'ur	To benefit or to have effect. In a contract, it means that if benefits accrue, they will take effect for or come to the party.	_____
13.	execute	'ek-si-kyüt	To carry out or put into effect. To execute a contract is to put it into effect by doing all the things that are necessary to make it valid and complete.	_____
14.	covenant	'kəv-nənt	An agreement between two or more persons that something will be or will not be done.	_____

Turn to page 218 and complete Quiz No. 2 before continuing this lesson.

Typing Legal Terms

Directions: Unless otherwise instructed, use a 70-space line and double spacing. Correct all errors. Follow one of the procedures below.

Words

Typing Procedure

On a separate sheet of paper, type the following words at least two times, concentrating on the correct spelling and pronunciation.

lease / lessee / lessor / landlord / tenant / demise /

demised premises / habitation / sublease / notice to

quit / eviction / inure / execute / covenant /

Shorthand Procedure

On a separate sheet of paper, type the following words once, concentrating on the correct spelling and pronunciation. Then write the shorthand outline for each word on the lines to the right or on your shorthand machine. Cover the printed words with a sheet of paper and transcribe from the shorthand outlines one time on your typewriter.

_____

_____

_____

Sentences

Typing Procedure

Type each of the following sentences one time. Concentrate on the correct spelling and pronunciation of each underlined legal term.

Shorthand Procedure

Write the correct shorthand outlines for the following sentences on the lines to the right or on your shorthand machine. Cover the printed material with a sheet of paper and transcribe from your shorthand outlines one time on the typewriter.

These sentences will be used for practice dictation on the cassettes.

A lease is an agreement whereby a tenant or person has possession of property belonging to a landlord for a specified period of time. A lessee is the one who leases the property from another, and the lessor is the one who owns the property which is leased. Thus, the tenant is a lessee, and the landlord is the lessor. The use of the term "demise" in a lease means that the lessee shall have full use and enjoyment of the leased premises. Demised premises are land and buildings which are leased. A person who occupies leased premises as a residence has the right of habitation. A sublease is one whereby the lessee lets another person occupy the leased premises. A notice to quit is a written notice to the tenant from the landlord which states that the tenant is to vacate the premises by a specified time if certain conditions are not met. If a tenant does not move from the demised premises after the landlord has served the notice to quit, the tenant is

subject to eviction. Eviction is the legal removal of

a tenant from leased property. Inure means to have

effect or to benefit. Inure, when used in a contract,

means that if benefits accrue, they will take effect

for or come to the party. To execute means to carry

out or put into effect. To execute a contract is to put

it into effect by doing all the things that are neces-

sary to make it valid and complete. A covenant is an

agreement between two or more persons that some-

thing will be or will not be done.

_____

_____

_____

_____

_____

_____

_____

_____

_____

Transcribing from Dictation

Directions: This dictation emphasizes and reinforces the legal terms and definitions you have studied. Listen carefully to the pronunciation of each of the legal terms. Unless otherwise directed, use a 70-space line and double spacing. Correct all errors. Follow one of the procedures below.

Typing Procedure

Using the cassette from Lesson 20, Part B, transcribe the dictation directly at your typewriter.

Shorthand Procedure

Using the cassette from Lesson 20, Part B, take the dictation using your shorthand system and then transcribe on the typewriter from your shorthand notes.

When you have finished transcribing Part B of the practice dictation, check your transcript with the printed copy. If you have made any mistakes in the transcription, you should practice those words several times before going on to Evaluation 10.

Check List

SUBMITTED TO INSTRUCTOR

	Part A, Date	Part B, Date	Yes	No
Terminology and Definitions				
*Typing Legal Terms				
Words				
Sentences				
*Transcribing from Dictation				
Quiz No. 1				
Quiz No. 2				

When you have successfully completed all the exercises in this lesson and submitted to your instructor those called for, you are ready to proceed with Evaluation 10.

*If you are using a shorthand system, turn in to your instructor your shorthand notes along with your transcript.

216

Quiz No. 1

Terminology and Definition Recall

Directions: In the Answers column write the letter from Column I that represents the word or phrase that best matches each item in Column II. After you have completed this quiz, check your answers with the key on page 337. Unless otherwise directed, turn in this quiz to your instructor upon completion of this lesson.

COLUMN I	COLUMN II	ANSWERS
A. bilateral contract	**1.** The failure to fulfill the terms of a contract.	1. _____
B. breach of contract	**2.** A contract in which a promise or obligation exists only on one side.	2. _____
C. default	**3.** The relationship of the parties to a contract.	3. _____
D. escalator clause	**4.** An agreement which arises from the actions or legal duties of the parties rather than from an actual contract.	4. _____
E. express clause		
F. express contract	**5.** A contract which involves mutual obligations for both sides of the contract.	5. _____
G. implied contract	**6.** To cancel or void a contract and to treat it as though no contract had ever been made.	6. _____
H. implied in fact		
I. implied in law	**7.** To destroy the legality of a contract.	7. _____
J. inchoate	**8.** An implied contract which is created by the actions of the parties.	8. _____
K. privity of contract		
L. rescind	**9.** Instruments which are required by law to be recorded but which have not been.	9. _____
M. unilateral contract	**10.** Failure to fulfill a legal duty.	10. _____
N. vitiate	**11.** An implied contract which is based on obligations created by law.	11. _____
	12. A clause in a contract which states that if costs increase or decrease, the payments may increase or decrease proportionately.	12. _____
	13. An actual agreement, not implied, which may be oral or written.	13. _____

Turn back to page 210 and continue with this lesson.

Quiz No. 2

Terminology and Definition Recall

Directions: In the Answers column write the legal term that is most representative of the corresponding statement. After you have completed this quiz, check your answers with the key on page 337. Unless otherwise directed, turn in this quiz to your instructor upon completion of this lesson.

ANSWERS

1. A word used in a contract to mean that if benefits accrue, they will take effect for or come to the party is _____.

1. _____

2. The owner of leased property or another name for a lessor is _____.

2. _____

3. An agreement whereby a tenant or person has possession of property belonging to a landlord for a specified period of time is a/an _____.

3. _____

4. To put a contract into effect by doing all the things that are necessary to make it valid and complete is to _____ it.

4. _____

5. A term used in a lease to mean that the lessee shall have full use and enjoyment of the leased premises is _____.

5. _____

6. Another name for a lessee is _____.

6. _____

7. A lease whereby the lessee lets another person occupy the leased premises is called a/an _____.

7. _____

8. A written notice to the tenant from the landlord which states that the tenant is to vacate the premises by a specified time if certain conditions are not met is a/an _____.

8. _____

9. The occupying of leased premises as a residence is called _____.

9. _____

10. The legal removal of a tenant from leased property is referred to as a/an _____

10. _____

11. One who leases the property of another and has possession of said property is a/an _____.

11. _____

12. An agreement between two or more persons that something will be or will not be done is a/an _____.

12. _____

13. Land and buildings which are leased are referred to as _____ premises.

13. _____

14. The one who owns property which is leased is the _____.

14. _____

Turn back to page 213 and continue with this lesson.

# EVALUATION No. 10

Student_____

Class_____Date_____

SCORING RECORD

	Perfect Score	Student's Score
Section A	50	
Section B	20	
Section C	30	
Total	100	

SECTION A

Directions: This dictation/transcription evaluation will test your spelling and transcription ability on the legal terms that you studied in the two preceding lessons. Use a 5-space paragraph indention, a 70-space line and double spacing unless otherwise instructed. Correct all errors. Follow one of the procedures below.

Typing Procedure

Using the cassette from Evaluation 10, transcribe the dictation directly at your typewriter.

Shorthand Procedure

Using the cassette from Evaluation 10, take the dictation using your shorthand system and then transcribe on the typewriter from your shorthand notes.

SECTIONS B AND C ARE AVAILABLE FROM YOUR INSTRUCTOR.

"Between those who are equally in the right, or equally in the wrong, the law does not interpose."

—Legal Maxim

LESSON 21

To Wit: Domestic Relations

The area of domestic relations encompasses marriages, divorces, annulments, and separations. Most court actions in domestic relations involve divorce proceedings. Grounds and procedures for divorce actions vary widely from state to state. In this lesson, the terms presented are those that will generally be encountered regardless of the jurisdiction. When you complete these exercises, you should have a knowledge and understanding of some of the terms used in reference to domestic relations.

Part A	Terminology and Definitions

Directions: Study the terms, pronunciations, and definitions until you are thoroughly familiar with them. In order to complete this lesson successfully, you must understand the meaning and usage of all the legal terms presented. If you are using shorthand, write your shorthand outline in the space provided or on your shorthand machine for each legal term.

	LEGAL TERM	PRONUNCIATION	DEFINITION	SHORTHAND OUTLINE
1.	domestic	də-'mes-tik	Refers to family affairs or to a home or household.	_____
2.	matrimony	'ma-trə-mō-nē	The marriage relationship between husband and wife.	_____
3.	religious ceremony	ri-'lij-əs 'ser-ə-mō-nē	A ceremony which creates a valid marriage and is performed by a duly ordained minister or a member of the clergy of any recognized religion.	_____
4.	civil ceremony	'siv-əl 'ser-ə-mō-nē	A ceremony which creates a valid marriage and is performed by a public official who is so authorized to perform marriages.	_____

5. common-law marriage   ′käm-ən ló ′mar-ij   A marriage which is not created by the usual ceremony required by law but exists between two people who agree to live together as husband and wife. It is not recognized as a valid marriage in some states.   _____

6. valid marriage   ′val-əd ′mar-ij   One which is created according to the requirements of the law.   _____

7. void marriage   vȯid ′mar-ij   One which is not valid and does not meet the requirements established by law for a valid marriage.   _____

8. voidable marriage   ′vȯid-ə-bəl ′mar-ij   One which exists for all practical purposes but contains a legal imperfection which could void the relationship in a court of law.   _____

9. annulment   ə-′nəl-mənt   The voiding of a marriage and treating it as though it never existed.   _____

10. nonage   ′nän-ij   Below the age of consent. In most states, nonage is a ground for obtaining an annulment.   _____

11. monogamy   mə-′näg-ə-mē   A marriage relationship between only one man and one woman at a time.   _____

12. bigamy   ′big-ə-mē   The state of having two husbands or two wives at any one time. A criminal offense in our country.   _____

Turn to page 229 and complete Quiz No. 1 before continuing this lesson.

Typing Legal Terms

Directions: Unless otherwise instructed, use a 70-space line and double spacing. Correct all errors. Follow one of the procedures below.

Words

Typing Procedure

On a separate sheet of paper, type the following words at least two times, concentrating on the correct spelling and pronunciation.

Shorthand Procedure

On a separate sheet of paper, type the following words once, concentrating on the correct spelling and pronunciation. Then write the shorthand outline for each word on the lines to the right or on your shorthand machine. Cover the printed words with a sheet of paper and transcribe from the shorthand outlines one time on your typewriter.

domestic / matrimony / religious ceremony / civil
ceremony / common-law marriage / valid marriage /
void marriage / voidable marriage / annulment /
nonage / monogamy / bigamy /

Sentences

Typing Procedure

Type each of the following sentences one time.
Concentrate on the correct spelling and pronunciation of each underlined legal term.

Shorthand Procedure

Write the correct shorthand outlines for the following sentences on the lines to the right or on your
shorthand machine. Cover the printed material with
a sheet of paper and transcribe from your shorthand
outlines one time on the typewriter.

These sentences will be used for practice dictation on the cassettes.

Domestic refers to family affairs or to a home or a
household. Domestic relations encompass the
areas of marriages, divorces, annulments, and
separations. Matrimony is the marriage relation between a husband and wife. Matrimony does not
refer to the ceremony itself. If a marriage is performed by a duly ordained minister or member of
the clergy of any recognized religion, it is a religious
ceremony. A civil ceremony creates a valid marriage and is performed by a public official who is
authorized to perform marriages. A common-law
marriage is one which is not created by the usual
ceremony required by law but exists between two
people who agree to live together as husband and
wife. Common-law marriages are not recognized in
many states. A valid marriage is one which is
created according to the requirements of the law. A
void marriage is one that is not valid and does not
meet the requirements established by law for a
valid marriage. A voidable marriage is one which
exists for all practical purposes but contains a legal
imperfection which could void the relationship in a
court of law. An annulment voids a marriage and
treats it as though it never existed. An annulment

means in effect that there was no marriage at all. _____

Nonage is below the age of consent. In most states, _____

nonage is a ground for obtaining an annulment. _____

Monogamy is a marriage relationship between only _____

one man and one woman at a time. Bigamy is the _____

state of having two husbands or two wives at the _____

same time. Bigamy is a criminal offense in our _____

country. _____

Transcribing from Dictation

Directions: This dictation emphasizes and reinforces the legal terms and definitions you have studied. Listen carefully to the pronunciation of each of the legal terms. Unless otherwise directed, use a 70-space line and double spacing. Correct all errors. Follow one of the procedures below.

Typing Procedure

Using the cassette from Lesson 21, Part A, transcribe the dictation directly at your typewriter.

Shorthand Procedure

Using the cassette from Lesson 21, Part A, take the dictation using your shorthand system and then transcribe on the typewriter from your shorthand notes.

When you have finished transcribing Part A of the practice dictation, check your transcript with the printed copy. If you made any mistakes in the transcription, you should practice those words several times before going on.

Part B | Terminology and Definitions

Directions: Study the terms, pronunciations, and definitions until you are thoroughly familiar with them. In order to complete this lesson successfully, you must understand the meaning and usage of all the legal terms presented. If you are using shorthand, write your shorthand outline in the space provided or on your shorthand machine for each legal term.

LEGAL TERM	PRONUNCIATION	DEFINITION	SHORTHAND OUTLINE
1. cohabitation	kō-hab-ə-'tā-shən	The state of living together as husband and wife.	_____
2. consanguinity	kän-san-'gwin-ət-ē	A blood relationship between two people.	_____
3. affinity	ə-'fin-ət-ē	The relationship of one spouse to the blood relatives of the other spouse because of the marriage.	_____
4. femme sole	fem sōl	French. A woman who is not married. A woman who is single, divorced, or widowed.	_____

5.	antenuptial agreement	ant-i-ˈnəp-shəl ə-gre-mənt	An agreement made between two people before they are married.	_____
6.	premarital	prē-ˈmar-ət-l	Before the marriage.	_____
7.	privileged communications	ˈpriv-lijd kə-myü-nə-ˈkā-shəns	A spouse is not permitted to testify as a witness against the other spouse in regard to matters revealed to the other because of the confidence which exists between them as a result of the marital relation.	_____
8.	counsel fee	ˈkau̇n-səl fē	Fees for legal counsel. In most states, the one filing for divorce is usually required to pay the counsel fees incurred by the spouse in the divorce action.	_____
9.	separation	sep-ə-ˈrā-shən	A partial or qualified divorce where the parties may not live together but are otherwise legally bound as husband and wife.	_____
10.	a mensa et thoro	ā ˈmen-sə et ˈthōr-ō	Latin. A legal separation.	_____
11.	separation agreement	sep-ə-ˈrā-shən ə-ˈgrē-mənt	A contract between a husband and wife who are living separately which clarifies the property rights, custody, and support for each party.	_____
12.	separate maintenance	ˈsep-rət ˈmānt-nəns	An amount granted by a court in a legal separation to one of the spouses for support and for the support of the children.	_____

Turn to page 230 and complete Quiz No. 2 before continuing this lesson.

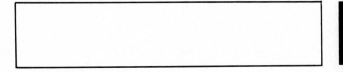

Typing Legal Terms

Directions: Unless otherwise instructed, use a 70-space line and double spacing. Correct all errors. Follow one of the procedures below.

Words

Typing Procedure

On a separate sheet of paper, type the following words at least two times, concentrating on the correct spelling and pronunciation.

Shorthand Procedure

On a separate sheet of paper, type the following words once, concentrating on the correct spelling and pronunciation. Then write the shorthand outline for each word on the lines to the right or on your shorthand machine. Cover the printed words with a sheet of paper and transcribe from the shorthand outlines one time on your typewriter.

cohabitation / consanguinity / affinity / femme sole / _____

antenuptial agreement / premarital / privileged _____

communications / counsel fee / separation / _____

a mensa et thoro / separation agreement / separate _____

maintenance / _____

Sentences

Typing Procedure

Type each of the following sentences one time. Concentrate on the correct spelling and pronunciation of each underlined legal term.

Shorthand Procedure

Write the correct shorthand outlines for the following sentences on the lines to the right or on your shorthand machine. Cover the printed material with a sheet of paper and transcribe from your shorthand outlines one time on the typewriter.

These sentences will be used for practice dictation on the cassettes.

Cohabitation is the state of living together as hus- _____

band and wife. Consanguinity is a blood relation- _____

ship between two people. Persons of the opposite _____

sex are forbidden, in most states, from living to- _____

gether unless they are related by consanquinity or _____

marriage. Affinity is the relationship of one spouse _____

to the blood relatives of the other spouse because _____

of marriage. Femme sole is a French term referring _____

to a single woman. Femme sole also includes those _____

women who are divorced or widowed. A premarital _____

or antenuptial agreement is an agreement made _____

between two people before they are married. _____

Privileged communications exist between a hus- _____

band and wife. Matters revealed to a spouse are _____

privileged communications, and the spouse is not _____

permitted to testify as a witness against the other _____

spouse in regard to those matters. In most states, _____

the one filing for a divorce is usually required to pay _____

the counsel fee incurred by the spouse in the di- _____

vorce action. A partial or qualified divorce where _____

the parties may not live together but are otherwise _____

legally bound as husband and wife is a separation. _____

A separation expressed in Latin is a mensa et thoro. _____

A mensa et thoro usually involves a separation _____

agreement between a husband and wife which _____

clarifies the property rights, custody, and support _____

for each party. The separation agreement may con- _____

tain provisions for separate maintenance which is _____

an allowance granted to one of the spouses for _____

support and for the support of the children. _____

Transcribing from Dictation

Directions: This dictation emphasizes and reinforces the legal terms and definitions you have studied. Listen carefully to the pronunciation of each of the legal terms. Unless otherwise directed, use a 70-space line and double spacing. Correct all errors. Follow one of the procedures below.

Typing Procedure

Using the cassette from Lesson 21, Part B, transcribe the dictation directly at your typewriter.

Shorthand Procedure

Using the cassette from Lesson 21, Part B, take the dictation using your shorthand system and then transcribe on the typewriter from your shorthand notes.

When you have finished transcribing Part B of the practice dictation, check your transcript with the printed copy. If you have made any mistakes in the transcription, you should practice those words several times before going on to Lesson 22.

Check List

SUBMITTED TO INSTRUCTOR

	PART A, DATE	PART B, DATE	YES	NO
Terminology and Definitions	_____	_____	____	____
*Typing Legal Terms	_____	_____	____	____
Words	_____	_____	____	____
Sentences	_____	_____	____	____
*Transcribing from Dictation	_____	_____	____	____
Quiz No. 1	_____	_____	____	____
Quiz No. 2	_____	_____	____	____

When you have successfully completed all the exercises in this lesson and submitted to your instructor those called for, you are ready to proceed with Lesson 22.

*If you are using a shorthand system, turn in to your instructor your shorthand notes along with your transcript.

Quiz No. 1

Terminology and Definition Recall

Directions: In the Answers column write the legal term that is most representative of the corresponding statement. After you have completed this quiz, check your answers with the key on page 337. Unless otherwise directed, turn in this quiz to your instructor upon completion of this lesson.

ANSWERS

1. A marriage relationship between only one man and one woman at a time is a/an _____.

1. _____

2. A marriage which is not created by the usual ceremony required by law but exists between two people who live together as husband and wife is a/an _____ marriage.

2. _____

3. A ceremony which creates a valid marriage and is performed by a duly ordained minister or member of the clergy of any recognized religion is a/an _____ ceremony.

3. _____

4. A ceremony which creates a valid marriage and is performed by a public official who is so authorized to perform marriages is a/an _____ ceremony.

4. _____

5. A marriage which is created according to the requirements of the law is a/an _____ marriage.

5. _____

6. The marriage relationship between a husband and wife is referred to as _____.

6. _____

7. A marriage which exists for all practical purposes but contains a legal imperfection which could void the relationship in a court of law is a/an _____ marriage.

7. _____

8. The voiding of a marriage and treating it as though it never existed is a/an _____.

8. _____

9. A term which refers to family affairs or to a home or household is _____.

9. _____

10. A marriage which is not valid and does not meet the requirements established by law for a valid marriage is a/an _____ marriage.

10. _____

11. The state of having two husbands or two wives at any one time is _____.

11. _____

12. A word meaning below the age of consent and a ground for annulment in most states is _____.

12. _____

Turn back to page 222 and continue with this lesson.

Quiz No. 2

Terminology and Definition Recall

Directions: In the Answers column write the letter from Column I that represents the word or phrase that best matches each item in Column II. After you have completed this quiz, check your answers with the key on page 337. Unless otherwise directed, turn in this quiz to your instructor upon completion of this lesson.

COLUMN I	COLUMN II	ANSWERS
A. a mensa et thoro	**1.** Fees for legal counsel usually paid by the one filing for the divorce.	1. _____
B. affinity		
C. antenuptial agreement	**2.** An amount granted by a court in a legal separation to one of the spouses for support and for the support of the children.	2. _____
D. cohabitation		
E. consanguinity	**3.** A Latin term for legal separation.	3. _____
F. counsel fee	**4.** The state of living together as husband and wife.	4. _____
G. femme sole	**5.** A French term for a woman who is not married.	5. _____
H. nonage		
I. premarital	**6.** A partial or qualified divorce where the parties may not live together but are otherwise legally bound as husband and wife.	6. _____
J. privileged communications		
K. separate maintenance	**7.** Before the marriage.	7. _____
L. separation	**8.** The relationship between husband and wife prohibits one from testifying against the other about matters revealed because of the marriage relationship.	8. _____
M. separation agreement		
	9. An agreement made between two people before they are married.	9. _____
	10. A contract between a husband and wife who are living separately which clarifies the property rights, custody, and support for each party.	10. _____
	11. The relationship of one spouse to the blood relatives of the other spouse because of the marriage.	11. _____
	12. A blood relationship between two people.	12. _____

Turn back to page 225 and continue with this lesson.

"One who consents to an act is not wronged by it."

—Legal Maxim

LESSON 22

To Wit: Domestic Relations

Many of the terms relating to the dissolution of marriage are introduced in this lesson. Divorce laws are changing rapidly and vary considerably from state to state. Therefore, the terms covered are those that are generally applicable to most states. For the successful completion of these exercises, you should be able to pronounce, define, and transcribe each of the terms that are presented.

Part A	Terminology and Definitions

Directions: Study the terms, pronunciations, and definitions until you are thoroughly familiar with them. In order to complete this lesson successfully, you must understand the meaning and usage of all the legal terms presented. If you are using shorthand, write your shorthand outline in the space provided or on your shorthand machine for each legal term.

LEGAL TERM	PRONUNCIATION	DEFINITION	SHORTHAND OUTLINE
1. dissolution of marriage	dis-ə-'lü-shən əv 'mar-ij	The termination of a marriage by a divorce.	_____
2. divorce	də-'vōrs	The dissolving of a marriage legally by an action of the court. Also includes a legal separation.	_____
3. no-fault divorce	nō-'folt də-'vōrs	A recently enacted change in the divorce laws of several states which does not require the one filing for divorce to prove the spouse at fault on grounds previously required for a divorce to be granted.	_____
4. absolute divorce	'ab-sə-lüt də-'vōrs	The total dissolution of a marriage.	_____
5. a vinculo matrimonii	ā vin-'kū-lō 'ma-trə-mō-nē-ī	Latin. "An absolute divorce."	_____

6.	limited divorce	'lim-ət-əd də-'vōrs	A legal separation which does not totally dissolve the marriage.	_____
7.	contested divorce	kən-'test-əd də-'vōrs	A divorce action in which one of the parties resists or opposes the granting of the divorce and challenges or defends the action.	_____
8.	uncontested divorce	ən-kən-'test-əd də-'vōrs	A divorce action in which the party being sued for divorce does not resist or oppose the grounds for the divorce and makes no defense thereto.	_____
9.	conciliation procedure	kən-sil-ē-'ā-shən prə-'sē-jər	A procedure whereby the judge meets with the parties to a divorce and attempts to work out their differences. The judge may make several recommendations to the parties that they attempt in trying to reconcile the marriage before granting the divorce.	_____
10.	grounds for divorce	graünds fər də-'vōrs	The foundation or basis for the granting of a divorce. The grounds for divorce will vary from state to state.	_____
11.	corespondent	kō-ri-'spän-dənt	The person charged with committing adultery with the respondent in a divorce action for which the grounds are adultery.	_____
12.	desertion	di-'zər-shən	The refusal without just cause of a husband or wife to continue a marital relationship.	_____
13.	Enoch Arden Law	'ē-nək ärd-n lȯ	A law in some states which specifies that the absence of a spouse for a lengthy and continuous period of time constitutes grounds for divorce.	_____

Turn to page 239 and complete Quiz No. 1 before continuing this lesson.

Typing Legal Terms

Directions: Unless otherwise instructed, use a 70-space line and double spacing. Correct all errors. Follow one of the procedures below.

Words

Typing Procedure

On a separate sheet of paper, type the following words at least two times, concentrating on the correct spelling and pronunciation.

Shorthand Procedure

On a separate sheet of paper, type the following words once, concentrating on the correct spelling and pronunciation. Then write the shorthand outline for each word on the lines to the right or on your shorthand machine. Cover the printed words with a sheet of paper and transcribe from the shorthand outlines one time on your typewriter.

dissolution of marriage / divorce / no-fault divorce / _____

absolute divorce / a vinculo matrimonii / limited _____

divorce / contested divorce / uncontested divorce / _____

conciliation procedure / grounds for divorce / _____

corespondent / desertion / Enoch Arden Law / _____

Sentences

Typing Procedure

Type each of the following sentences one time. Concentrate on the correct spelling and pronunciation of each underlined legal term.

Shorthand Procedure

Write the correct shorthand outlines for the following sentences on the lines to the right or on your shorthand machine. Cover the printed material with a sheet of paper and transcribe from your shorthand outlines one time on the typewriter.

These sentences will be used for practice dictation on the cassettes.

A dissolution of marriage is the act of terminating a marriage by divorce. A divorce is the dissolving of a marriage legally by an action of a court. A divorce may also include a legal separation. A divorce may be either limited or absolute. An absolute divorce is the total dissolution of the marriage. A limited divorce is a legal separation of husband and wife which does not totally dissolve the marriage. An absolute divorce expressed in Latin terms is a vinculo matrimonii. Recently, several states have enacted no-fault divorce laws. A no-fault divorce does not require the one filing for divorce to prove the spouse at fault on grounds that were previously required for a divorce action. A divorce action may be either contested or uncontested by the party against whom it is filed. In a contested divorce, the party against whom it is filed resists or opposes the granting of the divorce and challenges or defends the action. An uncontested divorce is one in which the party being sued for divorce does not resist or oppose the divorce and makes no defense thereto. If a judge feels that the marriage might possibly be reconciled, a conciliation procedure may be recommended. Grounds for divorce are the foundation or basis for the granting of a divorce as required by state law. A <u>corespondent</u> is a person charged with committing adultery with the respondent in a divorce action for which the grounds are adultery. <u>Desertion</u> is the refusal without just cause to continue a marital relationship. The <u>Enoch Arden Law</u> in some states permits divorce on the grounds of desertion.

_____

_____

_____

_____

_____

_____

_____

_____

Transcribing from Dictation

Directions: This dictation emphasizes and reinforces the legal terms and definitions you have studied. Listen carefully to the pronunciation of each of the legal terms. Unless otherwise directed, use a 70-space line and double spacing. Correct all errors. Follow one of the procedures below.

Typing Procedure

Using the cassette from Lesson 22, Part A, transcribe the dictation directly at your typewriter.

Shorthand Procedure

Using the cassette from Lesson 22, Part A, take the dictation using your shorthand system and then transcribe on the typewriter from your shorthand notes.

When you have finished transcribing Part A of the practice dictation, check your transcript with the printed copy. If you made any mistakes in the transcription, you should practice those words several times before going on.

Part B | Terminology and Definitions

Directions: Study the terms, pronunciations, and definitions until you are thoroughly familiar with them. In order to complete this lesson successfully, you must understand the meaning and usage of all the legal terms presented. If you are using shorthand, write your shorthand outline in the space provided or on your shorthand machine for each legal term.

LEGAL TERM	PRONUNCIATION	DEFINITION	SHORTHAND OUTLINE
1. alimony	'al-ə-mo̅-ne̅	A provision for the support and maintenance of a wife by her divorced husband. In recent years, some states have ruled that a wife who is financially able has to pay alimony to the husband.	_____
2. permanent alimony	'pərm-nənt 'al-ə-mo̅-ne̅	Alimony which is to continue during the lifetime of the spouse.	_____

3. temporary alimony	′tem-pə-rer-ē ′al-ə-mō-nē	An amount paid to the wife or husband while the divorce suit is pending.	_____
4. alimony pendente lite	′al-ə-mō-nē pen-′den-tē ′lī-tē	Latin. Temporary alimony paid while the divorce action is pending.	_____
5. property settlement	′präp-ərt-ē ′set-l-mənt	An agreement between the parties of a divorce action as to the division of property owned or acquired during the marriage.	_____
6. community property	kə-′myü-nət-ē ′präp-ərt-ē	Any property which is acquired by husband and wife during the marriage.	_____
7. domicile	′däm-ə-sīl	The legal place where a person or a family resides.	_____
8. necessaries	′nes-ə-ser-ēs	Generally means food, clothing, shelter, and medicines. Creditors who provide necessaries can file a claim for a judgment against alimony payments.	_____
9. earning capacity	′ərn-iŋ kə-′pas-ət-ē	The capacity or capability of one to earn money. A consideration in the awarding of alimony in a divorce action.	_____
10. support	sə-′pōrt	The payment of money in a divorce action which will provide the necessaries or maintain the lifestyle for the spouse and children.	_____
11. nonsupport	nän-sə-′pōrt	In some states, grounds for a divorce if the husband fails to support the wife. A husband's actual inability to provide for his wife is generally not sufficient grounds for divorce.	_____
12. custody	′kəs-təd-ē	The care and possession of minor children of a marriage which is in a state of separation or divorce.	_____
13. adoption	ə-′däp-shən	The taking of another person's child and giving the child all the rights and duties as though the child were the person's own.	_____

Turn to page 240 and complete Quiz No. 2 before continuing this lesson.

Typing Legal Terms

Directions: Unless otherwise instructed, use a 70-space line and double spacing. Correct all errors. Follow one of the procedures below.

Lesson 22, Part B

Words

Typing Procedure

On a separate sheet of paper, type the following words at least two times, concentrating on the correct spelling and pronunciation.

Shorthand Procedure

On a separate sheet of paper, type the following words once, concentrating on the correct spelling and pronunciation. Then write the shorthand outline for each word on the lines to the right or on your shorthand machine. Cover the printed words with a sheet of paper and transcribe from the shorthand outlines one time on your typewriter.

alimony / permanent alimony / temporary alimony / _____

alimony pendente lite / property settlement / _____

community property / domicile / necessaries / earning _____

capacity / support / nonsupport / custody / adoption / _____

Sentences

Typing Procedure

Type each of the following sentences one time. Concentrate on the correct spelling and pronunciation of each underlined legal term.

Shorthand Procedure

Write the correct shorthand outlines for the following sentences on the lines to the right or on your shorthand machine. Cover the printed material with a sheet of paper and transcribe from your shorthand outlines one time on the typewriter.

These sentences will be used for practice dictation on the cassettes.

Alimony is a provision for the support and maintenance of a wife by her divorced husband. In recent years, some states have ruled that a wife who is financially able has to pay alimony to the husband. Alimony may be either permanent or temporary. Permanent alimony is to continue during the lifetime of the spouse. Temporary alimony is an amount paid while the divorce suit is pending. Temporary alimony is referred to in Latin as alimony pendente lite. The parties to a divorce must come to an agreement as to a property settlement. A property settlement is an agreement as to the division of property owned or acquired during the marriage. Community property is property acquired by husband and wife during the marriage. A domicile is the legal place where a person or a family resides. <u>Necessaries</u> are generally food, clothing, shelter, and medicines. Creditors who provide necessaries can file a claim for a judgment against alimony payments. <u>Earning capacity</u>, which affects the amount of alimony payments, is the capability or capacity of a person to earn money. <u>Support</u> is the payment of money in a divorce action which will provide the necessaries or maintain the lifestyle for the spouse and children. In some states, if a husband fails to provide necessaries for a wife, it is called <u>nonsupport</u> and is grounds for divorce. <u>Custody</u> relates to the care and possession of minor children after a divorce. The taking of another person's child and giving a child all the rights and duties as though the child is the person's own is called <u>adoption</u>.

_____
_____
_____
_____
_____
_____
_____
_____
_____
_____
_____
_____
_____

Transcribing from Dictation

Directions: This dictation emphasizes and reinforces the legal terms and definitions you have studied. Listen carefully to the pronunciation of each of the legal terms. Unless otherwise directed, use a 70-space line and double spacing. Correct all errors. Follow one of the procedures below.

Typing Procedure

Using the cassette from Lesson 22, Part B, transcribe the dictation directly at your typewriter.

Shorthand Procedure

Using the cassette from Lesson 22, Part B, take the dictation using your shorthand system and then transcribe on the typewriter from your shorthand notes.

When you have finished transcribing Part B of the practice dictation, check your transcript with the printed copy. If you have made any mistakes in the transcription, you should practice those words several times before going on to Evaluation 11.

Check List

	PART A, DATE	PART B, DATE	SUBMITTED TO INSTRUCTOR	
			YES	NO
Terminology and Definitions	_____	_____	_____	_____
*Typing Legal Terms	_____	_____	_____	_____
Words	_____	_____	_____	_____
Sentences	_____	_____	_____	_____
*Transcribing from Dictation	_____	_____	_____	_____
Quiz No. 1	_____	_____	_____	_____
Quiz No. 2	_____	_____	_____	_____

When you have successfully completed all the exercises in this lesson and submitted to your instructor those called for, you are ready to proceed with Evaluation 11.

*If you are using a shorthand system, turn in to your instructor your shorthand notes along with your transcript.

Quiz No. 1

Terminology and Definition Recall

Directions: In the Answers column at the right of each statement, write the letter that represents the word, or group of words, that correctly completes the statement. After you have completed this quiz, check your answers with the key on page 338. Unless otherwise directed, turn in this quiz to your instructor upon completion of this lesson.

ANSWERS

1. The person charged with adultery with the respondent in a suit for divorce for that cause and joined as a defendant with such party is called a/an (a) Enoch Arden, (b) corespondent, (c) conciliation. . . . .   1. _____

2. A law in some states that the unexplained absence of a spouse for a lengthy and continuous period of time constitutes grounds for divorce is the (a) Enoch Arden Law, (b) corespondent, (c) desertion. . . . .   2. _____

3. An absolute divorce is (a) corespondent, (b) conciliation procedure, (c) a vinculo matrimonii. . . . .   3. _____

4. A procedure whereby the judge meets with the parties and endeavors to reconcile them is a/an (a) a vinculo matrimonii, (b) conciliation procedure, (c) dissolution of marriage. . . . .   4. _____

5. A legal separation which does not totally dissolve the marriage is a/an (a) no-fault divorce, (b) contested divorce, (c) limited divorce. . . . .   5. _____

6. The refusal without just cause of a husband or wife to continue a marital relationship is (a) corespondent, (b) desertion, (c) divorce. . . . .   6. _____

7. A divorce in which the one filing for the divorce does not have to prove the spouse at fault on grounds previously required in most states for a divorce to be granted is a (a) no-fault divorce, (b) limited divorce, (c) uncontested divorce.   7. _____

8. The dissolving of a marriage legally by an action of a court is a (a) divorce, (b) desertion, (c) corespondent. . . . .   8. _____

9. A divorce action in which one of the parties resists or opposes the granting of the divorce and challenges or defends the action is a/an (a) contested divorce, (b) limited divorce, (c) no-fault divorce. . . . .   9. _____

10. Termination of a marriage by divorce is (a) desertion, (b) corespondent, (c) dissolution of marriage. . . . .   10. _____

11. A divorce action in which the party being sued for divorce does not resist or oppose the grounds for the divorce and makes no defense thereto is a/an (a) absolute divorce, (b) contested divorce, (c) uncontested divorce. . . . .   11. _____

12. The foundation or basis for the granting of a divorce is referred to as (a) Enoch Arden Law, (b) grounds for divorce, (c) a vinculo matrimonii. . . . .   12. _____

13. The total dissolution of a marriage is a/an (a) absolute divorce, (b) uncontested divorce, (c) limited divorce. . . . .   13. _____

Turn back to page 232 and continue with this lesson.

Quiz No. 2

Terminology and Definition Recall

Directions: In the Answers column write the legal term that is most representative of the corresponding statement. After you have completed this quiz, check your answers with the key on page 338. Unless otherwise directed, turn in this quiz to your instructor upon completion of this lesson.

ANSWERS

1. The care and possession of minor children of a marriage which is in a state of separation or divorce is called _____.

1. _____

2. An agreement between the parties of a divorce action as to the division of property owned or acquired during the marriage is the _____.

2. _____

3. An amount paid to the wife or husband while the divorce suit is pending is referred to as _____ alimony.

3. _____

4. The capabilities of an individual to earn money less the necessary expense of the individual's own living which is considered in the awarding of alimony in a divorce action is called the _____.

4. _____

5. The legal place where a person or a family resides is called the _____.

5. _____

6. Food, clothing, shelter, and medicines are generally referred to as _____.

6. _____

7. The act of taking another's child into one's own family, treating the child as one's own, and giving the child all the rights and duties of one's own child is called _____.

7. _____

8. Any property which is acquired by husband and wife during the marriage is referred to as _____ property.

8. _____

9. Alimony which is to continue during the lifetime of the spouse is _____ alimony.

9. _____

10. If a husband has the ability to support his wife and does not, it is grounds for divorce in some states, and is referred to as _____.

10. _____

11. Temporary alimony paid while the divorce action is pending is expressed in Latin as alimony _____.

11. _____

12. A provision for the support and maintenance of a husband or wife by the divorced spouse is _____.

12. _____

13. The payment of money in a divorce action which will provide the necessaries or maintain the lifestyle for the spouse and children is _____.

13. _____

Turn back to page 235 and continue with this lesson.

EVALUATION No. 11

Student_____

Class_____Date_____

SCORING RECORD

	Perfect Score	Student's Score
Section A	50	
Section B	20	
Section C	30	
Total	100	

SECTION A

Directions: This dictation/transcription evaluation will test your spelling and transcription ability on the legal terms that you studied in the two preceding lessons. Use a 5-space paragraph indention, a 70-space line and double spacing unless otherwise instructed. Correct all errors. Follow one of the procedures below.

Typing Procedure

Using the cassette from Evaluation 11, transcribe the dictation directly at your typewriter.

Shorthand Procedure

Using the cassette from Evaluation 11, take the dictation using your shorthand system and then transcribe on the typewriter from your shorthand notes.

SECTIONS B AND C ARE AVAILABLE FROM YOUR INSTRUCTOR.

"Time does not confirm a void act."

—Legal Maxim

LESSON 23

To Wit: Commercial Paper

The extensive use of commercial paper in our society has resulted in uniform laws regulating commercial paper. The Uniform Commercial Code has been adopted in all states. This area of law affects the daily lives of individuals and businesses, and almost everyone has direct contact with commercial paper of some type. The terminology taught in the following exercises deals with the various trends of commercial paper. When you have satisfactorily completed the lesson, you will be able to spell, pronounce, define, and transcribe each of the terms presented in the area of commercial paper.

| Part A | Terminology and Definitions |

Directions: Study the terms, pronunciations, and definitions until you are thoroughly familiar with them. In order to complete this lesson successfully, you must understand the meaning and usage of all the legal terms presented. If you are using shorthand, write your shorthand outline in the space provided or on your shorthand machine for each legal term.

	LEGAL TERM	PRONUNCIATION	DEFINITION	SHORTHAND OUTLINE
1.	negotiable	ni-'gō-sh-ə-bəl	Capable of being transferred or assigned to another.	_____
2.	commercial paper	kə-'mər-shəl 'pā-pər	A written promise which is capable of being transferred or assigned to another.	_____
3.	Uniform Commercial Code (UCC)	'yü-nə-form kə-'mər-shəl kōd	Adopted by all states to govern and define commercial paper.	_____
4.	legal tender	'lē-gəl 'ten-dər	An accepted form of exchange which, according to law, must be accepted in the payment of a debt.	_____
5.	check	chek	A commercial paper which is used to transfer money from one person's bank account to another person.	_____

6. cashier's check	ka-'shirs chek	A check issued by a bank which promises to make payment on demand.	_____
7. promissory note	'präm-ə-sōr-ē nōt	An unconditional written commercial paper by which one promises to pay a certain amount of money to another at a definite time.	_____
8. demand note	di-'mənd nōt	A promissory note which has no specific payment date but must be paid upon demand.	_____
9. time note	tīm nōt	A promissory note which specifies the date on which it must be paid.	_____
10. collateral note	kə-'lat-ə-ral nōt	A note for which one has pledged security other than one's own promise to pay.	_____
11. judgment note	'jəj-mənt nōt	A promissory note in which the maker authorizes that a judgment may be made against the maker if the note is not paid when due.	_____
12. cognovit note	'kog-nō-vit nōt	Same as a judgment note.	_____
13. certificate of deposit	sər-'tif-i-kət əv di-'päz-ət	An instrument issued by a bank acknowledging the deposit of a specific sum of money and promising to pay the holder of the certificate that amount.	_____

Turn to page 251 and complete Quiz No. 1 before continuing this lesson.

Turn to page 251 and complete Quiz No. 1 before continuing this lesson.

Typing Legal Terms

Directions: Unless otherwise instructed, use a 70-space line and double spacing. Correct all errors. Follow one of the procedures below.

Words

Typing Procedure

On a separate sheet of paper, type the following words at least two times, concentrating on the correct spelling and pronunciation.

Shorthand Procedure

On a separate sheet of paper, type the following words once, concentrating on the correct spelling and pronunciation. Then write the shorthand outline for each word on the lines to the right or on your shorthand machine. Cover the printed words with a sheet of paper and transcribe from the shorthand outlines one time on your typewriter.

negotiable / commercial paper / Uniform
Commercial Code / legal tender / check / cashier's
check / promissory note / demand note / time note /
collateral note / judgment note / cognovit note /
certificate of deposit /

Sentences

Typing Procedure

Type each of the following sentences one time.
Concentrate on the correct spelling and pronunciation of each underlined legal term.

Shorthand Procedure

Write the correct shorthand outlines for the following sentences on the lines to the right or on your
shorthand machine. Cover the printed material with
a sheet of paper and transcribe from your shorthand
outlines one time on the typewriter.

These sentences will be used for practice dictation on the cassettes.

Negotiable means capable of being transferred or
assigned to another. Commercial paper is a written
promise which is capable of being transferred or
assigned to another. The requirements of commercial paper are defined under the Uniform
Commercial Code which has been adopted by all
states. Legal tender is an accepted form of exchange, usually money, which, according to law,
must be accepted in the payment of a debt. A
check is a commercial paper which is used to transfer money from one person's bank account to
another person. A cashier's check is a check issued
by a bank with a guarantee of payment on demand. A promissory note is a written commercial
paper by which one promises to pay a certain
amount of money to another at a definite time. A
demand note is a promissory note that has no
specific payment date but which must be paid
upon demand. A promissory note which specifies
the date on which it must be paid is a time note. If
security other than a promise to pay has been
pledged, the note is referred to as a collateral note.
A judgment note is a promissory note which authorizes that a judgment may be made against the
maker if the note is not paid when due. A cognovit

note is the same as a judgment note. A certificate of deposit is an instrument issued by a bank acknowledging the deposit of a specific sum of money and promising to pay the holder of the certificate that amount.

_____
_____
_____
_____
_____

Transcribing from Dictation

Directions: This dictation emphasizes and reinforces the legal terms and definitions you have studied. Listen carefully to the pronunciation of each of the legal terms. Unless otherwise directed, use a 70-space line and double spacing. Correct all errors. Follow one of the procedures below.

Typing Procedure

Using the cassette from Lesson 23, Part A, transcribe the dictation directly at your typewriter.

Shorthand Procedure

Using the cassette from Lesson 23, Part A, take the dictation using your shorthand system and then transcribe on the typewriter from your shorthand notes.

When you have finished transcribing Part A of the practice dictation, check your transcript with the printed copy. If you made any mistakes in the transcription, you should practice those words several times before going on.

Part B | Terminology and Definitions

Directions: Study the terms, pronunciations, and definitions until you are thoroughly familiar with them. In order to complete this lesson successfully, you must understand the meaning and usage of all the legal terms presented. If you are using shorthand, write your shorthand outline in the space provided or on your shorthand machine for each legal term.

LEGAL TERM	PRONUNCIATION	DEFINITION	SHORTHAND OUTLINE
1. draft	draft	A bill of exchange. A written order drawn by one person upon another requiring that person to pay a certain amount of money to a third party on demand or at a definite time. A check is a draft.	_____
2. bill of exchange	bil əv iks-'chānj	A draft.	_____
3. trade acceptance	trād ik-'sep-təns	A time draft drawn on the purchaser of goods by the one selling the goods and accepted by the purchaser.	_____
4. draft-varying acceptance	draft-'ver-ē-iŋ ik-'sep-təns	One in which the order of the instrument varies from the acceptor's agreement.	_____

5.	qualified acceptance	′kwäl-ə-fīd ik-′sep-təns	An acceptance which is only partial in that it varies the order of the draft in some way.	_____
6.	accommodation paper	ə-käm-ə-′dā-shən ′pā-pər	A paper, bill, or note signed by a person without consideration to accommodate another party to enable that party to obtain credit based on the paper.	_____
7.	payee	′pā-ē	The person to whom a check, promissory note, or draft is payable.	_____
8.	payer	′pā-ər	The one who pays a check, promissory note, or draft.	_____
9.	maker	′mā-kər	The one who orders payment on a check or draft or who makes a promissory note.	_____
10.	comaker	kō-′mā-kər	One who signs a commercial paper with others and is also responsible for its payment.	_____
11.	holder in due course	′hōl-dər in dü kōrs	One who has accepted a commercial paper for value on the condition that it is valid and not overdue.	_____
12.	bearer	′bar-ər	A person who is holding or in possession of a commercial paper which is made payable to bearer.	_____
13.	carte blanche	kärt blänsh	French. A blank instrument which is signed with the intention that it is to be filled in by another person.	

Turn to page 252 and complete Quiz No. 2 before continuing this lesson.

Typing Legal Terms

Directions: Unless otherwise instructed, use a 70-space line and double spacing. Correct all errors. Follow one of the procedures below.

Words

Typing Procedure

On a separate sheet of paper, type the following words at least two times, concentrating on the correct spelling and pronunciation.

Shorthand Procedure

On a separate sheet of paper, type the following words once, concentrating on the correct spelling and pronunciation. Then write the shorthand outline for each word on the lines to the right or on your shorthand machine. Cover the printed words with a sheet of paper and transcribe from the shorthand outlines one time on your typewriter.

draft / bill of exchange / trade acceptance /
draft-varying acceptance / qualified acceptance /
accommodation paper / payee / payer / maker /
comaker / holder in due course / bearer /
carte blanche /

_____

_____

_____

_____

Sentences

Typing Procedure

Type each of the following sentences one time.
Concentrate on the correct spelling and pronunciation of each underlined legal term.

Shorthand Procedure

Write the correct shorthand outlines for the following sentences on the lines to the right or on your
shorthand machine. Cover the printed material with
a sheet of paper and transcribe from your shorthand
outlines one time on the typewriter.

These sentences will be used for practice dictation on the cassettes.

A draft is a written order drawn by one person upon
another requiring that person to pay a certain
amount of money to a third party on demand. The
common term for a bill of exchange is draft. A trade
acceptance is a draft or bill of exchange drawn on
the purchaser of goods by the one selling the goods
and accepted by the purchaser. If the instrument
varies from the acceptor's agreement, it is called a
draft-varying acceptance. A qualified acceptance
is one which is only partial in that it varies the order
of the draft in some way. An accommodation paper
is a paper, bill, or note signed by a person, without
consideration, to accommodate another party to
enable that party to obtain credit based on the
paper. The person to whom a check, promissory
note, or bill of exchange is payable is the payee.
The payer is the one who pays. The one who makes
or executes a promissory note is called the maker.
A comaker is one who signs a commercial paper
with others and is also responsible for its payment.
A holder in due course is one who accepts a commercial paper for value on the condition that it is
valid and not overdue. A bearer is a person who
is holding or in possession of a commercial paper

which is payable to bearer. <u>Carte blanche</u> is a blank instrument which is signed with the intention that it is to be filled in by another person without restriction.

_____

_____

_____

_____

Transcribing from Dictation

Directions: This dictation emphasizes and reinforces the legal terms and definitions you have studied. Listen carefully to the pronunciation of each of the legal terms. Unless otherwise directed, use a 70-space line and double spacing. Correct all errors. Follow one of the procedures below.

Typing Procedure

Using the cassette from Lesson 23, Part B, transcribe the dictation directly at your typewriter.

Shorthand Procedure

Using the cassette from Lesson 23, Part B, take the dictation using your shorthand system and then transcribe on the typewriter from your shorthand notes.

When you have finished transcribing Part B of the practice dictation, check your transcript with the printed copy. If you have made any mistakes in the transcription, you should practice those words several times before going on to Lesson 24.

I have completed the following for Lesson 23:

	PART A, DATE	PART B, DATE	SUBMITTED TO INSTRUCTOR	
			YES	NO
Terminology and Definitions	_____	_____	_____	_____
*Typing Legal Terms	_____	_____	_____	_____
Words	_____	_____	_____	_____
Sentences	_____	_____	_____	_____
*Transcribing from Dictation	_____	_____	_____	_____
Quiz No. 1	_____	_____	_____	_____
Quiz No. 2	_____	_____	_____	_____

When you have successfully completed all the exercises in this lesson and submitted to your instructor those called for, you are ready to proceed with Lesson 24.

*If you are using a shorthand system, turn in to your instructor your shorthand notes along with your transcript.

Quiz No. 1

Terminology and Definition Recall

Directions: In the Answers column write the legal term that is most representative of the corresponding statement. After you have completed this quiz, check your answers with the key on page 338. Unless otherwise directed, turn in this quiz to your instructor upon completion of this lesson.

ANSWERS

1. Something that is capable of being transferred or assigned to another is referred to as being _____.

   1. _____

2. An accepted form of exchange which, according to law, must be accepted in the payment of a debt is _____.

   2. _____

3. A commercial paper which is used to transfer money from one person's bank to another person is a/an _____.

   3. _____

4. Another name for a judgment note is _____ note.

   4. _____

5. A promissory note which specifies the date on which it must be paid is a/an _____ note.

   5. _____

6. An unconditional commercial paper by which one promises to pay a certain amount of money to another at a given time is a/an _____.

   6. _____

7. A check issued by a bank that promises to make payment on demand is a/an _____ check.

   7. _____

8. A note by which one pledges security other than one's promise to pay is a/an _____.

   8. _____

9. A written promise which is capable of being transferred or assigned to another is a/an _____.

   9. _____

10. A uniform act which has been adopted by all states to govern and define commercial paper is the _____.

    10. _____

11. A promissory note which has no specific payment date but must be paid upon demand is a/an _____ note.

    11. _____

12. A promissory note in which the maker authorizes that a judgment may be made against the maker if the note is not paid when due is a/an _____ note.

    12. _____

Turn back to page 244 and continue with this lesson.

DATE _____ NAME _____

Quiz No. 2

Terminology and Definition Recall

Directions: In the Answers column at the right of each statement, write the letter that represents the word, or group of words, that correctly completes the statement. After you have completed this quiz, check your answers with the key on page 338. Unless otherwise directed, turn in this quiz to your instructor upon completion of this lesson.

ANSWERS

1. One who signs a commercial paper with others and is also responsible for its payment is a (a) maker, (b) payee, (c) comaker. .... 1. _____

2. A draft or bill of exchange in which the order of the instrument varies from the acceptor's agreement is a (a) draft-varying acceptance, (b) qualified acceptance, (c) trade acceptance. .... 2. _____

3. A person who is holding or in possession of a commercial paper which is made payable to bearer is a (a) holder, (b) bearer, (c) payer. .... 3. _____

4. A written order drawn by one person upon another person to pay a certain amount of money to a third party on demand or at a definite time is a/an (a) draft, (b) accommodation paper, (c) carte blanche. .... 4. _____

5. The person to whom a check, promissory note, or bill of exchange is payable is the (a) payer, (b) maker, (c) payee. .... 5. _____

6. An acceptance which is only partial in that it varies the order of the draft in some way is a (a) draft-varying acceptance, (b) qualified acceptance, (c) trade acceptance. .... 6. _____

7. The one who orders payment of a check or draft or who makes a promissory note is the (a) comaker, (b) maker, (c) payee. .... 7. _____

8. One who has accepted a commercial paper for value on the condition that it is valid and not overdue is a (a) holder in due course, (b) bearer, (c) comaker. 8. _____

9. A paper, bill, or note signed by a person without consideration to accommodate another party to enable that party to obtain credit based on the paper is a/an (a) qualified acceptance, (b) draft-varying acceptance, (c) accommodation paper. 9. _____

10. A time draft drawn on the purchaser of goods by the one selling the goods and accepted by the purchaser is a (a) draft-varying acceptance, (b) qualified acceptance, (c) trade acceptance. .... 10. _____

11. The one who pays a check, promissory note, or draft is the (a) bearer, (b) payee, (c) payer. .... 11. _____

12. Another name for a draft is (a) bill of exchange, (b) accommodation paper, (c) carte blanche. .... 12. _____

13. A blank instrument which is signed with the intention that it is to be filled in by another person without restriction is a (a) draft, (b) bill of exchange, (c) carte blanche. .... 13. _____

Turn back to page 247 and continue with this lesson.

*"One who grants a thing is presumed to grant also what-
ever is essential to its use."*

—Legal Maxim

LESSON 24

To Wit: Commercial Paper

Additional terms which relate to the area of commercial paper are presented in this lesson. Upon satisfactory completion of the following exercises, you will be able to spell, pronounce, define, and transcribe each of the terms introduced pertaining to commercial paper.

Part A	Terminology and Definitions

Directions: Study the terms, pronunciations, and definitions until you are thoroughly familiar with them. In order to complete this lesson successfully, you must understand the meaning and usage of all the legal terms presented. If you are using shorthand, write your shorthand outline in the space provided or on your shorthand machine for each legal term.

LEGAL TERM	PRONUNCIATION	DEFINITION	OUTLINE
1. delivery	di-ˈliv-rē	The act of transferring or placing a commercial paper in the possession or control of another person.	_____
2. maturity	mə-ˈtu̇r-ət-ē	The date or time on which a commercial paper comes due and is payable.	_____
3. interest	ˈin-trəst	An amount of money paid for the use of money belonging to another person.	_____
4. usury	ˈyüzh-rē	An illegal amount of interest charged for the use of money.	_____
5. accrue	ə-ˈkrü	To be added to or to increase. Interest on a note accrues to or is added to the principal.	_____
6. grace period	grās ˈpir-ē-əd	An extension of time after the due date for the payment of a commercial paper without defaulting on the obligation.	_____

7.	dishonor	dis-'än-ər	To refuse to pay a commercial paper when it is due or to refuse to accept a commercial paper.	_____
8.	value	'val-yü	The consideration involved in a contract. It may also be an abbreviation for "valuable consideration."	_____
9.	without recourse	with-'aut 'rē-kors	When used in an indorsement of a commercial paper, it means that the indorser cannot be held liable if the original makers of the instrument fail to make payment when due.	_____
10.	protest	'prō-test	A written notarized statement which certifies that a commercial paper was presented for payment and refused. Also refers to the payment of a debt which one does not feel that one owes with the intention of recovering the amount later. Such a debt is paid "under protest."	_____
11.	presentment	pri-'zent-mənt	The presentation of a commercial paper for payment to the one who has the responsibility for making such payment.	_____
12.	postdate	pōs-'dāt	To put a future date on a commercial paper instead of the date on which it is actually made.	_____

Turn to page 261 and complete Quiz No. 1 before continuing this lesson.

Typing Legal Terms

Directions: Unless otherwise instructed, use a 70-space line and double spacing. Correct all errors. Follow one of the procedures below.

Words

Typing Procedure

On a separate sheet of paper, type the following words at least two times, concentrating on the correct spelling and pronunciation.

Shorthand Procedure

On a separate sheet of paper, type the following words once, concentrating on the correct spelling and pronunciation. Then write the shorthand outline for each word on the lines to the right or on your shorthand machine. Cover the printed words with a sheet of paper and transcribe from the shorthand outlines one time on your typewriter.

delivery / maturity / interest / usury /   _____

accrue / grace period / dishonor / value / without   _____

recourse / protest / presentment / postdate /

Sentences

Typing Procedure

Type each of the following sentences one time. Concentrate on the correct spelling and pronunciation of each underlined legal term.

Shorthand Procedure

Write the correct shorthand outlines for the following sentences on the lines to the right or on your shorthand machine. Cover the printed material with a sheet of paper and transcribe from your shorthand outlines one time on the typewriter.

These sentences will be used for practice dictation on the cassettes.

Delivery is the act of transferring or placing an instrument in the possession or control of another person. Delivery is usually a requirement for the legal transfer of a commercial paper. Maturity is the date or time on which a commercial paper comes due and is payable. Interest is an amount of money paid for the use of money belonging to another person. Usury is an illegal amount of interest charged for the use of money. Accrue means to be added to or to increase. Interest on a note accrues to or is added to the principal. An extension of time after the due date of the payment of a commercial paper without defaulting on the obligation is called a grace period. Dishonor is to refuse to pay a commercial paper when it is due or to refuse to accept a commercial paper. Value is the consideration involved in a contract. Value is also an abbreviation for "valuable consideration." If an indorser writes "without recourse" when indorsing an instrument, it means the indorser cannot be held liable if the original makers of the instrument fail to make payment when due. A protest is a written notarized statement which certifies that a commercial paper was presented for payment and refused. A debt paid "under protest" is the payment of a debt that one feels is not owed with the intention of recovering the amount later. Presentment is the presentation of a commercial paper for payment to the one who has the responsibility for making such payment. To put a future date on a commercial paper instead of the date on which it is actually made is to <u>postdate</u>.

_____

_____

_____

_____

Transcribing from Dictation

Directions: This dictation emphasizes and reinforces the legal terms and definitions you have studied. Listen carefully to the pronunciation of each of the legal terms. Unless otherwise directed, use a 70-space line and double spacing. Correct all errors. Follow one of the procedures below.

Typing Procedure

Using the cassette from Lesson 24, Part A, transcribe the dictation directly at your typewriter.

Shorthand Procedure

Using the cassette from Lesson 24, Part A, take the dictation using your shorthand system and then transcribe on the typewriter from your shorthand notes.

When you have finished transcribing Part A of the practice dictation, check your transcript with the printed copy. If you made any mistakes in the transcription, you should practice those words several times before going on.

Part B Terminology and Definitions

Directions: Study the terms, pronunciations, and definitions until you are thoroughly familiar with them. In order to complete this lesson successfully, you must understand the meaning and usage of all the legal terms presented. If you are using shorthand, write your shorthand outline in the space provided or on your shorthand machine for each legal term.

LEGAL TERM	PRONUNCIATION	DEFINITION	SHORTHAND OUTLINE
1. indorsement*	in-'dȯr-smənt	The signing of one's name on the back of a commercial paper with the purpose of transferring or assigning it to another person.	_____
2. successive indorsement	sək-'ses-iv in-'dȯr-smənt	A series of indorsements following one after another on a commercial paper.	_____
3. special or full indorsement	'spesh-əl or fül in-'dȯr-smənt	An indorsement which specifically names the person to whom the instrument is being transferred.	_____
4. restrictive indorsement	ri-'strik-tiv in-'dȯr-smənt	One which contains restrictions as to any further transfer of a commercial paper.	_____

*The form *indorse* is used in the UCC. The form *endorse* is commonly used in business.

5.	qualified indorsement	'kwäl-ə-fīd in-'dòr-smənt	An indorsement which qualifies or restricts the liability of the indorser. Includes an indorsement which contains the words "without recourse."	_____
6.	blank indorsement	blaŋk in-'dòr-smənt	An indorsement which consists of only the indorsee's name.	_____
7.	allonge	a-'lōnzh	A piece of paper attached to a commercial paper to provide space for the indorsements when there is not enough space on the instrument itself.	_____
8.	spoliation	spō-lē-'ā-shən	An alteration or change made on a commercial paper by one who is not a party to the instrument. It does not affect the validity of the instrument if the terms can be determined.	_____
9.	bona fide	'bō-nə fīd	Latin. Genuine or real. In good faith without deceit or fraud.	_____
10.	bogus	'bō-gəs	Not genuine. Counterfeit.	_____
11.	kite	kīt	The securing temporary use of money by issuing worthless paper. Also refers to the worthless paper itself.	_____

Turn to page 262 and complete Quiz No. 2 before continuing this lesson.

Typing Legal Terms

Directions: Unless otherwise instructed, use a 70-space line and double spacing. Correct all errors. Follow one of the procedures below.

Words

Typing Procedure

On a separate sheet of paper, type the following words at least two times, concentrating on the correct spelling and pronunciation.

Shorthand Procedure

On a separate sheet of paper, type the following words once, concentrating on the correct spelling and pronunciation. Then write the shorthand outline for each word on the lines to the right or on your shorthand machine. Cover the printed words with a sheet of paper and transcribe from the shorthand outlines one time on your typewriter.

indorsement / successive indorsement / special or _____

full indorsement / restrictive indorsement / _____

qualified indorsement / blank indorsement / _____

allonge / spoliation / bona fide / bogus / kite / _____

Sentences

Typing Procedure

Type each of the following sentences one time. Concentrate on the correct spelling and pronunciation of each underlined legal term.

Shorthand Procedure

Write the correct shorthand outlines for the following sentences on the lines to the right or on your shorthand machine. Cover the printed material with a sheet of paper and transcribe from your shorthand outlines one time on the typewriter.

These sentences will be used for practice dictation on the cassettes.

An indorsement is the signing of one's name on the back of a commercial paper with the purpose of transferring or assigning it to another person. A successive indorsement is one in a series of indorsements which follow one after the other on a commercial paper. An indorsement which specifically names the person to whom the instrument is being transferred is a special or full indorsement. An indorsement which contains restrictions as to any further transfer of the instrument is a restrictive indorsement. If one wishes to qualify or restrict one's liability for the instrument, a qualified indorsement would be used. A qualified indorsement contains the words "without recourse." A blank indorsement consists only of the indorser's name. If there is not enough space on the instrument for the indorsements, an allonge or a piece of paper may be attached to the instrument to accommodate the indorsements. Spoliation is an alteration or change made on a commercial paper by one who is not a party to the instrument. Spoliation does not affect the validity of the instrument if the terms can be determined. Bona fide means genuine or real or in good faith and without deceit or fraud. If a commercial paper is not genuine or is a counterfeit, it is called a bogus

instrument. <u>Kite</u> is worthless paper used to secure
the temporary use of money. Kite also refers to the
worthless paper itself.

_____

_____

_____

Directions: This dictation emphasizes and reinforces the legal terms and definitions you have studied. Listen carefully to the pronunciation of each of the legal terms. Unless otherwise directed, use a 70-space line and double spacing. Correct all errors. Follow one of the procedures below.

Typing Procedure

Using the cassette from Lesson 24, Part B, transcribe the dictation directly at your typewriter.

Shorthand Procedure

Using the cassette from Lesson 24, Part B, take the dictation using your shorthand system and then transcribe on the typewriter from your shorthand notes.

When you have finished transcribing Part B of the practice dictation, check your transcript with the printed copy. If you have made any mistakes in the transcription, you should practice those words several times before going on to Evaluation 12.

Check List

	PART A, DATE	PART B, DATE	SUBMITTED TO INSTRUCTOR	
			YES	NO
Terminology and Definitions	_____	_____	_____	_____
*Typing Legal Terms	_____	_____	_____	_____
Words	_____	_____	_____	_____
Sentences	_____	_____	_____	_____
*Transcribing from Dictation	_____	_____	_____	_____
Quiz No. 1	_____	_____	_____	_____
Quiz No. 2	_____	_____	_____	_____

When you have successfully completed all the exercises in this lesson and submitted to your instructor those called for, you are ready to proceed with Evaluation 12.

*If you are using a shorthand system, turn in to your instructor your shorthand notes along with your transcript.

Quiz No. 1

Terminology and Definition Recall

Directions: In the Answers column write the legal term that is most representative of the corresponding statement. After you have completed this quiz, check your answers with the key on page 338. Unless otherwise directed, turn in this quiz to your instructor upon completion of this lesson.

ANSWERS

1. The presentation of a commercial paper for payment to the one who has the responsibility for making such payment is _____.

   1. _____

2. A term which means to be added to or to increase, such as interest on a note accrues to or is added to the principal, is _____.

   2. _____

3. A phrase used in an indorsement of a commercial paper which means that the indorser cannot be held liable if the original makers of the instrument fail to make payment when due is _____.

   3. _____

4. The date or time on which a commercial paper comes due and is payable is the _____ date.

   4. _____

5. The consideration involved in a contract is called _____.

   5. _____

6. To refuse to pay a commercial paper when it is due or to refuse to accept a commercial paper is to _____ it.

   6. _____

7. An amount of money paid for the use of money belonging to another person is called _____.

   7. _____

8. To put a future date on a commercial paper instead of the date on which it is actually made is to _____ the instrument.

   8. _____

9. An illegal amount of interest charged for the use of money is called _____.

   9. _____

10. A written notarized statement which certifies that a commercial paper was presented for payment and refused is a/an _____.

    10. _____

11. An extension of time after the due date for the payment of a commercial paper without defaulting on the obligation is referred to as a/an _____ period.

    11. _____

12. The act of transferring or placing an instrument in the possession or control of another person is the _____ of the instrument.

    12. _____

Turn back to page 254 and continue with this lesson.

Quiz No. 2

Terminology and Definition Recall

Directions: In the Answers column write the letter from Column I that represents the word or phrase that best matches each item in Column II. After you have completed this quiz, check your answers with the key on page 338. Unless otherwise directed, turn in this quiz to your instructor upon completion of this lesson.

COLUMN I	COLUMN II	ANSWERS
A. allonge	**1.** Securing temporary use of money by issuing worthless paper.	1. _____
B. blank indorsement		
C. bogus	**2.** An indorsement which specifically names the person to whom the instrument is being transferred.	2. _____
D. bona fide		
E. indorsement	**3.** An alteration or change made on a commercial paper by one who is not a party to the instrument.	3. _____
F. kite		
G. protest	**4.** An indorsement which consists of only the indorser's name.	4. _____
H. qualified indorsement		
I. restrictive indorsement	**5.** Genuine or real. In good faith without deceit or fraud.	5. _____
J. special or full indorsement	**6.** An indorsement which qualifies or restricts the liability of the indorser. Includes an indorsement which contains the words "without recourse."	6. _____
K. spoliation		
L. successive indorsement	**7.** A series of indorsements following one after another on a commercial paper.	7. _____
	8. A piece of paper attached to a commercial paper to provide space for the indorsements where there is not enough space on the instrument itself.	8. _____
	9. The signing of one's name on the back of a commercial paper with the purpose of transferring or assigning it to another person.	9. _____
	10. An indorsement which contains restrictions as to any further transfer of a commercial paper.	10. _____
	11. Not genuine, counterfeit.	11. _____

Turn back to page 257 and continue with this lesson.

⫸ EVALUATION No. 12

Student_____

Class_____Date_____

SCORING RECORD

	Perfect Score	Student's Score
Section A	50	
Section B	20	
Section C	30	
Total	100	

SECTION A

Directions: This dictation/transcription evaluation will test your spelling and transcription ability on the legal terms that you studied in the two preceding lessons. Use a 5-space paragraph indention, a 70-space line and double spacing unless otherwise instructed. Correct all errors. Follow one of the procedures below.

Typing Procedure

Using the cassette from Evaluation 12, transcribe the dictation directly at your typewriter.

Shorthand Procedure

Using the cassette from Evaluation 12, take the dictation using your shorthand system and then transcribe on the typewriter from your shorthand notes.

SECTIONS B AND C ARE AVAILABLE FROM YOUR INSTRUCTOR.

"One who takes the benefit must bear the burden."
—Legal Maxim

LESSON 25

To Wit: Bankruptcy

Due to changes in society and economic conditions, bankruptcy law is affecting more and more individuals and businesses. Bankruptcy proceedings are under the jurisdiction of the federal courts rather than the state courts. A person cannot be sent to jail for failure to pay his or her debts; however, the person's property may be taken to satisfy those debts. Bankruptcy is a branch of equity jurisprudence but, because of its increased importance, this lesson is devoted exclusively to the terms relating to bankruptcy. When you have satisfactorily completed these exercises, you will be able to spell, pronounce, define, and transcribe each of the terms presented which relate to the area of bankruptcy law.

| | *Part* A | **Terminology and Definitions** |

Directions: Study the terms, pronunciations, and definitions until you are thoroughly familiar with them. In order to complete this lesson successfully, you must understand the meaning and usage of all the legal terms presented. If you are using shorthand, write your shorthand outline in the space provided or on your shorthand machine for each legal term.

	LEGAL TERM	PRONUNCIATION	DEFINITION	SHORTHAND OUTLINE
1.	bankrupt	′baŋ-krəpt	A person who is declared by a court to be unable or unwilling to pay debts.	_____
2.	bankruptcy	′baŋ-krəp-sē	The process of declaring a person bankrupt and the taking of the person's assets and distributing them among the creditors.	_____
3.	bankruptcy court	′baŋ-krəp-sē kōrt	Federal courts which are established to administer the bankrupt laws.	_____
4.	voluntary bankruptcy	′väl-ən-ter-ē ′baŋ-krəp-sē	Bankruptcy proceedings which are started by the person who is bankrupt.	_____
5.	involuntary bankruptcy	in-′väl-ən-ter-ē ′baŋ-krəp-sē	Bankruptcy proceedings which are started by the creditors of the bankrupt person.	_____

6. petition for bankruptcy	pə-ˈtish-ən for ˈbaŋ-krəp-sē	The document filed in a bankruptcy court requesting that bankruptcy proceedings be started against a certain person. May be filed by the person declaring bankruptcy or by the creditors.	_____
7. referee	ref-ə-ˈrē	An officer of a bankruptcy court who is in charge of the proceedings in that court.	_____
8. solvent	ˈsäl-vənt	The ability or capacity to pay one's debts.	_____
9. insolvency	in-ˈsäl-vən-sē	The inability of a person to pay debts.	_____
10. ex parte application	eks ˈpärt-ē ap-lə-ˈkā-shən	Latin. An application by one side or one party. It is made by a creditor who is not a party to the bankruptcy proceeding but who has an interest in it.	_____
11. receiver	ri-ˈsē-vər	An impartial person appointed by the court to take charge of property involved in a bankruptcy proceeding and to follow the directions of the court in disposing of the property.	_____
12. trustee	trəs-ˈtē	A person who holds the property of a bankrupt for the benefit of the creditors.	_____
13. creditors	ˈkred-ət-ərs	One to whom a debt is owed.	_____

Turn to page 273 and complete Quiz No. 1 before continuing this lesson.

Typing Legal Terms

Directions: Unless otherwise instructed, use a 70-space line and double spacing. Correct all errors. Follow one of the procedures below.

Words

Typing Procedure

On a separate sheet of paper, type the following words at least two times, concentrating on the correct spelling and pronunciation.

Shorthand Procedure

On a separate sheet of paper, type the following words once, concentrating on the correct spelling and pronunciation. Then write the shorthand outline for each word on the lines to the right or on your shorthand machine. Cover the printed words with a sheet of paper and transcribe from the shorthand outlines one time on your typewriter.

bankrupt / bankruptcy / bankruptcy court / voluntary _____

bankruptcy / involuntary bankruptcy / petition _____

for bankruptcy / referee / solvent / insolvency / _____

ex parte application / receiver / trustee / creditors / _____

Sentences

Typing Procedure

Type each of the following sentences one time. Concentrate on the correct spelling and pronunciation of each underlined legal term.

Shorthand Procedure

Write the correct shorthand outlines for the following sentences on the lines to the right or on your shorthand machine. Cover the printed material with a sheet of paper and transcribe from your shorthand outlines one time on the typewriter.

These sentences will be used for practice dictation on the cassettes.

A bankrupt is a person who is declared by a court to be unable or unwilling to pay debts. Bankruptcy is the process of declaring a person bankrupt and the taking of the person's assets and distributing them among the creditors. A creditor is a person to whom a debt is owed. The bankrupt laws are administered in a federal court called a bankruptcy court. If a debtor initiates bankruptcy proceedings, it is called voluntary bankruptcy. However, if one is forced into bankruptcy on the petition of creditors, it is called involuntary bankruptcy. A petition for bankruptcy is the document filed in a bankruptcy court requesting that bankruptcy proceedings be started against a certain person. When a petition for bankruptcy is filed by a creditor for involuntary bankruptcy of a debtor, it is called an ex parte application. In bankruptcy courts, a referee is appointed by the court to assist in the bankruptcy proceedings. A referee is an officer of the bankruptcy court but not a judge. If a person is solvent, that person has the ability or capacity to pay debts. Insolvency is the inability of a person to pay debts. Insolvency exists when one's liabilities exceed one's assets. A receiver is an impartial person appointed by the court to take charge of and dispose of the property involved in a bankruptcy proceeding under the direction of the court. A trustee is a person who holds property of a bankrupt for the benefit of the creditors.

Directions: This dictation emphasizes and reinforces the legal terms and definitions you have studied. Listen carefully to the pronunciation of each of the legal terms. Unless otherwise directed, use a 70-space line and double spacing. Correct all errors. Follow one of the procedures below.

Typing Procedure

Using the cassette from Lesson 25, Part A, transcribe the dictation directly at your typewriter.

Shorthand Procedure

Using the cassette from Lesson 25, Part A, take the dictation using your shorthand system and then transcribe on the typewriter from your shorthand notes.

When you have finished transcribing Part A of the practice dictation, check your transcript with the printed copy. If you made any mistakes in the transcription, you should practice those words several times before going on.

Part B Terminology and Definitions

Directions: Study the terms, pronunciations, and definitions until you are thoroughly familiar with them. In order to complete this lesson successfully, you must understand the meaning and usage of all the legal terms presented. If you are using shorthand, write your shorthand outline in the space provided or on your shorthand machine for each legal term.

LEGAL TERM	PRONUNCIATION	DEFINITION	SHORTHAND OUTLINE
1. debtor's petition	′det-ərs pə-′tish-ən	A petition filed by the debtor requesting the benefit of the bankruptcy law. A petition for voluntary bankruptcy.	_____
2. insolvent debtor	in-′säl-vənt ′det-ər	A debtor who cannot pay debts.	_____
3. summary of debts and assets	′səm-ə-rē əv dets ən ′as-ets	A listing provided to the court containing all the debts and assets of the debtor in a bankruptcy proceeding.	_____
4. account stated	ə-′kaůnt ′stāt-əd	An agreement between the debtor and the creditor that the amount stated as owing to the creditor is accurate.	_____
5. account current	ə-′kaůnt ′kər-ənt	An open or unsettled account between a debtor and creditor. The opposite to account stated.	_____
6. assets	′as-ets	The property owned by a bankrupt which may be applied to pay debts.	_____

7.	liabilities	lī-ə-'bil-ət-ēs	Something which one owes to another and has an obligation to pay.	_____
8.	balance of funds	'bal-əns əv fənds	The amount remaining after the secured debts are paid which is to be divided among the other creditors.	_____
9.	liquidate	'lik-wə-dāt	To convert assets into cash to be used to pay the amounts owed to creditors.	_____
10.	composition	käm-pə-'zish-ən	An agreement between a debtor and a creditor in which the creditor agrees to accept less than the amount of the debt in settlement for the entire debt.	_____
11.	secured debts	si-'kyu̇rd dets	Debts which are guaranteed by pledged collateral such as a mortgage.	_____
12.	deficiency decree	di-'fish-ən-sē di-'krē	A judgment for a portion of a secured debt for which the sale of the property does not pay in full.	_____
13.	discharge	'dis-chärj	The release of a bankrupt from the obligation of paying former debts.	_____

Turn to page 274 and complete Quiz No. 2 before continuing this lesson.

Typing Legal Terms

Directions: Unless otherwise instructed, use a 70-space line and double spacing. Correct all errors. Follow one of the procedures below.

Words

Typing Procedure

On a separate sheet of paper, type the following words at least two times, concentrating on the correct spelling and pronunciation.

Shorthand Procedure

On a separate sheet of paper, type the following words once, concentrating on the correct spelling and pronunciation. Then write the shorthand outline for each word on the lines to the right or on your shorthand machine. Cover the printed words with a sheet of paper and transcribe from the shorthand outlines one time on your typewriter.

debtor's petition / insolvent debtor / summary of

debts and assets / account stated / account

current / assets / liabilities / balance of funds /

liquidate / composition / secured debts /

deficiency decree / discharge /

Sentences

Typing Procedure

Type each of the following sentences one time. Concentrate on the correct spelling and pronunciation of each underlined legal term.

Shorthand Procedure

Write the correct shorthand outline for the following sentences on the lines to the right or on your shorthand machine. Cover the printed material with a sheet of paper and transcribe from your shorthand outlines one time on the typewriter.

These sentences will be used for practice dictation on the cassettes.

A debtor's petition is one filed by the debtor requesting the benefit of the bankruptcy laws. A petition for voluntary bankruptcy is a debtor's petition. An insolvent debtor is a debtor who cannot pay debts. When a petition for bankruptcy is filed, a summary of debts and assets of the debtor must be provided to the bankruptcy court. A summary of debts and assets is a list containing all that a debtor owes and owns. Account stated refers to an agreement between the debtor and the creditor that the amount stated as owing to the creditor is accurate. However, an open or unsettled account between the debtor and creditor is referred to as an account current. Assets are the property owned by a bankrupt which may be applied to pay debts. Those debts are called liabilities. Balance of funds is the amount remaining after the secured debts are paid which is to be divided among the other creditors. To liquidate is to convert assets into cash to be used to pay the amounts owed to creditors. If the creditors agree to accept less than the total amount owed as settlement for the entire debt, it is called composition. Debts which are guaranteed by pledged collateral such as a mortgage are called secured debts. A deficiency decree may be entered for the portion of a secured debt for which the sale of the property does not pay in full. A discharge releases a bankrupt from the obligation of or liability for paying former debts.

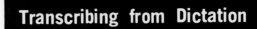

Directions: This dictation emphasizes and reinforces the legal terms and definitions you have studied. Listen carefully to the pronunciation of each of the legal terms. Unless otherwise directed, use a 70-space line and double spacing. Correct all errors. Follow one of the procedures below.

Typing Procedure

Using the cassette from Lesson 25, Part B, transcribe the dictation directly at your typewriter.

Shorthand Procedure

Using the cassette from Lesson 25, Part B, take the dictation using your shorthand system and then transcribe on the typewriter from your shorthand notes.

When you have finished transcribing Part B of the practice dictation, check your transcript with the printed copy. If you have made any mistakes in the transcription, you should practice those words several times before going on to Lesson 26.

Check List

	PART A, DATE	PART B, DATE	SUBMITTED TO INSTRUCTOR	
			YES	NO
Terminology and Definitions	_____	_____	_____	_____
*Typing Legal Terms	_____	_____	_____	_____
Words	_____	_____	_____	_____
Sentences	_____	_____	_____	_____
*Transcribing from Dictation	_____	_____	_____	_____
Quiz No. 1	_____	_____	_____	_____
Quiz No. 2	_____	_____	_____	_____

When you have successfully completed all the exercises in this lesson and submitted to your instructor those called for, you are ready to proceed with Lesson 26.

*If you are using a shorthand system, turn in to your instructor your shorthand notes along with your transcript.

Quiz No. 1

Terminology and Definition Recall

Directions: In the Answers column write the legal term that is most representative of the corresponding statement. After you have completed this quiz, check your answers with the key on page 339. Unless otherwise directed, turn in this quiz to your instructor upon completion of this lesson.

ANSWERS

1. The document filed in a bankruptcy court requesting that bankruptcy proceedings be started against a certain person is called a/an _____.

1. _____

2. One to whom a debt is owed is a/an _____.

2. _____

3. The ability or capacity to pay one's debts is referred to as being _____.

3. _____

4. Bankruptcy proceedings which are started by the person who is bankrupt are referred to as _____ bankruptcy proceedings.

4. _____

5. The inability of a person to pay debts is referred to as _____.

5. _____

6. An impartial person appointed by the court to take charge of property involved in a bankruptcy proceeding and to follow the directions of the court in disposing of the property is a/an _____.

6. _____

7. The process of declaring a person bankrupt and the taking of the person's assets and distributing them among the creditors is _____.

7. _____

8. A person who is declared by a court to be unable or unwilling to pay debts is a/an _____.

8. _____

9. An officer of a bankruptcy court who is in charge of the proceedings in that court is a/an _____.

9. _____

10. An application by one side or one party which, in a bankruptcy proceeding, is made by a creditor who is not a party to the bankruptcy proceeding but has an interest in it is a/an _____ application.

10. _____

11. Bankruptcy proceedings which are started by the creditors of the bankrupt person are called _____ bankruptcy proceedings.

11. _____

12. Federal courts which are established to administer the bankrupt laws are _____ courts.

12. _____

13. A person who holds the property of a bankrupt for the benefit of the creditors is a/an _____.

13. _____

Turn back to page 266 and continue with this lesson.

Quiz No. 2

Terminology and Definition Recall

Directions: In the Answers column at the right of each statement, write the letter that represents the word, or group of words, that correctly completes the statement. After you have completed this quiz, check your answers with the key on page 339. Unless otherwise directed, turn in this quiz to your instructor upon completion of this lesson.

ANSWERS

1. A judgment for a portion of a secured debt for which the sale of the property does not pay in full is (a) deficiency decree, (b) discharge, (c) account stated. ...

1. _____

2. A debtor who cannot pay debts is a/an (a) debtor's petition, (b) composition, (c) insolvent debtor..

2. _____

3. The release of a bankrupt from the obligation of paying former debts is the (a) composition, (b) balance of funds, (c) discharge.......................

3. _____

4. A petition filed by the debtor requesting the benefit of the bankruptcy laws is a (a) summary of debts and assets, (b) debtor's petition, (c) deficiency decree.

4. _____

5. An open or unsettled account between a debtor and a creditor is a/an (a) account stated, (b) account current, (c) secured debt................................

5. _____

6. The amount remaining after the secured debts are paid which is to be divided among the other creditors is the (a) balance of funds, (b) composition, (c) assets.

6. _____

7. A listing provided to the court containing all the debts and assets of the debtor in a bankruptcy proceeding is a (a) summary of debts and assets, (b) debtor's petition, (c) composition..

7. _____

8. An agreement between the debtor and the creditor that the amount stated as owing to the creditor is accurate is a/an (a) account current, (b) deficiency decree, (c) account stated..

8. _____

9. An agreement between a debtor and a creditor in which the creditor agrees to accept less than the amount of the debt in settlement for the entire debt is referred to as (a) discharge, (b) liquidate, (c) composition.................

9. _____

10. A debt which is guaranteed by pledged collateral such as a mortgage is a (a) secured debt, (b) debtor's petition, (c) liability.........................

10. _____

11. Something which one owes to another and has an obligation to pay is called (a) assets, (b) liabilities, (c) secured debts................................

11. _____

12. To convert assets into cash to be used to pay the amounts owed to creditors is to (a) liquidate, (b) discharge, (c) secure....................................

12. _____

13. The property owned by a bankrupt which may be applied to pay debts is the (a) liabilities, (b) assets, (c) balance of funds..............................

13. _____

Turn back to page 269 and continue with this lesson.

"No one can do that by another which one cannot do of oneself."

—Legal Maxim

 # LESSON 26

To Wit: Agency

In an agency relationship, a person grants another the authority to act for the person in the commission of certain acts. An agency relationship may exist, generally, for the doing of any lawful act unless the law deems such act so personal that another cannot do it, for example, the making of a will. Agency relationships include activities involving brokers, attorneys, bankers, and affect many day-to-day business transactions. When you have satisfactorily completed this lesson, you should be able to pronounce, define, spell, and transcribe the terms applicable to the principles of an agency.

Part A	**Terminology and Definitions**

Directions: Study the terms, pronunciations, and definitions until you are thoroughly familiar with them. In order to complete this lesson successfully, you must understand the meaning and usage of all the legal terms presented. If you are using shorthand, write your shorthand outline in the space provided or on your shorthand machine for each legal term.

LEGAL TERM	PRONUNCIATION	DEFINITION	SHORTHAND OUTLINE
1. agency	′ā-jən-sē	A relationship whereby one person gives permission to another person to act for or represent the person.	_____
2. principal	′prin-spəl	The one who gives permission to another person to act for or represent the person.	_____
3. agent	′ā-jənt	The one who acts for or represents a principal with the principal's permission.	_____
4. general agent	′jen-rəl ′ā-jənt	An agent who has permission to transact any and all affairs for a particular business for a principal.	_____
5. special agent	′spesh-əl ′ā-jənt	An agent who has permission to transact a specified act for the principal.	_____
6. universal agent	yü-nə-′vər-səl ′ā-jənt	An agent who has the authority to transact any and all business for the principal.	_____

7.	primary agent	'prī-mer-ē 'ā-jənt	An agent who is given direct and first authority by the principal to act as an agent.	_____
8.	subagent	səb-'ā-jənt	An agent given permission by a primary agent to transact business for the principal.	_____
9.	exclusive or irrevocable agency	iks-'klü-siv or ir-ev-ə-'kə-bəl 'ā-jən-sē	An agency which cannot be revoked by the principal while the agency contract or agreement is in effect.	_____
10.	implied agency	im-'plīd 'ā-jən-sē	An agency which is created by the actions of the parties in a particular situation.	_____
11.	del credere agent	del kre-'də-rē 'ā-jənt	Latin. An agent who guarantees or acts as a surety for the principal against the default of persons with whom the agent conducts business on behalf of the principal.	_____
12.	undisclosed principal	ən-dis-'klōzd 'prin-spəl	A principal who is not known to the party with whom an agent transacts business.	_____
13.	power of attorney	'pau̇r əv ə-'tər-nē	The instrument by which the principal gives the agent the authority to represent or act for the principal.	_____
14.	plenipotentiary	plen-ə-pə-'tench-rē	A person who has complete authority to do a certain thing or to act for another person.	_____

Turn to page 283 and complete Quiz No. 1 before continuing this lesson.

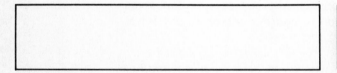

Typing Legal Terms

Directions: Unless otherwise instructed, use a 70-space line and double spacing. Correct all errors. Follow one of the procedures below.

Words

Typing Procedure

On a separate sheet of paper, type the following words at least two times, concentrating on the correct spelling and pronunciation.

Shorthand Procedure

On a separate sheet of paper, type the following words once, concentrating on the correct spelling and pronunciation. Then write the shorthand outline for each word on the lines to the right or on your shorthand machine. Cover the printed words with a sheet of paper and transcribe from the shorthand outlines one time on your typewriter.

agency / principal / agent / general agent / special
agent / universal agent / primary agent / subagent /
exclusive or irrevocable agency / implied agency /
del credere agent / undisclosed principal /
power of attorney / plenipotentiary /

Sentences

Typing Procedure

Type each of the following sentences one time.
Concentrate on the correct spelling and pronunciation of each underlined legal term.

Shorthand Procedure

Write the correct shorthand outlines for the following sentences on the lines to the right or on your
shorthand machine. Cover the printed material with
a sheet of paper and transcribe from your shorthand
outlines one time on the typewriter.

These sentences will be used for practice dictation on the cassettes.

An agency is a relationship whereby one person
gives permission to another person to act for or
represent the person. The principal is the person
who gives permission to an agent to act for or represent the principal. The person who acts for or
represents a principal with the principal's permission is an agent. A general agent is one who has
authorization to transact any or all affairs for a particular business for a principal; whereas, a special
agent is one who has permission to transact only an
act specified for the principal. A universal agent is
one who has the authority to transact any and all
business for the principal. A primary agent is one
who is given direct and first authority by the principal to act as an agent. A primary agent may give a
subagent the authority to transact business for the
primary agent's principal. An exclusive or irrevocable agency is an agency which cannot be
revoked by the principal while the agency contract
or agreement is in effect. An implied agency is one
which is created by the actions of the parties in the
situation. A del credere agent is one who guarantees or acts as a surety for the principal against the
default of persons with whom the agent conducts

business on behalf of the principal. If, at the time

of a transaction conducted by an agent, the third

party does not know who the principal is, the prin-

cipal is referred to as an <u>undisclosed principal</u>.

A <u>power of attorney</u> is the instrument by which the

principal gives the agent the authority to act.

A <u>plenipotentiary</u> is one who has authority to do a

certain thing or to act for another person.

Transcribing from Dictation

Directions: This dictation emphasizes and reinforces the legal terms and definitions you have studied. Listen carefully to the pronunciation of each of the legal terms. Unless otherwise directed, use a 70-space line and double spacing. Correct all errors. Follow one of the procedures below.

Typing Procedure

Using the cassette from Lesson 26, Part A, transcribe the dictation directly at your typewriter.

Shorthand Procedure

Using the cassette from Lesson 26, Part A, take the dictation using your shorthand system and then transcribe on the typewriter from your shorthand notes.

When you have finished transcribing Part A of the practice dictation, check your transcript with the printed copy. If you made any mistakes in the transcription, you should practice those words several times before going on.

Part B Terminology and Definitions

Directions: Study the terms, pronunciations, and definitions until you are thoroughly familiar with them. In order to complete this lesson successfully, you must understand the meaning and usage of all the legal terms presented. If you are using shorthand, write your shorthand outline in the space provided or on your shorthand machine for each legal term.

LEGAL TERM	PRONUNCIATION	DEFINITION	SHORTHAND OUTLINE
1. factor	′fak-tər	An agent who is employed by a principal to sell goods for the principal. The factor usually has possession of said goods and sells them in the factor's own name.	_____
2. delegation of authority	del-i-′gā-shən əv ə-′thär-ət-ē	One person giving or transferring that person's authority to another person.	_____

3. third party	thərd 'pärt-ē	The party with whom an agent transacts the business for a principal.	_____
4. ostensible authority or apparent authority	ä-'sten-sə-bəl ə-'thär-ət-ē or ə-'par-ənt ə-'thär-ət-ē	The authority which a principal, either intentionally or by want of due care, leads a third party to believe that the agent possesses.	_____
5. implied authority	im-'plīd ə-'thär-ət-ē	Authority of an agent which is implied by actions of the principal.	_____
6. incidental authority	in-sə-'dent-l ə-'thär-ət-ē	That which an agent must have in order to perform the business authorized by the principal.	_____
7. express authority	ik-'spres ə-'thär-ət-ē	Authority, either oral or written, which is definitely and explicitly given to an agent.	_____
8. ratification	rat-ə-fə-'kā-shən	The acceptance by the principal of the acts performed on the principal's behalf by an agent or another person.	_____
9. respondeat superior	ris-'pon-dē-at su̇-'pir-e-ər	Latin. "Let the master answer." The principal is responsible for the wrongful acts of an agent acting for the principal.	_____
10. fiduciary relationship	fə-'dü-shē-er-ē ri-'lā-shən-ship	A relationship which exists when one person trusts and relies upon another.	_____
11. nonfeasance	nän-'fēz-ns	The failure of an agent to perform the acts which the agent agreed to do for the principal.	_____
12. implied ratification	im-'plīd rat-ə-fə-'kā-shən	The presumed acceptance by the principal, because of the principal's actions, of the things done on the principal's behalf by the agent.	_____
13. mutual consent	'myüch-wəl kən-'sent	Agreement by both parties to the agent/principal relationship. An essential element of an agency.	_____
14. estoppel	e-'stäp-əl	A situation which arises when a principal is forbidden by law from alleging or denying certain things done by an agent because of the principal's action or lack of action in the past.	_____

Turn to page 284 and complete Quiz No. 2 before continuing this lesson.

Lesson 26, Part B

Directions: Unless otherwise instructed, use a 70-space line and double spacing. Correct all errors. Follow one of the procedures below.

Words

Typing Procedure

On a separate sheet of paper, type the following words at least two times, concentrating on the correct spelling and pronunciation.

Shorthand Procedure

On a separate sheet of paper, type the following words once, concentrating on the correct spelling and pronunciation. Then write the shorthand outline for each word on the lines to the right or on your shorthand machine. Cover the printed words with a sheet of paper and transcribe from the shorthand outlines one time on your typewriter.

factor / delegation of authority / third party /

ostensible authority or apparent authority / implied

authority / incidental authority / express authority /

ratification / respondeat superior / fiduciary

relationship / nonfeasance / implied ratification /

mutual consent / estoppel /

Sentences

Typing Procedure

Type each of the following sentences one time. Concentrate on the correct spelling and pronunciation of each underlined legal term.

Shorthand Procedure

Write the correct shorthand outlines for the following sentences on the lines to the right or on your shorthand machine. Cover the printed material with a sheet of paper and transcribe from your shorthand outlines one time on the typewriter.

These sentences will be used for practice dictation on the cassettes.

A factor is an agent who is employed by a principal to sell goods for the principal. One person giving or transferring his or her authority to another person is delegation of authority. A third party in an agency relationship is the one with whom an agent transacts the business for a principal. Ostensible authority or apparent authority is the authority which a principal, either intentionally or by want of due care, leads a third party to believe that the agent possesses. Implied authority is that of an agent which is implied by the principal's actions. <u>Express</u> <u>authority</u> is authority, either oral or written, which is definitely and explicitly given to an agent. <u>Incidental authority</u> is that which an agent must have in order to perform the business authorized by the principal. The acceptance by the principal of the acts which are performed on the principal's behalf by an agent or another person is called <u>ratification</u>. <u>Respondeat superior</u> is a Latin phrase for "let the master answer." Respondeat superior means that a principal is responsible for the wrongful acts of an agent acting for the principal. A relationship which exists when one person trusts and relies upon another is a <u>fiduciary relationship</u>. The failure of an agent to perform the acts which the agent agreed to do for the principal is called <u>nonfeasance</u>. <u>Implied ratification</u> is the presumed acceptance by the principal, because of the principal's actions, of the things done for the principal by an agent. <u>Mutual consent</u> is essential in a principal/agent relationship. Mutual consent is the agreement by both parties to the agency relationship. An <u>estoppel</u> arises when a principal is forbidden by law from alleging or denying certain things that have been done because of some action or lack of action in the past.

Transcribing from Dictation

Directions: This dictation emphasizes and reinforces the legal terms and definitions you have studied. Listen carefully to the pronunciation of each of the legal terms. Unless otherwise directed, use a 70-space line and double spacing. Correct all errors. Follow one of the procedures below.

Typing Procedure

Using the cassette from Lesson 26, Part B, transcribe the dictation directly at your typewriter.

Shorthand Procedure

Using the cassette from Lesson 26, Part B, take the dictation using your shorthand system and then transcribe on the typewriter from your shorthand notes.

When you have finished transcribing Part B of the practice dictation, check your transcript with the printed copy. If you have made any mistakes in the transcription, you should practice those words several times before going on to Evaluation 13.

Check List	I have completed the following for Lesson 26:

	PART A, DATE	PART B, DATE	SUBMITTED TO INSTRUCTOR	
			YES	NO
Terminology and Definitions	_____	_____	_____	_____
*Typing Legal Terms	_____	_____	_____	_____
Words	_____	_____	_____	_____
Sentences	_____	_____	_____	_____
*Transcribing from Dictation	_____	_____	_____	_____
Quiz No. 1	_____	_____	_____	_____
Quiz No. 2	_____	_____	_____	_____

When you have successfully completed all the exercises in this lesson and submitted to your instructor those called for, you are ready to proceed with Evaluation 13.

*If you are using a shorthand system, turn in to your instructor your shorthand notes along with your transcript.

Quiz No. 1

Terminology and Definition Recall

Directions: In the Answers column write the letter from Column I that represents the word or phrase that best matches each item in Column II. After you have completed this quiz, check your answers with the key on page 339. Unless otherwise directed, turn in this quiz to your instructor upon completion of this lesson.

COLUMN I	COLUMN II	ANSWERS

COLUMN I

A. agency
B. agent
C. del credere agent
D. exclusive or irrevocable agency
E. general agent
F. implied agency
G. plenipotentiary
H. power of attorney
I. primary agent
J. principal
K. secondary agent
L. special agent
M. subagent
N. undisclosed principal
O. universal agent

COLUMN II

1. The instrument by which the principal gives the agent the authority to represent or act for the principal.   1. _____

2. The one who acts for or represents a principal with the principal's permission.   2. _____

3. An agency which is created by the actions of the parties in a particular situation.   3. _____

4. An agency which cannot be revoked by the principal while the agency contract or agreement is in effect.   4. _____

5. An agent given permission by a primary agent to transact business for the principal.   5. _____

6. The one who is given direct and first permission by the principal to act as an agent.   6. _____

7. An agent who has permission to transact a specified act for the principal.   7. _____

8. An agent who has permission to transact any or all business for a principal.   8. _____

9. A principal who is not known to the party with whom an agent transacts business.   9. _____

10. The one who gives permission to another person to act for or represent the person.   10. _____

11. A relationship whereby one person gives permission to another person to act for or represent the person.   11. _____

12. An agent who guarantees or acts as a surety for the principal against the default of persons with whom the agent conducts business on behalf of the principal.   12. _____

13. An agent who has permission to transact any and all affairs for a particular business for the principal.   13. _____

14. A person who has complete authority to do a certain thing or to act for another person.   14. _____

Turn back to page 276 and continue with this lesson.

Quiz No. 2

Terminology and Definition Recall

Directions: In the Answers column write the legal term that is most representative of the corresponding statement. After you have completed this quiz, check your answers with the key on page 339. Unless otherwise directed, turn in this quiz to your instructor upon completion of this lesson.

ANSWERS

1. The acceptance by the principal of the acts performed on the principal's behalf by an agent or another person is _____.

    1. _____

2. The presumed acceptance by the principal, because of the principal's actions, of the things done on the principal's behalf by the agent, is referred to as _____ ratification.

    2. _____

3. A relationship which exists when one person trusts and relies upon another is a/an _____ relationship.

    3. _____

4. When one person gives or transfers authority to another person, it is called _____ of authority.

    4. _____

5. Authority, either oral or written, which is definitely and explicity given to an agent is _____ authority.

    5. _____

6. The authority which a principal, either intentionally or by want of due care, leads a third party to believe that the agent possesses is (a) _____ or (b) _____ authority.

    6. _____

7. A situation which arises when a principal is forbidden by law from alleging or denying certain things done by an agent because of the principal's action or lack of action in the past is a/an _____.

    7. _____

8. The party with whom an agent transacts the business for a principal is the _____.

    8. _____

9. The authority which an agent must have in order to perform the business authorized by the principal is referred to as _____ authority.

    9. _____

10. Authority of an agent which is implied by the principal's actions is _____ authority.

    10. _____

11. Agreement by both parties to the agent/principal relationship is called _____.

    11. _____

12. The failure of an agent to perform the acts which the agent agreed to do for the principal is _____.

    12. _____

13. An agent who is employed by a principal to sell goods for the principal is called a/an _____.

    13. _____

14. A Latin phrase which means that the principal is responsible for the wrongful acts of an agent is _____.

    14. _____

Turn back to page 280 and continue with this lesson.

EVALUATION No. 13

SCORING RECORD

	Perfect Score	Student's Score
Section A	50	
Section B	20	
Section C	30	
Total	100	

SECTION A

Directions: This dictation/transcription evaluation will test your spelling and transcription ability on the legal terms that you studied in the two preceding lessons. Use a 5-space paragraph indention, a 70-space line and double spacing unless otherwise instructed. Correct all errors. Follow one of the procedures below.

Typing Procedure

Using the cassette from Evaluation 13, transcribe the dictation directly at your typewriter.

Shorthand Procedure

Using the cassette from Evaluation 13, take the dictation using your shorthand system and then transcribe on the typewriter from your shorthand notes.

SECTIONS B AND C ARE AVAILABLE FROM YOUR INSTRUCTOR.

LESSON 27

To Wit: Equity

Equity law is based on rules of morality rather than on judicial laws. If there is no legal remedy available, relief may be granted under equity law. Equity is flexible and may be changed to meet the needs of each individual case. Since equity is administered in the same courts as common law, many of the terms dealing with equity are presented in other lessons. This lesson introduces terms relevant to equity which have not been taught in other areas of law. When you have successfully completed these exercises, you should be able to pronounce, spell, define, and transcribe the terms that are applicable to the principles of the law of equity.

| *Part* **A** | **Terminology and Definitions** |

Directions: Study the terms, pronunciations, and definitions until you are thoroughly familiar with them. In order to complete this lesson successfully, you must understand the meaning and usage of all the legal terms presented. If you are using shorthand, write your shorthand outline in the space provided or on your shorthand machine for each legal term.

	LEGAL TERM	PRONUNCIATION	DEFINITION	SHORTHAND OUTLINE
1.	equity	'ek-wət-ē	A system of law which is based on good conscience, justice, honesty, and right rather than common law.	_____
2.	maxims of equity	'mak-səms əv 'ek-wət-ē	General rules of conduct based upon reason and justice.	_____
3.	chancery	'chans-rē	Another word for equity.	_____
4.	chancery law	'chans-rē lȯ	The basis for equity law in the United States.	_____
5.	chancery court	'chans-rē kȯrt	A court of equity. Administers justice according to the rules of conscience and provides remedy for things not covered by common law.	_____

6.	concurrent jurisdiction	kən-'kər-ənt jur-əs-'dik-shən	Exists when a court of law or a court of equity can try both common law cases and equity cases.	_____
7.	preventive jurisdiction	pri-'vent-iv jur-əs-'dik-shən	Jurisdiction which a court of equity has to prevent future wrongs from being committed, as compared to courts of law that are concerned with wrongs which have already been committed.	_____
8.	bill quia timet	bil 'kwē-ə 'tīm-et	A bill filed with a court of equity which requests the court to exercise its preventive jurisdiction.	_____
9.	bill of interpleader	bil əv int-ər-'plēd-ər	A bill which provides that all persons who are interested in the same action will be joined together in a single lawsuit so as to prevent multiple suits for the same cause.	_____
10.	mistake of fact	mə-'stāk əv fakt	One that occurs unintentionally as to what the true facts are. A court of equity will grant relief on a mistake of fact.	_____
11.	mistake of law	mə-'stāk əv lo	Occurs when one who knows all the facts makes an error as to their legal effect. A court of equity will not usually grant relief on a mistake of law.	_____
12.	framed questions of fact	frāmd 'kwes-chəns əv fakt	Questions which a judge gives to a jury in an equity case for their determination.	_____
13.	advisory jury	əd-'vīz-rē 'jur-ē	A jury to which framed questions of fact are presented for their determination in an equity suit. The findings of an advisory jury are not binding on the court of equity.	_____
14.	laches (plural, laches)	'lach-əz	An unreasonable delay on the part of a plaintiff in asserting a right. A delay which causes a disadvantage to another and for which the court will not grant relief.	_____

Turn to page 295 and complete Quiz No. 1 before continuing this lesson.

Typing Legal Terms

Directions: Unless otherwise instructed, use a 70-space line and double spacing. Correct all errors. Follow one of the procedures below.

Words

Typing Procedure

On a separate sheet of paper, type the following words at least two times, concentrating on the correct spelling and pronunciation.

equity / maxims of equity / chancery / chancery law / chancery court / concurrent jurisdiction / preventive jurisdiction / bill quia timet / bill of interpleader / mistake of fact / mistake of law / framed questions of fact / advisory jury / laches /

Shorthand Procedure

On a separate sheet of paper, type the following words once, concentrating on the correct spelling and pronunciation. Then write the shorthand outline for each word on the lines to the right or on your shorthand machine. Cover the printed words with a sheet of paper and transcribe from the shorthand outlines one time on your typewriter.

_____

_____

_____

_____

_____

Sentences

Typing Procedure

Type each of the following sentences one time. Concentrate on the correct spelling and pronunciation of each underlined legal term.

Shorthand Procedure

Write the correct shorthand outlines for the following sentences on the lines to the right or on your shorthand machine. Cover the printed material with a sheet of paper and transcribe from your shorthand outlines one time on the typewriter.

These sentences will be used for practice dictation on the cassettes.

Equity is a system of law which is based on good conscience, justice, honesty, and rights rather than common law. Maxims of equity are general rules of conduct which are based upon reason and justice. Chancery is another term meaning equity. Chancery law is the basis for equity law in the United States. A chancery court administers justice according to the rules of conscience and provides a remedy for things not covered by common law. If courts of law and courts of equity can try both common law cases and equity cases, it is called concurrent jurisdiction. Preventive jurisdiction is the jurisdiction which a court of equity has to prevent future wrongs from being committed. Bill quia timet is a bill filed with a court of equity which requests the court to exercise its preventive jurisdiction. When two or more persons are interested in the same action, a <u>bill of interpleader</u> may be filed to join them together in one lawsuit so as to prevent multiple suits for the same cause. A <u>mistake of fact</u> is one that occurs unintentionally as to what the true facts are, and relief on a mistake of fact may be sought in a court of equity. A <u>mistake of law</u> occurs when one knows all the facts but makes an error as to their legal effect for which relief cannot be sought in a court of equity. <u>Framed questions of fact</u> are questions which a judge gives to a jury in an equity case for their determination. A jury in an equity suit serves only as an <u>advisory jury</u> to the judge, and its findings are not binding on the court. <u>Laches</u> is an unreasonable delay on the part of the plaintiff in asserting a right.

Transcribing from Dictation

Directions: This dictation emphasizes and reinforces the legal terms and definitions you have studied. Listen carefully to the pronunciation of each of the legal terms. Unless otherwise directed, use a 70-space line and double spacing. Correct all errors. Follow one of the procedures below.

Typing Procedure

Using the cassette from Lesson 27, Part A, transcribe the dictation directly at your typewriter.

Shorthand Procedure

Using the cassette from Lesson 27, Part A, take the dictation using your shorthand system and then transcribe on the typewriter from your shorthand notes.

When you have finished transcribing Part A of the practice dictation, check your transcript with the printed copy. If you made any mistakes in the transcription, you should practice those words several times before going on.

Part B   Terminology and Definitions

Directions: Study the terms, pronunciations, and definitions until you are thoroughly familiar with them. In order to complete this lesson successfully, you must understand the meaning and usage of all the legal terms presented. If you are using shorthand, write your shorthand outline in the space provided or on your shorthand machine for each legal term.

LEGAL TERM	PRONUNCIATION	DEFINITION	SHORTHAND OUTLINE
1. clean hands doctrine	klēn hands 'däk-trən	An equity maxim which states that one who comes into equity must come with clean hands. The one filing for equity must not be guilty of any wrongdoing.	_____
2. in pari delicto	in 'par-ī di-'likt-ō	Latin. "In equal fault." Equity relief will not be granted if both parties are at fault.	_____
3. reformation	ref-ər-'mā-shən	An equity remedy which provides for the amending or correcting a written document so that it conforms with the intentions of the parties.	_____
4. doctrine of doing complete justice	'däk-trən əv 'du-iŋ kəm-'plēt 'jəs-təs	The broad power of an equity court to dispose of all issues existing between the parties which are related to the main purpose of the suit.	_____
5. sua sponte	'swä 'spän-tə	Latin. Of one's own will or voluntarily.	_____
6. de minimis non curat lex	dā 'min-ə-mēs nōn kü-'rät leks	Latin. The law is not concerned with trifles. For example, an error involving a few cents will not be considered.	_____
7. rule of morality	rül əv mə-'ral-ət-ē	The rule of right and wrong conduct that forms the basis of the standards which people should follow in dealing with others.	_____
8. right and duty	rīt ən 'düt-ē	The foundation of equity jurisprudence.	_____
9. waiver	'wā-vər	Intentionally giving up of a right which one has.	_____
10. matter in pais	'mat-ər in pā	French. A matter of fact which is oral and not in writing. It is an estoppel which is created by the conduct of a party.	_____
11. estoppel in pais	e-'stäp-əl in pā	French. An estoppel which arises from the conduct of the party, laches, or negligence.	_____
12. finding of fact	'fīn-diŋ əv fakt	A statement made by the court pertaining to the conclusions reached which are based on the evidence in an equity case.	_____
13. declaratory judgment	di-'klar-ə-tōr-ē 'jej-mənt	A judgment which declares the existence of a right but does not provide any measures for enforcement.	_____
14. remedial	ri-'mēd-ē-əl	Providing a remedy.	_____

Turn to page 296 and complete Quiz No. 2 before continuing this lesson.

Lesson 27, Part B

Typing Legal Terms

Directions: Unless otherwise instructed, use a 70-space line and double spacing. Correct all errors. Follow one of the procedures below.

Words

Typing Procedure

On a separate sheet of paper, type the following words at least two times, concentrating on the correct spelling and pronunciation.

Shorthand Procedure

On a separate sheet of paper, type the following words once, concentrating on the correct spelling and pronunciation. Then write the shorthand outline for each word on the lines to the right or on your shorthand machine. Cover the printed words with a sheet of paper and transcribe from the shorthand outlines one time on your typewriter.

clean hands doctrine / in pari delicto / reformation/ _____

doctrine of doing complete justice / sua sponte / de _____

minimis non curat lex / rule of morality / right and _____

duty / waiver / matter in pais / estoppel in pais / _____

finding of fact / declaratory judgment / remedial / _____

Sentences

Typing Procedure

Type each of the following sentences one time. Concentrate on the correct spelling and pronunciation of each underlined legal term.

Shorthand Procedure

Write the correct shorthand outlines for the following sentences on the lines to the right or on your shorthand machine. Cover the printed material with a sheet of paper and transcribe from your shorthand outlines one time on the typewriter.

These sentences will be used for practice dictation on the cassettes.

The clean hands doctrine is an equity maxim which _____

states that one who comes into equity must not be _____

guilty of any wrongdoing. In pari delicto is a Latin _____

phrase meaning in equal fault. When both parties _____

are in pari delicto, equity relief will not be granted. _____

Reformation is a remedy which provides for the _____

amending or correcting of a written document so _____

that it conforms with the intentions of the parties. _____

The doctrine of doing complete justice is the broad _____

power of an equity court to dispose of all issues _____

existing between the parties which are related to _____

the main purpose of the suit. <u>Sua sponte</u> is a Latin phrase meaning of one's own will or voluntarily. <u>De minimis non curat lex</u> is a Latin phrase meaning the law is not concerned with trifles. The <u>rule of morality</u> is a rule of right and wrong conduct that forms the basis of the standards which people should follow in dealing with others. <u>Right and duty</u> form the foundation of equity jurisprudence. Whenever a right exists, there is also a duty. A <u>waiver</u> is intentionally giving up a right. A <u>matter in pais</u> is a matter of fact not in writing. An <u>estoppel in pais</u> is an estoppel which arises from the conduct of a party, laches, or negligence. A <u>finding of fact</u> is a statement by the court pertaining to the conclusions reached which are based on the evidence in an equity case. A <u>declaratory judgment</u> declares the existence of a right but does nothing to enforce it. <u>Remedial</u> means providing a remedy.

Transcribing from Dictation

Directions: This dictation emphasizes and reinforces the legal terms and definitions you have studied. Listen carefully to the pronunciation of each of the legal terms. Unless otherwise directed, use a 70-space line and double spacing. Correct all errors. Follow one of the procedures below.

Typing Procedure

Using the cassette from Lesson 27, Part B, transcribe the dictation directly at your typewriter.

Shorthand Procedure

Using the cassette from Lesson 27, Part B, take the dictation using your shorthand system and then transcribe on the typewriter from your shorthand notes.

When you have finished transcribing Part B of the practice dictation, check your transcript with the printed copy. If you have made any mistakes in the transcription, you should practice those words several times before going on to Lesson 28.

Check List

	PART A, DATE	PART B, DATE	SUBMITTED TO INSTRUCTOR YES	NO
Terminology and Definitions	_____	_____	_____	_____
*Typing Legal Terms	_____	_____	_____	_____
Words	_____	_____	_____	_____
Sentences	_____	_____	_____	_____
*Transcribing from Dictation	_____	_____	_____	_____
Quiz No. 1	_____	_____	_____	_____
Quiz No. 2	_____	_____	_____	_____

When you have successfully completed all the exercises in this lesson and submitted to your instructor those called for, you are ready to proceed with Lesson 28.

*If you are using a shorthand system, turn in to your instructor your shorthand notes along with your transcript.

Quiz No. 1

Terminology and Definition Recall

Directions: In the Answers column, write the legal term that is most representative of the corresponding statement. After you have completed this quiz, check your answers with the key on page 339. Unless otherwise directed, turn in this quiz to your instructor upon completion of this lesson.

ANSWERS

1. Another word for equity is _____.

   1. _____

2. A bill filed with a court of equity which requests the court to exercise its preventive jurisdiction is a/an _____.

   2. _____

3. An unreasonable delay on the part of a plaintiff in asserting a right which causes a disadvantage to another and for which the court will not grant relief is referred to as _____.

   3. _____

4. Jurisdiction which exists when a court of law or a court of equity can try both common-law cases and equity cases is referred to as _____.

   4. _____

5. A bill which provides that all persons who are interested in the same action will be joined together in a single lawsuit so as to prevent multiple suits for the same cause is a bill of _____.

   5. _____

6. A system of law based on good conscience, justice, honesty, and right rather than common law is _____.

   6. _____

7. A court of equity which administers justice according to the rules of conscience and provides remedy for things not covered by common law is a/an _____ court.

   7. _____

8. Questions which a judge gives to a jury in an equity case for their determination are _____.

   8. _____

9. A mistake which occurs unintentionally as to what the true facts are is called a mistake of _____.

   9. _____

10. Jurisdiction which a court of equity has to prevent future wrongs from being committed, as compared to courts of law which are concerned with wrongs which have already been committed, is _____ _____.

    10. _____

11. General rules of conduct based upon reason and justice are called _____.

    11. _____

12. The basis for equity law in the United States is called _____ law.

    12. _____

13. A jury to which framed questions of fact are presented for their determination in an equity suit is a/an _____ jury.

    13. _____

14. A mistake which occurs when one who knows all the facts makes an error as to their legal effect is a mistake of _____.

    14. _____

Turn back to page 288 and continue with this lesson.

Quiz No. 2

Terminology and Definition Recall

Directions: In the Answers column at the right of each statement, write the letter that represents the word, or group of words, that correctly completes the statement. After you have completed this quiz, check your answers with the key on page 339. Unless otherwise directed, turn in this quiz to your instructor upon completion of this lesson.

ANSWERS

1. Intentionally giving up of a right which one has is (a) reformation, (b) waiver, (c) right and duty. ....

   1. _____

2. An equity remedy which provides for the amending or correcting a written document so that it conforms with the intentions of the parties is (a) reformation, (b) waiver, (c) remedial. ....

   2. _____

3. A Latin phrase meaning in equal fault and for which equity will not be granted is (a) in pari delicto, (b) sua sponte, (c) de minimis non curat lex. ....

   3. _____

4. A term which means providing a remedy is (a) matter in pais, (b) remedial, (c) reformation. ....

   4. _____

5. The broad power of an equity court to dispose of all issues existing between the parties which are related to the main purpose of the suit is the (a) rule of morality, (b) clean hands doctrine, (c) doctrine of doing complete justice. ...

   5. _____

6. An equity maxim which states that one who comes into equity must not be guilty of any wrongdoing is (a) rule of morality, (b) clean hands doctrine, (c) doctrine of doing complete justice. ....

   6. _____

7. A judgment which declares the existence of a right but does not provide any measure for enforcement is a (a) remedial judgment, (b) finding of fact, (c) declaratory judgment. ....

   7. _____

8. The rule of right and wrong conduct which forms the basis of the standards which people should follow in dealing with others is the (a) rule of morality, (b) clean hands doctrine, (c) doctrine of doing complete justice. ....

   8. _____

9. The foundation of equity jurisprudence is (a) right and duty, (b) finding of fact, (c) reformation. ....

   9. _____

10. A Latin phrase meaning of one's own will or voluntarily is (a) in pari delicto, (b) sua sponte, (c) de minimis non curat lex. ....

    10. _____

11. A Latin phrase meaning the law is not concerned with trifles is (a) in pari delicto, (b) sua sponte, (c) de minimis non curat lex. ....

    11. _____

12. A statement made by the court pertaining to the conclusions reached which are based on the evidence in an equity case is a/an (a) finding of fact, (b) waiver, (c) estoppel in pais. ....

    12. _____

13. A matter of fact which is oral and not in writing which creates an estoppel based on the conduct of a party is (a) matter in pais, (b) estoppel in pais, (c) reformation. ....

    13. _____

Turn back to page 292 and continue with this lesson.

*"One who can and does not forbid that which is done
on his or her behalf, is deemed to have bidden it."*

—Legal Maxim

LESSON 28

To Wit: Partnerships

The sole proprietorship, the partnership, and
the corporation are the three most common types
of business organizations. Partnerships and corporations involve more legalities than single pro-
prietorships, thus, the terms in this lesson will deal
mainly with partnerships and the next two lessons
with corporations. When you complete these exercises, you should be able to spell, pronounce,
define, and transcribe the terms which are introduced herein.

Part A	Terminology and Definitions

Directions: Study the terms, pronunciations, and definitions until you are thoroughly familiar with them.
In order to complete this lesson successfully, you must understand the meaning and usage of all the legal
terms presented. If you are using shorthand, write your shorthand outline in the space provided or on your
shorthand machine for each legal term.

LEGAL TERM	PRONUNCIATION	DEFINITION	SHORTHAND OUTLINE
1. proprietor	prə-'prī-ət-ər	One who is the sole owner of something, such as a business.	_____
2. sole proprietorship	sōl prə-'prī-ət-ər-ship	A business owned by one person who has the legal right to the business.	_____
3. severalty	'sev-rəl-tē	Sole ownership of property. Owned by one person.	_____
4. partnership	'pärt-nər-ship	A business owned by two or more persons for their common benefit and who share in the profits and losses.	_____
5. articles of partnership	'ärt-i-kəls əv 'pärt-nər-ship	The agreement which contains the terms of a partnership.	_____
6. Uniform Partnership Act	'yü-nə-form 'pärt-nər-ship akt	Uniform laws adopted in most states to define the legalities and requirements for the formation and operation of partnerships.	_____

7.	limited partnership	'lim-ət-əd 'pärt-nər-ship	A partnership which consists of a general partner who conducts the business and one or more limited partners who contribute capital and share in profits.	_____
8.	Uniform Limited Partnership Act	'yü-nə-form 'lim-ət-əd 'pärt-nər-ship akt	Uniform laws which have been adopted in most states to define the legalities and requirements for the formation and operation of limited partnerships.	_____
9.	general partner	'jen-rəl 'pärt-nər	One who conducts the business of a partnership and has unlimited liability.	_____
10.	limited partner	'lim-ət-əd 'pärt-nər	One who contributes capital and shares in the profits of a limited partnership but whose liability is limited to the amount of the person's investment.	_____
11.	senior partner	'sē-nyər 'pärt-nər	Usually one who has a greater investment, seniority, and plays a major role in the management of the business.	_____
12.	junior partner	'jün-yər 'pärt-nər	Usually one who has a lesser investment, seniority, and role in the management of the business than the senior partner.	_____
13.	silent partner	'sī-lənt 'pärt-nər	One who is not publicly known as being a partner but who shares in the profits. Sometimes called a dormant or sleeping partner.	_____

Turn to page 305 and complete Quiz No. 1 before continuing this lesson.

Typing Legal Terms

Directions: Unless otherwise instructed, use a 70-space line and double spacing. Correct all errors. Follow one of the procedures below.

Words

Typing Procedure

On a separate sheet of paper, type the following words at least two times, concentrating on the correct spelling and pronunciation.

Shorthand Procedure

On a separate sheet of paper, type the following words once, concentrating on the correct spelling and pronunciation. Then write the shorthand outline for each word on the lines to the right or on your shorthand machine. Cover the printed words with a sheet of paper and transcribe from the shorthand outlines one time on your typewriter.

proprietor / sole proprietorship / severalty /
partnership / articles of partnership / Uniform
Partnership Act / limited partnership /
Uniform Limited Partnership Act / general partner /
limited partner / senior partner / junior partner /
silent partner /

_____

_____

_____

_____

_____

_____

Sentences

Typing Procedure

Type each of the following sentences one time.
Concentrate on the correct spelling and pronunciation of each underlined legal term.

Shorthand Procedure

Write the correct shorthand outlines for the following sentences on the lines to the right or on your
shorthand machine. Cover the printed material with
a sheet of paper and transcribe from your shorthand
outlines one time on the typewriter.

These sentences will be used for practice dictation on the cassettes.

A proprietor is one who is the sole owner of something. A sole proprietorship is a business owned by
one person who has the legal right to the business.
Sole ownership of property is also called severalty.
A partnership is a business owned by two or more
persons for their common benefit and who share in
the profits and losses. When parties enter into a
partnership, the written agreement stating the
terms and conditions is called the articles of
partnership. The Uniform Partnership Act consists
of uniform laws which have been adopted by most
states to define the legalities and requirements for
the formation and operation of partnerships. A limited partnership is a partnership which consists of
a general partner who conducts the business and
one or more limited partners who contribute capital
and share in profits. Most states have adopted the
Uniform Limited Partnership Act to define the
legalities and requirements for the formation and
operation of limited partnerships. A general partner
is one who conducts the business of a partnership
and has unlimited liability; whereas, a limited part-

ner is one who contributes capital and shares in the profits but whose liability is limited to the amount of the person's investment. The <u>senior partner</u> has a greater investment, seniority, and plays a greater role in the management of the business than the <u>junior partner</u>. A <u>silent partner</u> is one whose name is not publicly known as being a partner, but who shares in the profits.

_____
_____
_____
_____
_____
_____
_____
_____

Transcribing from Dictation

Directions: This dictation emphasizes and reinforces the legal terms and definitions you have studied. Listen carefully to the pronunciation of each of the legal terms. Unless otherwise directed, use a 70-space line and double spacing. Correct all errors. Follow one of the procedures below.

Typing Procedure

Using the cassette from Lesson 28, Part A, transcribe the dictation directly at your typewriter.

Shorthand Procedure

Using the cassette from Lesson 28, Part A, take the dictation using your shorthand system and then transcribe on the typewriter from your shorthand notes.

When you have finished transcribing Part A of the practice dictation, check your transcript with the printed copy. If you made any mistakes in the transcription, you should practice those words several times before going on.

Part B — Terminology and Definitions

Directions: Study the terms, pronunciations, and definitions until you are thoroughly familiar with them. In order to complete this lesson successfully, you must understand the meaning and usage of all the legal terms presented. If you are using shorthand, write your shorthand outline in the space provided or on your shorthand machine for each legal term.

LEGAL TERM	PRONUNCIATION	DEFINITION	SHORTHAND OUTLINE
1. assumed name	ə-'sümd nām	A name other than one's own under which business is transacted. The law usually requires the name to be filed so that the persons operating under the assumed name are known.	_____
2. D/B/A	'dü-iŋ 'biz-nəs əz	Abbreviation for "doing business as." Used when identifying a person who is doing business under an assumed name.	_____

3. joint venture	joint 'ven-chər	Where two or more persons join together in a business venture without forming an actual partnership or corporation.	_____
4. secret partner	'sē-krət 'pärt-nər	A dormant or silent partner.	_____
5. nominal partner	'näm-ən-l 'pärt-nər	One who permits one's name to be used as though the person were a partner but really has no financial interest in the business.	_____
6. syndicate	'sin-di-kət	A joint venture composed of individuals who have the purpose of conducting a specific business transaction.	_____
7. underwriting syndicate	'ən-də-rīt-iŋ 'sin-di-kət	A joint venture which consists of investment banking companies and whose purpose is to sell large issues of stocks and bonds.	_____
8. Securities and Exchange Commission	si-'kyur-ət-ēs ən iks-'chānj kə-'mish-ən	A commission formed to regulate the exchange of securities. Stocks, securities, and shares in limited partnerships must comply with SEC requirements.	_____
9. prospectus	prə-'spek-təs	A printed document issued by a company or corporation which describes a proposed business venture, such as a limited partnership.	_____
10. subscription	səb-'skrip-shən	A written contract by which one agrees to purchase shares, debentures, or other securities issued by a company or corporation.	_____
11. capital	'kap-ət-l	The assets of a company or corporation. The money which partners are required to invest in a business venture.	_____
12. commingle	kə-'miŋ-gəl	Putting two different persons' money together into one account.	_____

Turn to page 306 and complete Quiz No. 2 before continuing this lesson.

Typing Legal Terms

Directions: Unless otherwise instructed, use a 70-space line and double spacing. Correct all errors. Follow one of the procedures below.

Words

Typing Procedure

On a separate sheet of paper, type the following words at least two times, concentrating on the correct spelling and pronunciation.

Shorthand Procedure

On a separate sheet of paper, type the following words once, concentrating on the correct spelling and pronunciation. Then write the shorthand outline for each word on the lines to the right or on your shorthand machine. Cover the printed words with a sheet of paper and transcribe from the shorthand outlines one time on your typewriter.

assumed name / D/B/A / joint venture / secret partner / nominal partner / syndicate / underwriting syndicate / Securities and Exchange Commission / prospectus / subscription / capital / commingle /

_____

_____

_____

_____

Typing Procedure

Type each of the following sentences one time. Concentrate on the correct spelling and pronunciation of each underlined legal term.

Shorthand Procedure

Write the correct shorthand outlines for the following sentences on the lines to the right or on your shorthand machine. Cover the printed material with a sheet of paper and transcribe from your shorthand outlines one time on the typewriter.

These sentences will be used for practice dictation on the cassettes.

An assumed name is a name other than one's own under which business is transacted. The abbreviation for "doing business as" is D/B/A which is used to identify a person who is doing business under an assumed name; for example, Sally and Jerry Bates D/B/A Bates Enterprises. A joint venture is where two or more persons join together in a business venture without forming an actual partnership or corporation. A secret partner is a dormant or silent partner. A nominal partner permits one's name to be used as though one were a partner but really has no financial interest in the business. A syndicate is a joint venture composed of individuals who have the purpose of conducting a specific business transaction. An underwriting syndicate is a group of investment banking companies who enter into a joint venture for the purpose of selling large issues of stocks and bonds. The Securities and Exchange

Commission regulates the exchange of securities. Stocks, securities, and shares in limited partnerships must comply with SEC requirements. A company or corporation which invites the public to subscribe to shares, debentures, or other securities publishes a prospectus. The prospectus describes the proposed business venture. A subscription is a written contract by which one agrees to purchase shares, debentures, or other securities issued by a company or corporation. The assets of a corporation or company are referred to as capital. Capital is also the money required of partners when entering into a business arrangement. To commingle is to put two different persons' money into one account.

Transcribing from Dictation

Directions: This dictation emphasizes and reinforces the legal terms and definitions you have studied. Listen carefully to the pronunciation of each of the legal terms. Unless otherwise directed, use a 70-space line and double spacing. Correct all errors. Follow one of the procedures below.

Typing Procedure

Using the cassette from Lesson 28, Part B, transcribe the dictation directly at your typewriter.

Shorthand Procedure

Using the cassette from Lesson 28, Part B, take the dictation using your shorthand system and then transcribe on the typewriter from your shorthand notes.

When you have finished transcribing Part B of the practice dictation, check your transcript with the printed copy. If you have made any mistakes in the transcription, you should practice those words several times before going on to Evaluation 14.

Check List

	PART A, DATE	PART B, DATE	SUBMITTED TO INSTRUCTOR YES	NO
Terminology and Definitions	_____	_____	_____	_____
*Typing Legal Terms	_____	_____	_____	_____
Words	_____	_____	_____	_____
Sentences	_____	_____	_____	_____
*Transcribing from Dictation	_____	_____	_____	_____
Quiz No. 1	_____	_____	_____	_____
Quiz No. 2	_____	_____	_____	_____

When you have successfully completed all the exercises in this lesson and submitted to your instructor those called for, you are ready to proceed with Evaluation 14.

*If you are using a shorthand system, turn in to your instructor your shorthand notes along with your transcript.

Quiz No. 1

Terminology and Definition Recall

Directions: In the Answers column write the letter from Column I that represents the word or phrase that best matches each item in Column II. After you have completed this quiz, check your answers with the key on page 340. Unless otherwise directed, turn in this quiz to your instructor upon completion of this lesson.

COLUMN I	COLUMN II	ANSWERS
A. articles of partnership	**1.** The agreement which contains the terms of a partnership.	1. _____
B. general partner	**2.** Usually one who has a greater investment, seniority, and plays a major role in the management of the business.	2. _____
C. junior partner		
D. limited partner	**3.** A business owned by one person who has the legal right to the business.	3. _____
E. limited partnership		
F. nominal partner	**4.** A partnership which consists of a general partner who conducts the business and one or more limited partners who contribute capital and share in profits.	4. _____
G. partnership		
H. proprietor		
I. senior partner	**5.** Uniform laws adopted by most states to define the legalities and requirements for the formation and operation of partnerships.	5. _____
J. severalty		
K. silent partner		
L. sole proprietorship	**6.** A business owned by two or more persons for their common benefit and who share in the profits and losses.	6. _____
M. Uniform Limited Partnership Act		
N. Uniform Partnership Act	**7.** Sole ownership of property. Owned by one person.	7. _____
	8. One who is the sole owner of something, such as a business.	8. _____
	9. One who conducts the business of a partnership and has unlimited liability.	9. _____
	10. One who contributes capital and shares in the profits of a limited partnership but whose liability is limited to the amount of the person's investment.	10. _____
	11. Usually one who has a lesser investment, seniority, and role in the management of the business than the senior partner.	11. _____
	12. Uniform laws which have been adopted by most states to define the legalities and requirements for the formation and operation of limited partnerships.	12. _____

Turn back to page 298 and continue with this lesson.

Quiz No. 2

Terminology and Definition Recall

Directions: In the Answers column write the legal term that is most representative of the corresponding statement. After you have completed this quiz, check your answers with the key on page 340. Unless otherwise directed, turn in this quiz to your instructor upon completion of this lesson.

ANSWERS

1. A printed document issued by a company or corporation which describes a proposed business venture, such as a limited partnership, is a/an _____.

1. _____

2. A name other than one's own under which business is transacted is a/an _____.

2. _____

3. The assets of a company or corporation or the money which partners are required to invest in a business venture is called _____.

3. _____

4. An abbreviation for "doing business as" which is used when identifying a person who is doing business under an assumed name is _____.

4. _____

5. A commission formed to regulate the exchange of securities is the _____.

5. _____

6. One who permits one's name to be used as though the person were a partner but who really has no financial interest in the business is a/an _____ partner.

6. _____

7. To put two different persons' money together into one account is to _____.

7. _____

8. A joint venture composed of individuals who have the purpose of conducting a specific business transaction is called a/an _____.

8. _____

9. A written contract by which one engages to purchase shares, debentures, or other securities issued by a company or corporation is a/an _____.

9. _____

10. When two or more persons join together in a business venture without forming an actual partnership or corporation, it is referred to as a/an _____.

10. _____

11. A dormant or silent partner is also called a/an _____ partner.

11. _____

12. A joint venture which consists of investment banking companies and whose purpose is to sell large issues of stocks and bonds is a/an _____.

12. _____

Turn back to page 301 and continue with this lesson.

# EVALUATION
No. 14

Student _____

Class _____ Date _____

SCORING RECORD

	Perfect Score	Student's Score
Section A	50	
Section B	20	
Section C	30	
Total	100	

SECTION A

Directions: This dictation/transcription evaluation will test your spelling and transcription ability on the legal terms that you studied in the two preceding lessons. Use a 5-space paragraph indention, a 70-space line and double spacing unless otherwise instructed. Correct all errors. Follow one of the procedures below.

Typing Procedure

Using the cassette from Evaluation 14, transcribe the dictation directly at your typewriter.

Shorthand Procedure

Using the cassette from Evaluation 14, take the dictation using your shorthand system and then transcribe on the typewriter from your shorthand notes.

SECTIONS B AND C ARE AVAILABLE FROM YOUR INSTRUCTOR.

"The law respects form less than substance."

—Legal Maxim

LESSON 29

To Wit: Corporations

Of the three types of businesses, corporations are the most complex legally. Corporate law is a specialty for some law firms and involves many different legal activities. Even though corporate law varies from state to state, most of the terminology presented is used in most states. When you have satisfactorily completed the following exercises, you will be able to spell, pronounce, define, and transcribe the terms that are introduced relating to the field of corporate law.

Part A	Terminology and Definitions

Directions: Study the terms, pronunciations, and definitions until you are thoroughly familiar with them. In order to complete this lesson successfully, you must understand the meaning and usage of all the legal terms presented. If you are using shorthand, write your shorthand outline in the space provided or on your shorthand machine for each legal term.

	LEGAL TERM	PRONUNCIATION	DEFINITION	SHORTHAND OUTLINE
1.	corporation	kōr-pə-'rā-shən	An artificial being created by law.	_____
2.	articles of incorporation	'ärt-i-kəls əv in-kōr-pə-'rā-shən	The instrument which provides for the organization of a corporation.	_____
3.	charter	'chärt-ər	The authority granted by a legislature which gives a corporation the right to exist.	_____
4.	legal entity	'lē-gəl 'en-ət-ē	Legal being or existence.	_____
5.	board of directors	bōrd əv də-'rek-tərs	The group of persons who are responsible for governing a corporation.	_____
6.	chairperson	'cher-pərs-n	The presiding officer of the board of directors of a corporation.	_____

7. president	'prez-əd-ənt	The chief officer of a corporation who implements the policies established by the board of directors.	_____
8. domestic corporation	də-'mes-tik kōr-pə-'rā-shən	One created by the laws of the state in which it is transacting business.	_____
9. foreign corporation	'fȯr-ən kōr-pə-'rā-shən	One created by the laws of another state, government, or country other than the one in which it is transacting business.	_____
10. de jure corporation	dē 'jur-ē kōr-pə-'rā-shən	One which is in total compliance with the laws of the state in which it is organized.	_____
11. de facto corporation	dī 'fak-tō kōr-pə-'rā-shən	One existing in fact and which, in good faith, has made an effort to comply with state law but has failed to meet one or more of the requirements of the law.	_____
12. eleemosynary corporation	el-i-'mäs-ən-er-ē kōr-pə-'rā-shən	One organized for a charitable or benevolent purpose.	_____
13. subsidiary corporation	səb-'sid-ē-er-ē kōr-pə-'rā-shən	One that is under the control of another corporation which owns a majority of the shares.	_____
14. franchise	'fran-chīz	A special privilege granted by the government to an individual or a corporation and which does not belong to the general public. A corporation is a franchise.	_____

Turn to page 317 and complete Quiz No. 1 before continuing this lesson.

Typing Legal Terms

Directions: Unless otherwise instructed, use a 70-space line and double spacing. Correct all errors. Follow one of the procedures below.

Words

Typing Procedure

On a separate sheet of paper, type the following words at least two times, concentrating on the correct spelling and pronunciation.

Shorthand Procedure

On a separate sheet of paper, type the following words once, concentrating on the correct spelling and pronunciation. Then write the shorthand outline for each word on the lines to the right or on your shorthand machine. Cover the printed words with a sheet of paper and transcribe from the shorthand outlines one time on your typewriter.

corporation / articles of incorporation / charter /

legal entity / board of directors / chairperson /

president / domestic corporation / foreign

corporation / de jure corporation / de facto

corporation / eleemosynary corporation /

subsidiary corporation / franchise /

_____

_____

_____

_____

_____

_____

Sentences

Typing Procedure

Type each of the following sentences one time. Concentrate on the correct spelling and pronunciation of each underlined legal term.

Shorthand Procedure

Write the correct shorthand outlines for the following sentences on the lines to the right or on your shorthand machine. Cover the printed material with a sheet of paper and transcribe from your shorthand outlines one time on the typewriter.

These sentences will be used for practice dictation on the cassettes.

A corporation is an artificial being created by law. The instrument which provides for the organization of a corporation is called articles of incorporation. A charter is the authority granted by a legislature which gives a corporation the right to exist. A legal entity refers to a legal being or existence. A private corporation is governed by a board of directors. The presiding officer of the board of directors of a corporation is the chairperson. The president is the chief officer of a corporation who implements the policies established by the board of directors. A domestic corporation is one created by the laws of the state in which it is transacting business; whereas, a foreign corporation is one created by the laws of another state, government, or country other than the one in which it is transacting business. A corporation which is in total compliance with the laws of the state in which it is organized is a de jure corporation. If a corporation exists in fact and has made a good faith effort to comply with the state laws but has failed to meet one or more of the re-

quirements of the law, it is called a <u>de facto corpo-</u>
<u>ration</u>. An <u>eleemosynary corporation</u> is one which is
organized for a charitable or benevolent purpose.
A <u>subsidiary corporation</u> is one that is under the
control of another corporation which owns a majority of the shares. A special privilege granted by the
government to an individual or a corporation and
which does not belong to the general public is a
<u>franchise</u>. A corporation is a franchise.

Transcribing from Dictation

Directions: This dictation emphasizes and reinforces the legal terms and definitions you have studied.
Listen carefully to the pronunciation of each of the legal terms. Unless otherwise directed, use a 70-space
line and double spacing. Correct all errors. Follow one of the procedures below.

Typing Procedure

Using the cassette from Lesson 29, Part A, transcribe the dictation directly at your typewriter.

Shorthand Procedure

Using the cassette from Lesson 29, Part A, take the
dictation using your shorthand system and then
transcribe on the typewriter from your shorthand
notes.

When you have finished transcribing Part A of the practice dictation, check your transcript with
the printed copy. If you made any mistakes in the transcription, you should practice those
words several times before going on.

Part B | Terminology and Definitions

Directions: Study the terms, pronunciations, and definitions until you are thoroughly familiar with them.
In order to complete this lesson successfully, you must understand the meaning and usage of all the legal
terms presented. If you are using shorthand, write your shorthand outline in the space provided or on your
shorthand machine for each legal term.

LEGAL TERM	PRONUNCIATION	DEFINITION	SHORTHAND OUTLINE
1. share	sher	A specific part or portion of the capital of a company or a corporation.	
2. stock	stäk	Shares of ownership in a corporation.	
3. shareholder (stockholder)	'sher-hōl-dər 'stäk-hōl-dər	One who owns shares of stock in a corporation.	

4.	stock certificate	stäk sər-'tif-i-kət	A written document which states that the named person owns a certain number of shares of stock in a corporation.	_____
5.	common stock	'käm-ən stäk	The ordinary stock of a corporation which has no preference or special rights.	_____
6.	preferred stock	pri-'ferd stäk	Stock which has priority as to dividends over the common stock of the corporation.	_____
7.	par value	pär 'val-yü	Face value of all shares of stock in a particular class.	_____
8.	book value	bůk 'val-yü	The net worth of a share of stock.	_____
9.	treasury stock	'trezh-rē stäk	Stock which belongs to the corporation.	_____
10.	watered stock	'wȯt-ərd stäk	Stock which is issued as paid-up stock but which is not and is issued below par value.	_____
11.	promoters	prə-'mōt-ərs	The persons who organize a corporation.	_____
12.	transfer agent	'trans-fər 'ā-jənt	A bank or other institution which handles the transfer of stock for a corporation.	_____

Turn to page 318 and complete Quiz No. 2 before continuing this lesson.

Typing Legal Terms

Directions: Unless otherwise instructed, use a 70-space line and double spacing. Correct all errors. Follow one of the procedures below.

Words

Typing Procedure

On a separate sheet of paper, type the following words at least two times, concentrating on the correct spelling and pronunciation.

Shorthand Procedure

On a separate sheet of paper, type the following words once, concentrating on the correct spelling and pronunciation. Then write the shorthand outline for each word on the lines to the right or on your shorthand machine. Cover the printed words with a sheet of paper and transcribe from the shorthand outlines one time on your typewriter.

share / stock / shareholder (stockholder) / _____

stock certificate / common stock / preferred _____

stock / par value / book value / treasury stock / _____

watered stock / promoters / transfer agent / _____

Sentences

Typing Procedure

Type each of the following sentences one time. Concentrate on the correct spelling and pronunciation of each underlined legal term.

Shorthand Procedure

Write the correct shorthand outlines for the following sentences on the lines to the right or on your shorthand machine. Cover the printed material with a sheet of paper and transcribe from your shorthand outlines one time on the typewriter.

These sentences will be used for practice dictation on the cassettes.

Shares of ownership in a corporation are called stock. A share is a specific part or portion of the capital of a company or a corporation. One who owns shares of stock in a corporation is called a shareholder or a stockholder. A stock certificate is a written document which states that the named person owns a certain number of shares of stock in the corporation. The ordinary stock of a corporation which has no preference or special rights is known as common stock. Preferred stock is a stock which has priority as to dividends over the common stock of the corporation. Par value is the face value of all shares of stock in a particular class. Par value is the value of the stock listed on the stock certificate regardless of the amount actually paid for the stock. The net worth of a share of stock is the book value. The book value is determined by deducting the liabilities from the assets. Stock that is owned by the corporation is referred to as treasury stock. Stock which is issued by a corporation as fully paid-up stock when in fact it is not and is sold below par value is called watered stock. Promoters are persons who organize a corporation. A transfer agent is a bank or other institution which handles the transfer of stock for a corporation.

Directions: This dictation emphasizes and reinforces the legal terms and definitions you have studied. Listen carefully to the pronunciation of each of the legal terms. Unless otherwise directed, use a 70-space line and double spacing. Correct all errors. Follow one of the procedures below.

Typing Procedure

Using the cassette from Lesson 29, Part B, transcribe the dictation directly at your typewriter.

Shorthand Procedure

Using the cassette from Lesson 29, Part B, take the dictation using your shorthand system and then transcribe on the typewriter from your shorthand notes.

When you have finished transcribing Part B of the practice dictation, check your transcript with the printed copy. If you have made any mistakes in the transcription, you should practice those words several times before going on to Lesson 30.

	PART A, DATE	PART B, DATE	SUBMITTED TO INSTRUCTOR	
			YES	NO
Terminology and Definitions	_____	_____	_____	_____
*Typing Legal Terms	_____	_____	_____	_____
Words	_____	_____	_____	_____
Sentences	_____	_____	_____	_____
*Transcribing from Dictation	_____	_____	_____	_____
Quiz No. 1	_____	_____	_____	_____
Quiz No. 2	_____	_____	_____	_____

When you have successfully completed all the exercises in this lesson and submitted to your instructor those called for, you are ready to proceed with Lesson 30.

*If you are using a shorthand system, turn in to your instructor your shorthand notes along with your transcript.

Quiz No. 1

Terminology and Definition Recall

Directions: In the Answers column write the legal term that is most representative of the corresponding statement. After you have completed this quiz, check your answers with the key on page 340. Unless otherwise directed, turn in this quiz to your instructor upon completion of this lesson.

ANSWERS

1. The presiding officer of the board of directors of a corporation is the _____.

   1. _____

2. An artificial being created by law is a/an _____.

   2. _____

3. The instrument which provides for the organization of a corporation is the _____.

   3. _____

4. A legal being or existence is referred to as a legal _____.

   4. _____

5. The authority granted by a legislature which gives a corporation the right to exist is the _____.

   5. _____

6. A corporation created by or organized under the laws of the state in which it is transacting business is a/an _____ corporation.

   6. _____

7. The chief officer of a corporation who implements the policies established by the board of directors is the _____.

   7. _____

8. A corporation organized for a charitable or benevolent purpose is a/an _____ corporation.

   8. _____

9. The group of persons who are responsible for governing a corporation is the _____.

   9. _____

10. A corporation that is under the control of another corporation which owns a majority of the shares is called a/an _____ corporation.

    10. _____

11. A special privilege granted by the government to an individual or a corporation and which does not belong to the general public is a/an _____.

    11. _____

12. A corporation created by or under the laws of another state, government, or country other than the state in which it is transacting business is a/an _____ corporation.

    12. _____

13. A corporation which exists in fact and has made an effort to comply with state law but has failed to meet one or more of the requirements of the law is a/an _____ corporation.

    13. _____

14. A corporation which is organized in total compliance with the laws of the state in which it is organized is a/an _____ corporation.

    14. _____

Turn back to page 310 and continue with this lesson.

Quiz No. 2

Terminology and Definition Recall

Directions: In the Answers column at the right of each statement, write the letter that represents the word, or group of words, that correctly completes the statement. After you have completed this quiz, check your answers with the key on page 340. Unless otherwise directed, turn in this quiz to your instructor upon completion of this lesson.

ANSWERS

1. A person who owns shares of stock in a corporation is a (a) shareholder, (b) promoter, (c) transfer agent. .... 1. _____

2. Stock which has priority as to dividends over other stock of the corporation is (a) watered stock, (b) common stock, (c) preferred stock. .... 2. _____

3. The net worth of a share of stock is the (a) par value, (b) treasury stock, (c) book value. .... 3. _____

4. Stock which is issued as paid-up stock but is not and which is issued below par value is (a) watered stock, (b) common stock, (c) preferred stock. .... 4. _____

5. A bank or other institution which handles the transfer of stock for a corporation is a (a) promoter, (b) transfer agent, (c) shareholder. .... 5. _____

6. A written instrument stating or acknowledging that the named person is owner of a designated number of shares of stock in the corporation is a (a) treasury stock, (b) stock certificate, (c) book value. .... 6. _____

7. The ordinary stock of a corporation which has no preference or special rights is (a) common stock, (b) preferred stock, (c) watered stock. .... 7. _____

8. The persons who organize a corporation are known as the (a) shareholders, (b) promoters, (c) transfer agents. .... 8. _____

9. Shares of ownership in a corporation are referred to as (a) stock, (b) book value, (c) par value. .... 9. _____

10. The face value of all shares of stock in a particular class is the (a) par value, (b) book value, (c) watered stock. .... 10. _____

11. A definite part or portion of the capital of a company or a corporation is called a (a) stock, (b) book value, (c) share. .... 11. _____

12. Stock which belongs to the corporation is called (a) common stock, (b) preferred stock, (c) treasury stock. .... 12. _____

Turn back to page 313 and continue with this lesson.

"Acquiescence in error takes away the right of objecting to it."

—Legal Maxim

LESSON 30

To Wit: Corporations

This lesson continues the study of some of the terms relating to corporate law. A knowledge of these terms will assist your understanding of corporations and the laws that govern them. You will be able to spell, define, pronounce, and transcribe the legal terms presented in the following exercises when you have satisfactorily completed the lesson.

Part A	Terminology and Definitions

Directions: Study the terms, pronunciations, and definitions until you are thoroughly familiar with them. In order to complete this lesson successfully, you must understand the meaning and usage of all the legal terms presented. If you are using shorthand, write your shorthand outline in the space provided or on your shorthand machine for each legal term.

	LEGAL TERM	PRONUNCIATION	DEFINITION	SHORTHAND OUTLINE
1.	antitrust acts	ant-i-'trəst akts	Laws to prevent monopolies. A corporation cannot own or control so much of the market as to eliminate competition.	_____
2.	merger	'mər-jər	The joining of one corporation with another which continues in existence as one corporation.	_____
3.	blue-sky laws	'blü-'skī lȯs	Laws to protect persons from investing in fraudulent companies.	_____
4.	bylaws	'bī-lȯs	The rules or regulations by which a corporation is managed.	_____
5.	ultra vires	'əl-trə 'vī-rēz	Latin. Acts which are not within the powers of a corporation as defined in its charter.	_____

6. annual report	'an-yəl ri-'pōrt	A report to the shareholders of a corporation at the end of a fiscal year which presents financial statements and operational information for the corporation for the preceding year.	_____
7. minutes	'min-əts	A written record of the proceedings which took place at a board of directors' or shareholders' meeting.	_____
8. quorum	'kwōr-əm	A majority. The number of members required to be present at a meeting for business to be transacted.	_____
9. proxy	'präk-sē	A person who is designated to represent or act for another in a meeting. Also refers to the instrument which gives the authority.	_____
10. goodwill	'gud-'wil	The favorable reputation of an established business with its customers.	_____
11. liquidation	lik-wə-'dā-shən	The distribution of the assets of a business to settle accounts with creditors.	_____
12. dissolution	dis-ə-'lü-shən	The termination of the legal existence of a corporation.	_____

Turn to page 327 and complete Quiz No. 1 before continuing this lesson.

Typing Legal Terms

Directions: Unless otherwise instructed, use a 70-space line and double spacing. Correct all errors. Follow one of the procedures below.

Words

Typing Procedure

On a separate sheet of paper, type the following words at least two times, concentrating on the correct spelling and pronunciation.

Shorthand Procedure

On a separate sheet of paper, type the following words once, concentrating on the correct spelling and pronunciation. Then write the shorthand outline for each word on the lines to the right or on your shorthand machine. Cover the printed words with a sheet of paper and transcribe from the shorthand outlines one time on your typewriter.

antitrust acts / merger / blue-sky laws / bylaws / _____

ultra vires / annual report / minutes / quorum / _____

proxy / goodwill / liquidation / dissolution / _____

Sentences

Typing Procedure

Type each of the following sentences one time. Concentrate on the correct spelling and pronunciation of each underlined legal term.

Shorthand Procedure

Write the correct shorthand outlines for the following sentences on the lines to the right or on your shorthand machine. Cover the printed material with a sheet of paper and transcribe from your shorthand outlines one time on the typewriter.

These sentences will be used for practice dictation on the cassettes.

Antitrust acts are laws to prevent monopolies. The antitrust acts prevent a corporation from controlling so much of the market as to eliminate competition. The joining of two or more corporations into one corporation is a merger. Blue-sky laws are to protect persons from investing in fraudulent companies. The rules and regulations which govern the operations of a corporation are the bylaws. Ultra vires is a Latin term which refers to acts which are not within the powers of a corporation as defined in its charter. A corporation makes an annual report to its shareholders at the end of a fiscal year which presents financial statements and operational information for the corporation for the preceding year. The written record of the proceedings which took place at a board of directors' or shareholders' meeting is the minutes. A quorum is a majority of the number of members required to be present at a meeting for business to be transacted. A proxy is a person who is designated to represent or act for another in a meeting. A proxy is also the instrument which gives such authority. Goodwill refers to the favorable reputation of an established business with its customers. Liquidation is the distribution of the assets of a business to settle accounts with creditors. The dissolution of a corporation is the termination of its legal existence.

Directions: This dictation emphasizes and reinforces the legal terms and definitions you have studied. Listen carefully to the pronunciation of each of the legal terms. Unless otherwise directed, use a 70-space line and double spacing. Correct all errors. Follow one of the procedures below.

Typing Procedure

Using the cassette from Lesson 30, Part A, transcribe the dictation directly at your typewriter.

Shorthand Procedure

Using the cassette from Lesson 30, Part A, take the dictation using your shorthand system and then transcribe on the typewriter from your shorthand notes.

When you have finished transcribing Part A of the practice dictation, check your transcript with the printed copy. If you made any mistakes in the transcription, you should practice those words several times before going on.

Part B — Terminology and Definitions

Directions: Study the terms, pronunciations, and definitions until you are thoroughly familiar with them. In order to complete this lesson successfully, you must understand the meaning and usage of all the legal terms presented. If you are using shorthand, write your shorthand outline in the space provided or on your shorthand machine for each legal term.

LEGAL TERM	PRONUNCIATION	DEFINITION	SHORTHAND OUTLINE
1. financial reports	fə-'nan-chəl ri-'pōrts	Statements of the financial condition of a company or corporation which include the balance sheet, the income statement, the statement of retained earnings, and other statements relating to the financial condition of a corporation.	_____
2. balance sheet	'bal-əns shēt	A statement which summarizes the net worth of a business at the end of a fiscal period and shows the assets and liabilities of the company.	_____
3. income statement	'in-kəm 'stāt-mənt	Shows the income of the business, the cost of goods sold, the expenses, and the net income which resulted from the operation of the business for a specified fiscal period.	_____
4. net worth	net wərth	The worth of a business after deducting the liabilities from the assets.	_____
5. liability	lī-ə-'bil-ət-ē	A debt or obligation of a business or company. That which is owed.	_____

6. dividends	'div-ə-dends	A portion of the profits of a corporation which is to be divided among the shareholders.	_____
7. retained earnings	ri-'tānd 'ər-niŋz	That portion of the earnings which the company keeps for operations or additional capital investments.	_____
8. earnings per share	'ər-niŋz pər sher	The average earnings based on the number of shares of stock issued by the corporation.	_____
9. working capital	'wərk-iŋ 'kap-ət-l	Cash or other assets which are readily available for the use of a corporation.	_____
10. sinking fund	'sink-iŋ fənd	A sum of money set aside by a corporation to pay off a debt.	_____
11. debenture	di-'ben-chər	An instrument which acknowledges a debt of a corporation.	_____
12. auditor	'òd-ət-ər	A person who examines the financial accounts and statements of a corporation or a company and verifies their accuracy.	_____

Turn to page 328 and complete Quiz No. 2 before continuing this lesson.

Typing Legal Terms

Directions: Unless otherwise instructed, use a 70-space line and double spacing. Correct all errors. Follow one of the procedures below.

Words

Typing Procedure

On a separate sheet of paper, type the following words at least two times, concentrating on the correct spelling and pronunciation.

Shorthand Procedure

On a separate sheet of paper, type the following words once, concentrating on the correct spelling and pronunciation. Then write the shorthand outline for each word on the lines to the right or on your shorthand machine. Cover the printed words with a sheet of paper and transcribe from the shorthand outlines one time on your typewriter.

financial reports / balance sheet / income

statement / net worth / liability / dividends /

retained earnings / earnings per share / working

capital / sinking fund / debenture / auditor /

Sentences

Typing Procedure

Type each of the following sentences one time. Concentrate on the correct spelling and pronunciation of each underlined legal term.

Shorthand Procedure

Write the correct shorthand outlines for the following sentences on the lines to the right or on your shorthand machine. Cover the printed material with a sheet of paper and transcribe from your shorthand outlines one time on the typewriter.

These sentences will be used for practice dictation on the cassettes.

Financial reports consist of statements of the financial condition of a company or corporation. Financial reports include the balance sheet, the income statement, the statement of retained earnings, and other statements relating to the financial condition of a corporation. A balance sheet summarizes the net worth of a business at the end of a fiscal period and shows the assets and liabilities of the company. Net worth is the worth of a business after deducting the liabilities from the assets. An income statement shows the income of the business, the cost of goods sold, the expenses, and the net income which resulted from the operation of the business for a specified period of time. A liability is a debt or obligation of a business or company. Dividends are a portion of the profits of a corporation and are to be divided among the shareholders. Retained earnings is that portion of the earnings which the company keeps for operations or additional capital investments. The earnings of a corporation prorated according to the number of shares of stock issued by the corporation are referred to as earnings per share. Working capital is cash and other assets which the corporation has readily available for use. A sinking fund is a sum of money set aside by a corporation to pay off a debt. A debenture is an instrument which acknowledges a debt of a corporation. A person who examines the financial accounts and financial statements of a

corporation or a company and verifies their accu-

racy is an <u>auditor</u>.

_____

_____

_____

Directions: This dictation emphasizes and reinforces the legal terms and definitions you have studied. Listen carefully to the pronunciation of each of the legal terms. Unless otherwise directed, use a 70-space line and double spacing. Correct all errors. Follow one of the procedures below.

Typing Procedure

Using the cassette from Lesson 30, Part B, transcribe the dictation directly at your typewriter.

Shorthand Procedure

Using the cassette from Lesson 30, Part B, take the dictation using your shorthand system and then transcribe on the typewriter from your shorthand notes.

When you have finished transcribing Part B of the practice dictation, check your transcript with the printed copy. If you have made any mistakes in the transcription, you should practice those words several times before going on to Evaluation 15.

	PART A, DATE	PART B, DATE	SUBMITTED TO INSTRUCTOR	
			YES	NO
Terminology and Definitions	_____	_____	_____	_____
*Typing Legal Terms	_____	_____	_____	_____
Words	_____	_____	_____	_____
Sentences	_____	_____	_____	_____
*Transcribing from Dictation	_____	_____	_____	_____
Quiz No. 1	_____	_____	_____	_____
Quiz No. 2	_____	_____	_____	_____

When you have successfully completed all the exercises in this lesson and submitted to your instructor those called for, you are ready to proceed with Evaluation 15.

*If you are using a shorthand system, turn in to your instructor your shorthand notes along with your transcript.

Quiz No. 1

Terminology and Definition Recall

Directions: In the Answers column write the legal term that is most representative of the corresponding statement. After you have completed this quiz, check your answers with the key on page 340. Unless otherwise directed, turn in this quiz to your instructor upon completion of this lesson.

ANSWERS

1. A report to the shareholders of a corporation at the end of a fiscal year which presents financial statements and operational information for the corporation for the preceding year is a/an _____.

1. _____

2. The termination of the legal existence of a corporation is known as _____.

2. _____

3. The joining of one corporation with another which continues in existence as one corporation is referred to as a/an _____.

3. _____

4. The rules or regulations by which a corporation is managed are _____.

4. _____

5. The favorable reputation, of an established business with its customers is referred to as _____.

5. _____

6. A written record of the proceedings which took place at a board of directors' or shareholders' meeting is the _____.

6. _____

7. The distribution of the assets of a business to settle accounts with creditors is called _____.

7. _____

8. The Latin term for acts which are not within the powers of a corporation as defined in its charter is _____.

8. _____

9. A person who is designated to represent or act for another in a meeting, or the instrument which gives the authority is called a/an _____.

9. _____

10. Laws which are for the purpose of preventing monopolies are called _____.

10. _____

11. A majority or the number required to be present at a meeting for business to be conducted is a/an _____.

11. _____

12. Laws which are designed to protect persons from investing in fraudulent companies are _____ laws.

12. _____

Turn back to page 320 and continue with this lesson.

Quiz No. 2

Terminology and Definition Recall

Directions: In the Answers column write the letter from Column I that represents the word or phrase that best matches each item in Column II. After you have completed this quiz, check your answers with the key on page 340. Unless otherwise directed, turn in this quiz to your instructor upon completion of this lesson.

COLUMN I	COLUMN II	ANSWERS
A. assets	1. A debt or obligation of a business or company or that which is owed.	1. _____
B. auditor		
C. balance sheet	2. A statement which summarizes the net worth of a business at the end of a fiscal period which shows the assets and liabilities.	2. _____
D. debenture		
E. dividends		
F. earnings per share	3. A person who examines the financial accounts and statements of a corporation or a company and verifies their accuracy.	3. _____
G. financial reports		
H. income statement	4. An instrument which acknowledges a debt of a corporation.	4. _____
I. liability		
J. net worth	5. A statement which shows the income of the business, the cost of goods sold, the expenses, and the net income which resulted from the operation of the business for a specified fiscal period.	5. _____
K. retained earnings		
L. sinking fund		
M. working capital	6. Statements of the financial condition of a company or corporation.	6. _____
	7. That portion of the earnings which the company keeps for operations or additional capital investments.	7. _____
	8. The earnings of a corporation prorated according to the number of shares of stock issued by the corporation.	8. _____
	9. A portion of the profits of a corporation which is to be divided among the shareholders.	9. _____
	10. A sum of money set aside by a corporation to pay off a debt.	10. _____
	11. Cash or other assets which are readily available for the use of a corporation.	11. _____
	12. The worth of a business after deducting the liabilities.	12. _____

Turn back to page 323 and continue with this lesson.

# EVALUATION No. 15

Student_____

Class_____Date_____

SCORING RECORD

	Perfect Score	Student's Score
Section A	50	
Section B	20	
Section C	30	
Total	100	

SECTION A

Directions: This dictation/transcription evaluation will test your spelling and transcription ability on the legal terms that you studied in the two preceding lessons. Use a 5-space paragraph indention, a 70-space line and double spacing unless otherwise instructed. Correct all errors. Follow one of the procedures below.

Typing Procedure

Using the cassette from Evaluation 15, transcribe the dictation directly at your typewriter.

Shorthand Procedure

Using the cassette from Evaluation 15, take the dictation using your shorthand system and then transcribe on the typewriter from your shorthand notes.

SECTIONS B AND C ARE AVAILABLE FROM YOUR INSTRUCTOR.

KEY

1. supreme court
2. U.S. Supreme Court
3. eight
4a. trial court
4b. courts of original jurisdiction
5. courts not of record
6. probate court
7. courts of record
8. lower or inferior courts
9a. courts of appeal
9b. appellate courts
10a. U.S. Court of Appeals
10b. 11
11. U.S. District Court
12. may not
13. special
14. are not
15. are

1. administrative
2. common
3. public
4. Napoleonic Code
5. State
6. statutory
7a. Substantive
7b. procedural
8. constitutional
9. federal
10a. local
10b. municipal
11. case
12. private

1. A
2. M
3. B
4. L
5. E
6. J
7. H
8. K
9. C
10. I
11. O
12. F
13. N
14. G

1. c
2. b
3. a
4. b
5. c
6. a
7. b
8. a
9. c
10. c
11. a
12. a
13. b
14. a

1. a
2. b
3. b
4. c
5. c
6. b
7. c
8. a
9. a
10. b
11. a
12. c
13. b
14. a
15. c

1. minor
2. alias
3. allege
4. statute of limitations
5. malfeasance
6. double jeopardy
7. is not
8. statute of frauds
9. feasance
10. jointly and severally
11. sui juris
12. malicious prosecution
13. ignorantia legis non excusat
14. per se
15. act of God

Lesson 4 Quiz No. 1
Page 41

1. K
2. C
3. E
4. J
5. B
6. I
7. D
8. O
9. G
10. H
11. L
12. A
13. N
14. F

Lesson 4 Quiz No. 2
Page 42

1. chose in action
2. malice
3. penal
4. fraud
5. collusion
6. turpitude
7. ensue
8. irrevocable
9. quasi
10. recidivist
11. duress
12. mens rea
13. incriminate

Lesson 5 Quiz No. 1
Page 53

1. doe clause
2. prayer for relief
3. service
4. case title
5. caption
6. summons
7. answer
8. demurrer to complaint
9. jurisdiction
10. filed
11. venue
12. bill of particulars
13. appearance
14. ad damnum clause

Lesson 5 Quiz No. 2
Page 54

1. crossclaim
2. counterclaim
3. motion
4. recrimination
5. affiant
6. intervener
7. cross complainant
8. verification
9. omnibus clause
10. reply
11. cross defendant
12. jurat
13. court docket
14. affidavit

Lesson 6 Quiz No. 1
Page 63

1. c
2. a
3. b
4. b
5. c
6. b
7. a
8. a
9. a
10. c
11. b
12. c

Lesson 6 Quiz No. 2
Page 64

1. A
2. F
3. I
4. G
5. L
6. N
7. J
8. K
9. H
10. C
11. D
12. E
13. B

1. peremptory challenge	1. D	1. c
2. challenge	2. J	2. a
3. oath	3. B	3. b
4. voir dire	4. M	4. a
5. jury	5. L	5. a
6. challenge for cause	6. A	6. a
7. foreman or forewoman	7. O	7. a
8. impanel	8. C	8. a
9. trial	9. I	9. c
10. challenge to the array	10. G	10. b
11. veniremen	11. N	11. c
12. juror	12. K	12. c
13. counsel	13. F	13. b
	14. H	14. b

1. amicus curiae	1. res judicata	1. M
2. alibi	2. dictum	2. O
3. pendente lite	3. advisement	3. N
4. credible evidence	4. verdict	4. A
5. bailiff	5. exonerate	5. J
6. causal	6. judgment	6. F
7. preponderance of evidence	7. opinion	7. D
8. sequestered	8. polling the jury	8. K
9. charge to the jury	9. hung jury	9. L
10. prima facie	10. judgment by default	10. B
11. burden of proof	11. per curiam	11. C
12. deliberations	12. guilty	12. E
13. closing arguments	13. acquittal	13. G
		14. H

Lesson 10 Quiz No. 1 Page 107	Lesson 10 Quiz No. 2 Page 108	Lesson 11 Quiz No. 1 Page 119
1. H	1. a	1. tortious
2. A	2. a	2. allegation
3. F	3. b	3. intent
4. C	4. c	4. replevin
5. E	5. a	5. willful tort
6. L	6. b	6. ex delicto
7. G	7. b	7. grievance
8. K	8. a	8. tortfeasor
9. I	9. c	9. actio civilis
10. D	10. b	10. tort
11. M	11. b	11. civil law
12. N	12. b	12. actio in personam
13. B	13. c	
	14. a	

Lesson 11 Quiz No. 2 Page 120	Lesson 12 Quiz No. 1 Page 129	Lesson 12 Quiz No. 2 Page 130
1. c	1. last clear chance	1. H
2. b	2. licensee	2. M
3. a	3. attractive nuisance	3. E
4. b	4. intervening	4. B
5. b	5. nominal	5. N
6. c	6a. punitive	6. G
7. c	6b. exemplary	7. C
8. a	7. tangible	8. D
9. a	8. invitee	9. A
10. c	9. mental anguish	10. L
11. b	10. trespasser	11. J
12. a	11. nonfeasance	12. I
13. b	12. misfeasance	
	13. proximate cause	

1. felony
2. information
3. offense
4. habeas corpus
5. crime
6. warrant
7. extradition
8. indictment
9. grand jury
10. arrest
11. arraignment
12. corpus delicti
13. misdemeanor
14. preliminary examination

1. b
2. b
3. c
4. a
5. c
6. a
7. b
8. a
9. a
10. c
11. b
12. a
13. a

1. pardon
2. reprieve
3. parole
4. bail
5. sentence
6. incarcerate
7. reasonable
8. imprisonment
9. conviction
10. accomplice
11. accessory
12. aid and abet
13. principal

1. L
2. G
3. M
4. K
5. H
6. J
7. I
8. C
9. N
10. F
11. E
12. O
13. D
14. B

1. nuncupative
2. testamentary capacity
3. testate
4. will
5. attestation
6. formal
7. intestate
8. probate
9. holographic
10. codicil
11. testator/testatrix
12. petition for probate
13. animus testandi

1. J
2. G
3. C
4. E
5. M
6. A
7. D
8. I
9. B
10. F
11. L
12. K
13. H

Lesson 16 Quiz No. 1
Page 173

1. cy pres doctrine
2. cestui que trust
3. per stirpes
4. escheat
5. succession
6. ademption
7. citation
8. legacy
9. precatory words
10. beneficiary
11. pretermitted heir
12. heir
13. trust

Lesson 16 Quiz No. 2
Page 174

1. c
2. b
3. b
4. c
5. a
6. a
7. c
8. b
9. b
10. a
11. a
12. b

Lesson 17 Quiz No. 1
Page 185

1. warranty
2. real
3. premises
4. realty
5. habendum
6. quitclaim
7. fee simple
8. seisin
9. title
10. defeasible title
11. defective title
12. deed

Lesson 17 Quiz No. 2
Page 186

1. I
2. B
3. A
4. D
5. J
6. C
7. N
8. M
9. L
10. E
11. H
12. F
13. K

Lesson 18 Quiz No. 1
Page 195

1. a
2. c
3. a
4. a
5. a
6. c
7. a
8. c
9. b
10. a
11. b
12. c
13. a

Lesson 18 Quiz No. 2
Page 196

1. collateral
2. foreclosure
3. encumbrance
4. escrow
5. ad valorem
6. hypothecate
7. release
8. land contract
9. mortgage
10. acceleration clause
11. recording
12. lien
13. assessment

Lesson 19   Quiz No. 1
Page 207

1. option
2. caveat emptor
3. contract
4. offer
5. acceptance
6. counteroffer
7. ex contractu
8. bailment
9. parol evidence
10. contract law
11. binder
12. surety

Lesson 19   Quiz No. 2
Page 208

1. b
2. b
3. a
4. a
5. a
6. b
7. c
8. a
9. b
10. b
11. c
12. c
13. a

Lesson 20   Quiz No. 1
Page 217

1. B
2. M
3. K
4. G
5. A
6. L
7. N
8. H
9. J
10. C
11. I
12. D
13. F

Lesson 20   Quiz No. 2
Page 218

1. inure
2. landlord
3. lease
4. execute
5. demise
6. tenant
7. sublease
8. notice to quit
9. habitation
10. eviction
11. lessee
12. covenant
13. demised
14. lessor

Lesson 21   Quiz No. 1
Page 229

1. monogamy
2. common-law
3. religious
4. civil
5. valid
6. matrimony
7. voidable
8. annulment
9. domestic
10. void
11. bigamy
12. nonage

Lesson 21   Quiz No. 2
Page 230

1. F
2. K
3. A
4. D
5. G
6. L
7. I
8. J
9. C
10. M
11. B
12. E

Lesson 22   Quiz No. 1
Page 239

1. b
2. a
3. c
4. b
5. c
6. b
7. a
8. a
9. a
10. c
11. c
12. b
13. a

Lesson 22   Quiz No. 2
Page 240

1. custody
2. property settlement
3. temporary
4. earning capacity
5. domicile
6. necessaries
7. adoption
8. community
9. permanent
10. nonsupport
11. pendente lite
12. alimony
13. support

Lesson 23   Quiz No. 1
Page 251

1. negotiable
2. legal tender
3. check
4. cognovit note
5. time
6. promissory note
7. cashier's
8. collateral
9. commercial paper
10. Uniform Commercial Code
11. demand
12. judgment

Lesson 23   Quiz No. 2
Page 252

1. c
2. a
3. b
4. a
5. c
6. b
7. b
8. a
9. c
10. c
11. c
12. a
13. c

Lesson 24   Quiz No. 1
Page 261

1. presentment
2. accrue
3. without recourse
4. maturity
5. value
6. dishonor
7. interest
8. postdate
9. usury
10. protest
11. grace
12. delivery

Lesson 24   Quiz No. 2
Page 262

1. F
2. J
3. K
4. B
5. D
6. H
7. L
8. A
9. E
10. I
11. C

Lesson 25 Quiz No. 1
Page 273

1. petition for bankruptcy
2. creditor
3. solvent
4. voluntary
5. insolvency
6. receiver
7. bankruptcy
8. bankrupt
9. referee
10. ex parte
11. involuntary
12. bankruptcy
13. trustee

Lesson 25 Quiz No. 2
Page 274

1. a
2. c
3. c
4. b
5. b
6. a
7. a
8. c
9. c
10. a
11. b
12. a
13. b

Lesson 26 Quiz No. 1
Page 283

1. H
2. B
3. F
4. D
5. M
6. I
7. L
8. O
9. N
10. J
11. A
12. C
13. E
14. G

Lesson 26 Quiz No. 2
Page 284

1. ratification
2. implied
3. fiduciary
4. delegation
5. express
6a. ostensible
6b. apparent
7. estoppel
8. third party
9. incidental
10. implied
11. mutual consent
12. nonfeasance
13. factor
14. respondeat superior

Lesson 27 Quiz No. 1
Page 295

1. chancery
2. bill quia timet
3. laches
4. concurrent jurisdiction
5. interpleader
6. equity
7. chancery
8. framed questions of fact
9. fact
10. preventive jurisdiction
11. maxims of equity
12. chancery
13. advisory
14. law

Lesson 27 Quiz No. 2
Page 296

1. b
2. a
3. a
4. b
5. c
6. b
7. c
8. a
9. a
10. b
11. c
12. a
13. a

Lesson 28 Quiz No. 1
Page 305

1. A
2. I
3. L
4. E
5. N
6. G
7. J
8. H
9. B
10. D
11. C
12. M

Lesson 28 Quiz No. 2
Page 306

1. prospectus
2. assumed name
3. capital
4. D/B/A
5. Securities and Exchange Commission
6. nominal
7. commingle
8. syndicate
9. subscription
10. joint venture
11. secret
12. underwriting syndicate

Lesson 29 Quiz No. 1
Page 317

1. chairperson
2. corporation
3. articles of incorporation
4. entity
5. charter
6. domestic
7. president
8. eleemosynary
9. board of directors
10. subsidiary
11. franchise
12. foreign
13. de facto
14. de jure

Lesson 29 Quiz No. 2
Page 318

1. a
2. c
3. c
4. a
5. b
6. b
7. a
8. b
9. a
10. a
11. c
12. c

Lesson 30 Quiz No. 1
Page 327

1. annual report
2. dissolution
3. merger
4. bylaws
5. goodwill
6. minutes
7. liquidation
8. ultra vires
9. proxy
10. antitrust acts
11. quorum
12. blue-sky

Lesson 30 Quiz No. 2
Page 328

1. I
2. C
3. B
4. D
5. H
6. G
7. K
8. F
9. E
10. L
11. M
12. J

INDEX OF TERMS

lex, 11
lexicon, 11
lex loci contractus, 200
liabilities, 269
liability, 115, 322
licensee, 122
lien, 190
limited divorce, 232
limited partner, 298
limited partnership, 298
liquidate, 269
liquidation, 320
litigant, 15
litigation, 15
local and municipal ordinances, 5
locus sigilli, 34
lower or inferior courts, 2

M

maker, 247
mala in se (malum in se), 146
mala prohibita (malum prohibitum),
  146
malfeasance, 27
malice, 37
malice aforethought, 147
malicious prosecution, 27
mandamus, 103
manslaughter, 147
matrimony, 221
matter in pais, 291
maturity, 253
maxims of equity, 287
mens rea, 37
mental anguish, 122
merger, 319
metes and bounds, 180
minor, 27
minutes, 320
misdemeanor, 134
misfeasance, 121
mistake of fact, 288
mistake of law, 288
mistrial, 71
M'Naghten Rule, 137
monogamy, 222
moot, 59
mortgage, 190
motion, 49
motion to strike out, 71
murder, 146
mutual consent, 279
mutual obligations, 203

N

Napoleonic Code, 5
narratio, 24
necessaries, 235
negligence, 114
negotiable, 243
net worth, 322
no-fault divorce, 231
nolo contendere, 137
nominal damages, 122
nominal partner, 301
nonage, 222
non compos mentis, 137
nonfeasance, 121, 279
nonsuit, 92
nonsupport, 235
notary public, 34
notice of lis pendens, 59
notice to quit, 213
nudum pactum, 203
nunc pro tunc, 100
nuncupative will, 155

O

oath, 67
objections, 71
offense, 134
offer, 199
omnibus clause, 49
opening statement, 70
opinion, 90
opinion evidence, 77
option, 200
order, 93
ordinary, reasonable person, 125
ostensible authority, 279
overruled, 71

P

pardon, 144
parole, 144
parol evidence rule, 199
partnership, 297
party, 15
par value, 313
payee, 247
payer, 247
penal, 37
pendente lite, 80
per curiam, 90
peremptory challenge, 68
performance, 203
perjury, 78

permanent alimony, 234
per se, 27
per stirpes, 165
petition, 23
petition for bankruptcy, 266
petition for probate, 155
petit jury, 67
physically expunge, 71
plaintiff, 15
plat, 180
plea, 136
pleadings, 23
plenipotentiary, 276
polling the jury, 89
possession, 187
postdate, 254
power of attorney, 276
prayer for relief, 46
precatory words, 165
precedent, 59
preferred stock, 313
preliminary examination, 134
premarital, 225
premises, 177
preponderance of evidence, 81
prescription, 188
prescriptive rights, 188
presentment, 254
president, 310
pretermitted heir, 166
pretrial conference, 59
pretrial stipulations, 56
preventive jurisdiction, 288
prima facie, 81
primary agent, 276
principal, 143, 275
private law, 5
privileged communications, 225
privity of contract, 210
probable consequences, 125
probate, 155
probate courts, 2
procedural law, 6
proceeding, 14
promissory note, 244
promoters, 313
property settlement, 235
proprietor, 297
prosecuting attorney, 12
prospectus, 301
pro tanto, 203
protest, 254
proximate cause, 121
proxy, 320
publication, 158

public domain, 187
public law, 5
punitive damages, 122

Q

qualified acceptance, 247
qualified indorsement, 257
quantum meruit, 203
quasi, 36
quid pro quo, 203
quitclaim deed, 178
quorum, 320

R

ratification, 279
real property, 177
realty, 177
reasonable doubt, 144
rebuttal, 78
receiver, 266
recidivist, 37
recognizance, 59
recording, 191
recrimination, 49
recusation, 59
redress, 100
referee, 266
reformation, 291
rehearing, 103
release, 191
religious ceremony, 221
remedial, 291
remittitur, 103
replevin, 112
reply, 49
reprieve, 144
rescind, 210
res gestae, 78
residuary estate, 159
res ipsa loquitur, 126
res judicata, 90
respondeat superior, 279
respondent, 102
restraining order, 93
restrictive indorsement, 256
retained earnings, 323
retainer, 24
reverse, 102
reversion, 168
reversionary interest, 188
review, 102
revocation, 169
right, 114
right and duty, 291

riparian owner, 188
robbery, 147
rule of morality, 291

S

scienter, 137
scilicet, 34
seal, 34
secret partner, 301
secured debts, 269
Securities and Exchange Commission, 301
seisin—also seizin, 178
senior partner, 298
sentence, 144
separate maintenance, 225
separation, 225
separation agreement, 225
sequestered, 81
service, 46
servitude, 180
severalty, 297
share, 312
shareholder, 312
silent partner, 298
sine die, 93
sine qua non, 137
sinking fund, 323
sole proprietorship, 297
solvent, 266
sovereign immunity, 126
special agent, 275
special courts, 2
special indorsement, 256
spoliation, 257
stare decisis, 92
state law, 5
status quo, 100
statute, 11
statute of frauds, 26
statute of limitations, 26
statutory law, 5
stay, 99
stock, 312
stock certificate, 313
stockholder, 312
sua sponte, 291
subagent, 276
sublease, 213
subpoena, 56
subpoena duces tecum, 56
subrogation, 203
subscription, 301
subsidiary corporation, 310

substantive law, 5
succession, 166
successive indorsement, 256
sudden emergency doctrine, 125
sui generis, 33
sui juris, 26
suit, 15
summary of debts and assets, 268
summons, 46
supersedeas, 99
support, 235
suppress, 99
supreme court, 2
surety, 200
surety bond, 59
sustained, 71
syndicate, 301

T

tangible damages, 121
temporary alimony, 235
tenancy by the entirety, 181
tenancy in common, 181
tenant, 213
testamentary capacity, 156
testate, 156
testator—testatrix, 156
testimonium clause, 34
testimony, 70
third party, 279
time note, 244
title, 177
tort, 111
tortfeasor, 112
tortious activity, 112
to wit, 33
trade acceptance, 246
transcript, 55
transfer agent, 313
treasury stock, 313
trespasser, 122
trial, 67
trial courts, 2
trial de novo, 103
tribunal, 24
trust, 166
trustee, 266
trust estate, 168
turpitude, 37

U

ultra vires, 319
uncontested divorce, 232
underwriting syndicate, 301